P9-CQM-299

Welcome to
DUNDER MIFFLIN

Welcome to
DUNDER MIFFLIN

THE ULTIMATE ORAL HISTORY OF
THE OFFICE

Brian Baumgartner
and Ben Silverman

FOREWORD BY GREG DANIELS

CUSTOM
HOUSE

WELCOME TO DUNDER MIFFLIN. Copyright © 2021 by Propagate Content. All rights reserved. Printed in Canada. No part of this book may be used or reproduced in any manner whatsoever without written permission except in the case of brief quotations embodied in critical articles and reviews. For information, address HarperCollins Publishers, 195 Broadway, New York, NY 10007.

HarperCollins books may be purchased for educational, business, or sales promotional use. For information, please email the Special Markets Department at SPsales@harpercollins.com.

FIRST EDITION

Designed by Michelle Crowe

Background art and illustrations by David Smart, Devita ayu silvianingtyas, magiccoven, MMPhotos, P-fotography/ Shutterstock, Inc.

Photo credits: Grateful acknowledgment is made to the following parties for the use of the images that appear in this book: Pages 60, 161, 267, 395, 399, 402–403 courtesy of Brian Baumgartner. Pages xii, 246 courtesy of Greg Daniels. Pages 5, 26 courtesy of Teri Weinberg. Page 64 courtesy of Propagate Content. Page 7 courtesy of BBC. All other photos © Universal Television LLC. All Rights Reserved.

Library of Congress Cataloging-in-Publication Data

Names: Baumgartner, Brian, author. | Silverman, Benjamin, 1970– author. | Daniels, Greg, writer of foreword.

Title: Welcome to Dunder Mifflin : the ultimate oral history of The office / Brian Baumgartner and Ben Silverman ; foreword by Greg Daniels.

Description: First edition. | New York : Custom House, [2021]

Identifiers: LCCN 2021026348 (print) | LCCN 2021026349 (ebook) | ISBN 9780063082199 (hardcover) | ISBN 9780063217065 (hardcover) | ISBN 9780063217041 (hardcover) | ISBN 9780063217058 (hardcover) | ISBN 9780063082205 (trade paperback) | ISBN 9780063082212 (ebook)

Subjects: LCSH: Office (Television program : U.S.) | Situation comedies (Television programs)—United States—History and criticism. | Television remakes—United States—History and criticism. | Television actors and actresses—United States—Interviews.

Classification: LCC PN1992.77.O34 B38 2021 (print) | LCC PN1992.77.O34 (ebook) | DDC 791.45/72—dc23

LC record available at https://lccn.loc.gov/2021026348

LC ebook record available at https://lccn.loc.gov/2021026349

ISBN 978-0-06-308219-9

21 22 23 24 25 TC 10 9 8 7 6 5 4 3 2 1

For our fans and *Office* family

Contents

Foreword

BY GREG DANIELS

It's May 2004. A small company called Netflix only mails you movies on DVD. NBC, the home of "Must See TV," is throwing a bash in a Manhattan restaurant for the new shows of the 2004–2005 season. I'm standing unnoticed, wearing my only suit, as the casts and producers of the pilots NBC loves are celebrating with executives. The party is packed with the teams from *Joey* and *Father of the Pride*, a cartoon sitcom about the pet tigers of Las Vegas magicians Siegfried & Roy. NBC is incredibly confident in *Father of the Pride*, despite the fact the real Roy has recently been mauled by his tiger, which is a whiff of oncoming doom that someone should be sniffing. Their schedule is built around this sure thing, which was picked up weeks ago, giving its team plenty of time to book hotel rooms and make plans. *The Office* was picked up only hours before, and I have just arrived in New York to represent the show at the party. That night I will sleep on my parents' couch.

The previous day I was desperately arguing to the execs that *The Office*, with its relatable setting, observational humor, and bittersweet tone, was classic NBC—and that testing poorly with audiences only showed we were delivering something fresh, that we would follow the same trajectory as *Cheers* or *Seinfeld*. After much courageous tenacity from programming chief Kevin Reilly and persuasive begging from producer Ben Silverman, Jeff Zucker, the head of NBC, finally agreed to give us a tiny weak order: we could make five episodes past the pilot for a midseason launch.

To be fair, the negativity is not only coming from the network top. A *New Yorker* writer wanted to follow me around during the shooting of the pilot, and literally told me the piece "wouldn't make *you* look bad, it would be about how stupid NBC is."

I wander the party alone, wishing the team was there to share this weird experience. Sixteen months have passed since I first met Ricky Gervais and Stephen Merchant in Ben's office. When we wrapped the week of shooting our U.S. adaptation, the cast and crew felt if all we got to make was that pilot, it was still so worth it. But now we will be able to shoot five more. The show will get a chance to grow and find a life.

At the party, ignored by the brass, I start getting to know the ordinary NBC office workers in sales and marketing and affiliate relations that I'll be working with, and I find they have all seen the pilot in internal screenings and they love it. They get it. They have their own Michael Scotts to deal with, and they give me reassurance that we're not crazy; this show is special and deserves its break.

I wait in line to thank Jeff Zucker for the five episodes. He pulls me in for a quick handshake before moving on to someone else, muttering only "Okay, Greg, I'm giving you a chance. Don't fuck it up."

Are you still reading? If so, you must have an interest in backstage stories about our show. Or else maybe you're in a bookstore, pretending to be fascinated, while secretly glancing over the top of the page at your office crush, who you convinced to walk to the mall with you. Either way works for me.

I have a lot of backstage stories about *The Office,* beginning in 2002 when my agent sent me a VHS tape of season one of the brilliant British show to consider adapting, through to turning in the final cut of our series finale, which reunited the team with our adored number one Steve Carell. As the showrunner for most of the run (I started relying on Paul Lieberstein and Jen Celotta in the middle of season five, and Paul took the reins himself in seven and eight), I selected which stories we told from hundreds of ideas pitched, which scenes or lines made it into the script, and which actor improvs or moments made it into the cuts. That means my brain is stuffed with all the false starts, weird clunkers, and paths not traveled. I think one of Michael Scott's funniest talking heads was a long rant about his shower curtain and a novelty gift bull penis he uses to hold his shampoo. That never made it out of the writers' room, for good reason, but we laughed for hours in season two wording it every which way. Working on the show was fun, which you would hope would be the case making any TV comedy, but often isn't.

To guide us with tone, I wrote three words on index cards and taped them to my computer: **original** • **funny** • **poignant**. (The Netflix algo- rithm has three different words for the show: **witty** • **sitcom** • **comedy**, which is basically **funny** • **funny** • **funny**. Good job, robot!) When I think back about our cast and crew, the words that come to mind are **talent** • **passion** • **love**. They had mad skills, they cared deeply about every de- tail, and they supported each other.

Two early decisions contributed to the behind-the-scenes spirit of the show. The first was blurring the lines between people's jobs. Writ- ers acted, actors wrote, editors directed. I asked the accountants their opinions on the edits and listened to story feedback from prop master Phil Shea or set painter Shelley Adajian. The second was finding a tiny lot for us in the middle of nowhere instead of renting stages at a Holly- wood studio with a lot of other shows. I mostly wanted a real building and parking lot to shoot, but the best part turned out to be that every day of production the cast and crew ate lunch together. Over the years, over many wonderful meals from our caterer mensch Sergio Giacoman, we bonded into a strong team, maybe even, if I can say it without sound- ing too much like a deluded Michael Scott . . . a family?

Steve was the dad who went to work every day and provided for us, brought home the bacon with his unique talent and was the moral center, the pillar of integrity. I was the stay-at-home dad, raising the kids (writers?) and running things behind the scenes. One nice thing about my partnership with Steve was that we were the same age and had come up in similar worlds. While most of the cast and writing staff were younger and hipper, our references and instincts worked great for Michael, like the late-eighties *SNL* sketches we remembered verbatim that made the others scratch their heads. Steve accessed his humanity to make Michael a lovable character despite his flaws; I gave the writers ideas for Michael's stupidity just by being their boss. Like the time Mindy was depressed about a breakup, and I asked to hold her cell phone and pretended to call her ex as a joke. Halfway through, I blundered and actually connected and then panicked and hung up, as she watched in mounting horror. No wonder she could write Pam so well.

Many times the real experiences we had in our production office went straight into the show. Jen made a game out of the bouncing DVD icon screensaver on a TV . . . boom! Cold open. That's how a writers' room is supposed to work. But sometimes it's more random. Staff writer Caroline Williams was anxious that her grandmother was going to watch her first episode, "Phyllis' Wedding," so to tease her during the rewrite, we pretended to put in a fart joke. But fart jokes are powerful magic, and as writers will, we fell in love with it, and pretty soon the joke had put down roots and couldn't be dislodged. (Sorry, Granny Williams.) Once we even put in stuff that made no sense whatsoever, as when B.J. and Mike Schur had an intense conflict in the writers' room over a long-sleeve T-shirt. It is memorialized on-screen by Ryan asking "Will I be too warm in a long-sleeve T?" in "Safety Training." This line is utterly pointless in the episode, but I left it in to remind us of the hilarious super-articulate fury Mike brought to this inconsequential issue. I still have no idea what it was about.

This book is full of the memories and stories of the cast and crew and how we all found our way to each other, from everyone's point of view. I loved hearing so many of their voices, guided expertly by Brian in his podcast. The benefit of the show's early lack of success was how

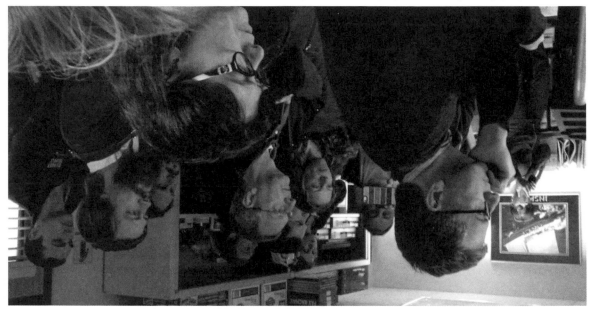

Greg Daniels (left) and team watch the last take of the series finale.

it screened out the cautious and political, and attracted adventurous people who were all-in to make something new. My ten years of working with these vivid personalities were the best of times. Please cue up U2's "With or Without You" under my slow-mo memory montage: Going to London with baller Ben and trying out my first ideas on the gracious and supportive Ricky and Stephen at the Groucho Club. Meeting Steve for the first time at a deli off Mulholland and finding out in moments we would be comedy brothers and friends. Long huddles with John and Jenna sharing our romantic histories in service of greater truthfulness for Jim and Pam. Giggle fits with Rainn directing his talking heads or poring over his family albums looking for a weird Dwight backstory. Oscar, Angela, and Brian calling me over to preview the show-within-a-show they were producing in Accountants' Corner. Kicking Dave Roger's chair legs to make "'Watson'' edit faster. Jeff Blitz and I trying to get the cat wrangler to put a cash value on the rest of a cat's acting career in case it didn't want to return to a set after being thrown (safely) through the ceiling in "Stress Relief." The detective show we wrote in Video Village for scripty Veda Semarne (Liar! This morning your hair was on your left shoulder!). Standing with Ken Kwapis in the Schrute wedding-graves on a windswept farm as it all came full circle. . . .

The Office boiled down a decade of all our best work into seventy-odd hours of entertaining moments. When you watch it, you're participating in a great game of human behavior, the sport of people watching. You're tracking the characters' delusions and obsessions and noticing them play out in their faces and behaviors, judging how close it is to life or our wishes about life. Those of us who worked on the show were playing that same game, and so you share that connection with everyone Brian interviewed whose stories are in this book. We all find individual humans and their quirks so interesting.

The real story in this book of how we made the show might not be as entertaining as the show itself, but it's also pretty great: a small band of passionate practitioners of a certain style of comedy coming together as a team, being mocked and criticized, fighting unlikely odds, figuring out how to let our lights shine, and finally coming out on top, still friends, reminiscing for the next generation as the credits roll. Where did it take place? A basketball court in Indiana? The fields of Watership Down? A Shaolin monastery? Or in this case, an undistinguished lot by the railroad tracks, down a street of stonecutters and upholsterers, on the border of Van Nuys and Panorama City. The adventure of my life happened in the most ordinary place in the world. If that isn't on brand for the show, I don't know what is.

Preface

HOW DID WE GET HERE?

BY BRIAN BAUMGARTNER

In 2007, just days after our season three finale, Angela Kinsey and I traveled from New York to Scranton, Pennsylvania. We had booked a series of appearances there in town. Fairly straightforward stuff. . . . We were to sign autographs at the Steamtown Mall, a shopping center built on an old abandoned railroad yard; have a VIP breakfast at the "Rad," the Radisson Hotel that used to be the railway station; and finally have a "block party" that was to take place in the center of town. I was so excited. This was my first time visiting the real city where our fictional world was based. I wanted to see it all.

At my urging, a few folks in town (who have now become like family to me) took us to many of the familiar locations from *The Office*. At Poor Richard's Pub I signed a bowling pin (I didn't even know it was in a bowling alley!); at Cooper's Seafood House I donned an elegant felt crab hat; and at The Bog, Angela and I ended up tending bar into the wee hours of the night. But the fans . . . it is hard even now to describe. Looking back, this trip to Scranton was the moment I realized how deeply *The Office* had connected with its fans. While we were there, Angela said it best: "We now know how the Beatles must have felt in Liverpool."

I knew that our little show was successful—I'd seen the ratings—but that's mostly theoretical. It is one thing to intellectually understand a show is becoming a hit. It is quite another to FEEL it—to be in a confined space with a throng of fans, all of them staring right at you, hunger in their eyes, as they press forward to shake your hand or get a photo with you. It's lovely, but I'll be honest, it's also a little scary. For the first time in my life I had a full police escort. Jenn Gerrity (again, now I consider her family) was the police officer assigned to me. I remember turning to her . . . fear in my eyes and in my voice . . . and saying, "You have my back, right? 'Cause this feels like it could get out of control." Words I would never have thought I would speak in regard to me and fans.

The next day, Angela and I were safely in the lobby bar in the Rad, and Tim Holmes, the city's regional director of marketing and events, told me there was a wedding reception happening at the hotel. The bride, he said, was a "really big fan of Kevin." He asked if I'd be willing to stop by and say hello. Of course I was willing, but at this point in the trip, I wasn't sure HOW. I couldn't just walk in the front door of the ballroom—there could be a scene. No problem, he said, they had already gotten clearance from the hotel that I could walk through the "employees only" door, down a flight of stairs, through the service entrance, around back through the kitchen to an unlocked door on the side of the ballroom where they would have the bride there to meet me. This was all a little 007 to me, but whatever—I went with it. The moment I walked inside the ballroom, the bride—still in her white wedding dress, mind you—walked straight over and threw her arms around me and started crying.

"This is the best moment of my life," she told me.

I'm sorry, what?

I tried to smile and deflect. This could get awkward. Her new husband was standing RIGHT THERE. "No," I told her. "This cannot be the best moment of your life. You just got MARRIED like an hour ago?!?"

But she was unfazed. "Best moment of my life," she insisted, as her new husband took photos of US.

For a while, I convinced myself that our show's popularity was fleeting. Sure, we'd have a second life in syndication, but it'd never be this huge again. We connected with the right audience at the right time in history, but tapping into the cultural zeitgeist is a fleeting, once-in-a-lifetime thing.

But instead, something strange and wonderful has happened. Years after we stopped making new episodes of *The Office*, the show is more popular than ever. People were rediscovering us—and in some cases, discovering us for the first time—on streaming services like Netflix and Peacock. Nielsen, the company that measures TV ratings, found that audiences watched 57.1 billion minutes of *The Office* in 2020. Not millions, *billions*.

A few years ago, I went back to The Westminster Schools, my high school in Atlanta. Ed Helms went to the same school, and though he looks way older than me, I graduated one year earlier. They asked if I'd sit down for a Q&A with students, and I thought, "Why not, this might be fun." I was expecting a small crowd at most—I mean, these are teenagers we're talking about. Teens are supposed to be preoccupied with their phones, making memes, and taking selfies. What interest could they possibly have in a decade-old TV show about middle-aged office workers in a dying paper industry?

But when I showed up, the theater was packed. There were students sitting in the aisles, and (I will swear to this) they were hanging from the rafters. I'd performed in plenty of shows in that theater, and I'd never seen so many bodies squeezed inside. And what really struck me was, these kids couldn't possibly have watched *The Office* during its initial run. Many of them were in diapers or yet to be born. They'd found it on streaming services, where they somehow picked our show out of literally thousands of other options.

One of the students asked me what my favorite episode was. My answer changes depending on my mood, but on that particular day, I picked "Diversity Day" from season one. The moment I said it, I like literally the words "Diversity Day" there was like a wave of laughter that erupted from the crowd. It was the laughter of recognition, the delight of being reminded of an episode of television that makes you happy.

It blew my mind. That episode came out in 2005, the year YouTube launched and Netflix still did most of its business in DVDs. How in the world did they connect so deeply with this show that might as well have been from another century? I remember when I was eighteen, and I guarantee you that my favorite show wasn't from fifteen years earlier. And I can DOUBLY guarantee you that I would not have known a particular episode by the TITLE OF THE EPISODE.

Why is *The Office* different? How did we make a show that has a larger and more loyal following today than it did when we first created it?

These are the questions we set out to answer in this book, which grew out of hundreds of hours of interviews. I asked everybody involved in making the show—the cast, the writers, the directors and film crew, producers, casting agents, makeup, and our fearless leader, Greg Daniels—to weigh in on this riddle.

What you're about to read in *Welcome to Dunder Mifflin* isn't just a behind-the-scenes account of how *The Office* was created, although it's certainly that too. Yes, we're going to show you how the sausage gets made, and unlike a sausage factory, our process was a lot more fun (and considerably less gross, chili aside). Michael Scott used to insist that Dunder Mifflin was like a family. Well, it's debatable whether any of his employees agreed with that sentiment, but what is most certainly true is that the cast and crew of *The Office* were family, and we still feel that way about each other.

But this is about more than just war stories from the TV trenches. When I started work on this oral history, I thought of it as a true crime podcast. There weren't any dead bodies or seedy, nefarious characters or an undercurrent of danger. But the mystery was just as compelling.

How did we get here? What did *The Office* do right? Could we find the clues, retrace our steps, and figure out how we stumbled onto a formula that resonates stronger today than it ever did?

I have some theories. And it turns out, many of my old *Office* mates do, too. And, oh boy it was fun to explore these questions with them. But even more than that, it was fun to just see everyone again. To relive the collective experiences we had in the context of these questions and the show's popularity today. On set for the pilot. Our terrible ratings in the beginning. That first Golden Globe Awards. Our first Emmys. Our multiple all-night shoots for "Booze Cruise." Steve leaving. Jim and Pam's wedding. Our finale together after ten years. And over and over as I talked with my old pals I just kept thinking about what that bride said . . .

"This is the best moment of my life."

Let's start at the beginning. . . .

Welcome to
DUNDER MIFFLIN

WELCOME TO DUNDER MIFFLIN: THE FAMOUS *OFFICE* SIGN ON THE DOOR OF THE "SCRANTON BUSINESS PARK."

1

"Okay, Here's the Pitch"

THE OFFICE TRAVELS
ACROSS THE ATLANTIC

BEN SILVERMAN (EXECUTIVE PRODUCER): It was the summer of 2001, and I was staying with my friend [TV producer] Henrietta Conrad in London. She was out one night, and I was sitting in her living room, flipping through the TV for something to watch, and I came across this show. I remember just being mesmerized by it.

Ben Silverman was not used to being surprised by TV shows. Since 1995, he'd worked at esteemed agency William Morris, where he'd been promoted to head of the international packaging division. Which means he found successful TV shows in other countries and "repackaged" them for American audiences.

BEN SILVERMAN: I would travel around the world, looking for ideas and cultural nuggets that could be brought to life in America. I found everything from *Who Wants to Be a Millionaire* to a myriad of other shows, like *Big Brother* and *Queer as Folk*.

In 2001, Silverman left William Morris to launch his own TV production company, Reveille. It was during a trip to London to find potential projects that he first stumbled upon this mysterious show.

BEN SILVERMAN: At first, I was wondering if it was comedy or for real, but I pretty quickly figured it out. And I was laughing, which I almost never do anymore. Because I work in television, a lot of the visceral enjoyment of episodic television goes away for me. But this show, whatever it was, it was just so brilliant and funny, and I immediately connected. Then Henrietta came home, and I was like, "What the hell is this? How do I not know about this? This is my job." And she's like, "Oh, it just came on the air."

That show, which was so new that most Londoners weren't even aware of it yet, was a single-camera "mockumentary" called *The Office*, by the then mostly unknown (at least in the U.S.) comedy duo Ricky Gervais and Stephen Merchant. The show followed a suburban London branch of a fictional paper supply company, Wernham Hogg, starring Gervais as a needy, narcissistic middle manager named David Brent who described himself as "basically a chilled-out entertainer."

BEN SILVERMAN: Henrietta told me that the best way to Ricky was probably Dan Mazer, who at the time was Sacha Baron Cohen's partner. So we organized and had dinner with Dan that night. I started peppering Dan with questions about *The Office*, and he gave me Ricky's cell phone number.

BRIAN BAUMGARTNER: Within twenty-four hours of seeing *The Office* for the first time, you somehow manage to get Ricky Gervais's phone number?

BEN SILVERMAN: [*Laughs.*] Well, I am in the business of show.

He called Ricky the next morning.

Ben Silverman

Job Title: Executive producer of *The Office*; cochairman of NBC Universal Entertainment (2007–2009)

Hometown: Manhattan

Training: Tufts University, Class of 1992, history major

Previous Employment: Warner Bros. intern, head of the international packaging division for the William Morris Agency (1995–2002), founder of Reveille production company

Post-*Office* Credits: Founded Electus production company (2009); executive producer for shows like *Jane the Virgin* (2014–2019), *Fameless* (2015–2017), and *Charmed* (2018–2021)

Honors: Youngest division head ever employed at William Morris

Special Skills: Packaging international shows for American audiences

Personal History: Proposed to his future wife on a golf course (the ring was hidden in the cup)

RICKY GERVAIS (COCREATOR OF THE OFFICE): I was walking down the street in London—I think I was going to see my agent—and the phone rang. "Hi, it's Ben Silverman. You don't know me, but I want to remake The Office for America." And I went, "Okay."

BEN SILVERMAN: I said, "I'd love to meet you. Are you in town?"

RICKY GERVAIS: I looked up and said, "I'm right outside the Starbucks on Wardour Street." He went, "Wait there, I'll be there in fifteen minutes."

BEN SILVERMAN: As somebody who travels the world, I hate going to chains. But I almost thought that Ricky was testing me. Like, "Oh, you're an American, you'll love this."

STEPHEN MERCHANT (COCREATOR OF THE OFFICE): Whenever they have a producer character in a Hollywood movie, he's always like, "We're gonna make you a star, kid." Ben is like the Hollywood producer cliché you see in movies, but it works.

BEN SILVERMAN: We talked for two hours. [Ricky and I] very quickly got along because we both love television. We talked about the shows that inspired him, like The Simpsons and [the 1960 Jack Lemmon movie] The Apartment. We talked about reality television, which I'd been a pioneer of in America.

STEPHEN MERCHANT: At the time in the UK, there was a spate of what I guess you'd now call reality TV. Fly-on-the-wall documentaries about everyday subjects. There was a very famous one about a driving school.

Driving School, which aired on BBC One during the summer of 1997, featured student drivers in Bristol and South Wales. It created one of the first household-name British reality stars, Maureen Rees, who repeatedly failed her driving tests.

STEPHEN MERCHANT: It was just following normal people doing driving lessons. And these types of shows were incredibly popular. Nobody had seen everyday people on-screen in that way before.

RICKY GERVAIS: It was ordinary people trying to get their fifteen minutes of fame. Of course, now fame is a different beast. They'd try and get their own game show and make the most of it. But back in the nineties, it was more quaint.

STEPHEN MERCHANT: When we did *The Office*, we had those shows in our mind.

Ben Silverman and Stephen Merchant,
cocreator of *The Office* (UK).

BEN SILVERMAN: All these vérité reality shows set in these workplace environments in the UK clearly had informed Ricky on what he was mocking, I was explaining to him, we don't yet have those formats to mock. So as we look at the show, we need to ensure where the characters are grounded and where the comedy comes from. It can't just be through the faux documentary lens.

BRIAN BAUMGARTNER: Are you also asking him, "Is the show for sale?"

BEN SILVERMAN: No, I'm not asking that, because you don't sell in our business. It's not like the shoe business. It's more like, "Are you interested in adapting your great work for America? And would you like to collaborate with me on this process? I know everything about getting a television show made in America. Which part of that process would you like to learn about? How much would you like to be involved?" He clearly had chosen this Starbucks for a reason, because he says to me, "Oh, good news. My agent is right around the corner. Let's go meet with him."

Even before talking to Ricky, Ben had reached out to the BBC (British Broadcasting Corporation). After all, this wasn't the first time he'd negotiated to bring a British TV show to American shores.

BEN SILVERMAN: It helped one hundred percent not only knowing where to go but who to call at BBC Worldwide and having those relationships already.

BRIAN BAUMGARTNER: Was there pushback from the BBC?

BEN SILVERMAN: The BBC is a wonderful cultural institution, and I am a huge fan of it. But they're also a giant government bureaucracy. It was literally like dealing with characters from *The Office*, trying to get them to move forward on this. They were not used to the pace and process I wanted to follow. They're much more sophisticated now, but at the time it took a lot of explaining and educating to show them what was possible.

RICKY GERVAIS: When we were pitching our version of *The Office* to [BBC producer] Jon Plowman, he said, "I've got one question. This guy who's the boss, if he's so terrible at his job, how does he keep it?" And I said, "Let's take a little walk around the BBC, shall we?" He just started laughing and went, "Okay, let's do it." [*Laughs.*]

BEN SILVERMAN: I began a three-month process to secure the rights. And I ended up engaging with the BBC for a long time around it. It wasn't until Duncan [Hayes, Ricky's agent at the time] helped me unlock it that I realized both the BBC and Ricky controlled the rights. And neither one could do it without the other. In dealing with the BBC, I realized quickly I needed Ricky and Stephen Merchant to actually get it done. And from there, it was negotiations and conversations.

There was another problem. Ricky and Stephen weren't convinced yet that an American adaptation could work.

Ricky Gervais on the set of *The Office* (UK).

RICKY GERVAIS: I'd mostly heard of all the failures, like when they tried to remake *Fawlty Towers* and it was dreadful.

There were actually three attempts to re-create the John Cleese classic *Fawlty Towers* in America, including sitcoms starring Harvey Korman (in 1978), Bea Arthur (1983), and John Larroquette (1999). They were all critical and ratings flops.

STEPHEN MERCHANT: *The Office* was a quirky show even in the UK. The idea that this weird, downbeat sitcom from the UK would somehow translate to American television, where everyone was supposed to be beautiful and a winner, was hard to fathom.

BEN SILVERMAN: Ricky had shared with me that he wanted to end the UK *Office*.

Ricky had just wrapped the British *Office*'s second and final season, which aired in the autumn of 2002. The decision to end after just twelve episodes was Ricky's call, not a cancellation by the BBC.

BEN SILVERMAN: I told him, "We'll make twenty-five times more episodes than you'll ever make in the UK, and it will be far more valuable to you than what you do in the UK." Both of those things became true.

It took months of negotiating, but Ben finally got the blessing of Ricky, Stephen, and the BBC. How did he do it?

STEPHEN MERCHANT: Ben's a force of nature. He's like a man who drinks fifteen espressos directly before a meeting. And he has such a real enthusiasm. He was passionate about the show and his enthusiasm was very infectious. He definitely moved that train forward.

BEN SILVERMAN: In my business, if you don't go after it with perseverance and conviction, you can't get it done. I had a premonition about this show. You know when you know. I knew when I heard the title of *Who Wants to Be a Millionaire*, I didn't even need to see the game show. I knew when I saw five frames of *The Office*, it was fresh and genre breaking. That's why I kept pushing forward to make this deal.

"Moving the Ship of Comedy in a Different Direction"
The Office Finds Its Captain

Although Ben had found the show, he wasn't a showrunner, the person who creates and oversees a television program. With nothing else on TV quite like *The Office*, it was difficult to envision who would be a perfect fit for the job.

BEN SILVERMAN: I immediately looked at Larry David and what he was doing. 'Cause I thought it was the closest in format and we could maybe work with his director. So, we met with Larry Charles, we met with Bob Weide, we met with a lot of people in the Larry David world. I was also a huge fan of Greg Daniels, even though I didn't know him from a hole in the wall.

GREG DANIELS (DEVELOPED *THE OFFICE* FOR AMERICAN TV): I'd just come off a very intense eight years at *King of the Hill,* and it was the first time I'd worked as a showrunner.

　　After *King of the Hill* became successful, I was looking for what to do next and I took all sorts of interesting meetings. Like, I had

Greg Daniels

Job Title: Creator and original showrunner of the American Office

Hometown: Manhattan

Training: Harvard University, Class of 1985, concentration in history and literature

Previous Employment: Cocreator of King of the Hill (1997-2010), a critically beloved animated show (which managed to feel more realistic and true to life than most live-action shows) about a propane salesman and his quirky family and friends living in a small Texas town; writer for Not Necessarily the News (1985-1987), Saturday Night Live (1987-1990), The Simpsons (1994-1995); three-time Emmy winner prior to The Office (SNL, The Simpsons, and King of the Hill)

Post-Office Credits: Cocreator, executive producer, and writer for Parks and Recreation (2009-2020); creator, director, and executive producer of Upload (2020-) and Space Force (2020-)

Completed Project Work: Six hundred-ish half-hour television episodes (to date)

Managerial Style: Collaborative, encourages improv and numerous field trips for employees

Special Skills: Ability to recite the "Knights Who Say 'Ni!'" Monty Python sketch by memory

Emergency Contact: Conan O'Brien, former writing partner at the Harvard Lampoon

a meeting about possibly redoing *The Muppet Show*. Right around Christmas of 2003, I believe, my agent Ari Emanuel—he's the guy that the Ari Gold character on *Entourage* was based on—sent me a VHS cassette of the British *Office*. I didn't watch it, and he called me after the holidays and said, "Hey, I'm gonna send this to the next guy on my list if you don't watch it." I said, "All right, all right, I'll try and watch it tonight." So I popped the cassette in at like nine P.M. or something, and I stayed up till one in the morning watching it all and absolutely loved it. I couldn't even figure out how it was done. It didn't feel scripted at all. It was just so alive and cool.

Greg called Ari, who put him in touch with Ben.

BEN SILVERMAN: I immediately connected with Greg. I just felt his genius and his thoughtfulness and real rigorous approach.

GREG DANIELS: Ben and I both grew up in New York, in the same kind of brainy, city-life environment.

BEN SILVERMAN: I think we both had a real respect for our parents' intellect, which is something not every kid has. A lot of kids strive for something beyond their parents.

Greg's father ran a commercial radio network in New York and his mom worked for the New York Public Library. Ben's father is an award-winning composer and his mother is an actress and programming executive.

BEN SILVERMAN: Greg's father now plays bridge with my mother's best friends, fifty years later. It's pretty incredible.

GREG DANIELS: Ben's got an enthusiasm and an energy that I don't have. I like to carefully plot how I approach stuff, but Ben is like mercury. He zooms in. He's also able to draw pieces in from all over the place and make a coherent vision.

BEN SILVERMAN: The experience that we both had in connecting on this show was about the architecture of television and the architecture of the idea, because so much about it was newly conceived. We kept talking about it with a shared love of television. We were people who grew up loving TV.

BRIAN BAUMGARTNER: Did it concern you at all that he was mostly involved in the animated world at that point?

BEN SILVERMAN: Not at all. The characters he had created in those animated worlds were very accessible and real in a way that the characters in *The Office* work. And knowing that *The Simpsons* had actually informed Ricky and Stephen made me feel like there would be a good correlation.

GREG DANIELS: *The Simpsons* was really good training in many ways, but there were a lot of things I wanted to do differently. When I got to *The Simpsons,* it was at the end of season four. The show was getting a little wilder. For *King of the Hill,* I wanted to keep it contained and realistic. There were a lot of shows around that time trying to re-create *The Simpsons'*s success and they moved at a very frenetic pace. I was a believer in the value of slowness. A big part of *King of the Hill* was trying to slow everything down. Like in the pilot, the first couple of minutes were just these guys standing around a truck, just going, "Yep. Yep." Really slow. That freaked out everybody at Fox. They'd recently done a show called *The Critic*, which was just *bam, bam, bam* with the jokes. And here we come with this slow-paced show that was either gonna work or it was going to be a disaster and we'd be dropped out of the business.

It wasn't a disaster. *King of the Hill* became one of Fox's highest-rated programs and won an Emmy in 1999 for Outstanding Animated Program. But to land the job as the *Office* showrunner, Greg needed the blessing of Ricky Gervais and Stephen Merchant. So in February 2003, Ben invited everyone to his office to meet.

GREG DANIELS: I wanted to meet people who I thought were doing the best work, whether or not I would ever work with them. It was really important for me to sell an episode to *Seinfeld* so that I could work with Larry David and see what was up. Ricky and Stephen had created something amazing, and I wanted to figure it out. But I didn't really think it was plausible that it would come to American TV or that I would get the job. I just wanted to meet them and ask them about it.

Ben, Greg, Stephen, and Ricky gathered together at a bungalow on the Universal lot.

GREG DANIELS: It turned out that, number one, they loved *The Simpsons*. Number two, Ricky's favorite *Simpsons* episode was one I'd written called "Homer Badman."

The 1994 episode involved Homer being accused of sexual harassment after he retrieves a gummy *Venus de Milo* stuck to a babysitter's butt.

LISA: Dad, I don't understand. What is she saying you did?

HOMER: Well, Lisa, remember that postcard Grampa sent us from Florida of that alligator biting that woman's bottom?

BART: Oh yeah, that was brilliant!

HOMER: That's right, we all thought it was hilarious. But it turns out we were wrong: that alligator was sexually harassing that woman.

GREG DANIELS: So we started vibing nicely. I talked to them about what I saw in the show and how I would adapt it. A lot of it came from *King of the Hill*, being realistic and slow and poignant.

STEPHEN MERCHANT: The thing which charmed us about Greg was he realized that the beating heart of the show was the will-they-won't-they romance.

RICKY GERVAIS: We met with a lot of amazing showrunners from some of my favorite programs of all time. We chose Greg not just because of his body of work, which was as good as anyone's, or because he was a nice chap. It was because he was the only one that brought up that he thought it was a love story. That was very important to me, the love story.

STEPHEN MERCHANT: That was the thing that you really need to get right. People tuned in for the David Brent/Michael Scott character, but they *stayed* for the love affair.

Greg, however, didn't share their confidence that he could pull it off.

BEN SILVERMAN: He was so anxious about doing it. He kept saying to me, "I can't make it better than the British one." I'd done a show that aired while I was working on this called *Coupling*, which was an adaptation of a British show that was in the *Friends* vein. It was almost as if *Friends* had been adapted to the UK and then adapted back. The show had been perceived poorly in America.

The U.S. adaptation of *Coupling*, about a group of thirtysomething friends living in Chicago, premiered in September 2003 and lasted just four episodes before being canceled. Even NBC president Jeff Zucker admitted publicly that it "just sucked."

BEN SILVERMAN: Greg was concerned the same thing was going to happen this time.

GREG DANIELS: The biggest thing I was worried about was taking this little jewel of a TV show and messing it up. I'd have these anxiety dreams where it was like a comedy court, and all the good people in comedy were judging me for remaking *The Office* and saying I had ruined it.

BRIAN BAUMGARTNER: Wow. Did you usually have anxiety dreams before starting a new project?

GREG DANIELS: Well, at the very beginning of my career, I was writing partners with Conan O'Brien. And he used to say to me, "When you overthink, you start to stink." [Laughs.] He kind of pegged me as an overthinker.

BEN SILVERMAN: Greg was who I really wanted to do it. And he was suddenly getting cold feet based on the concern of adapting something so critically beloved. And I said, "No one in America has seen this one. It's too dark, too narrow, and not gonna play to a wide American audience unless we do a more optimistic adaptation informed by *your* vision and *your* ownership of the world."

GREG DANIELS: Ben can be very persuasive.

BEN SILVERMAN: I told him there are millions of great books that are adapted all the time. Do you want to adapt the worst piece of shit? Or do you want to try and adapt a Pulitzer Prize–winning novel?

They had their showrunner. They had the blessing of Gervais and Merchant. They had the rights to produce it in the U.S. There was just one small problem.

BEN SILVERMAN: No one fucking wanted it. So all of this, everything we'd done, it was like spitting into the air. I mean, there's nothing. We had no traction at all.

Ben reached out to everyone he knew in television, trying to drum up excitement and gauge who might be ready for a groundbreaking television show based on a cult hit from the UK that nobody in the U.S. had heard of (yet).

BEN SILVERMAN: I went to Les Moonves [the CEO of CBS], he passed. Gail Berman [president of entertainment for Fox], she passed immediately. Didn't get it. HBO said, "We'll never do a remake of a show." Showtime wasn't doing shows like this. HBO, with their typical foo-foo-ness, "we're too cool for you, buddy," they just wanted rarefied air and weren't trying to reach as many people as I was. I'm really culture focused and culture piercing and I wanted scale, so I was worried about it behind a subscription paywall anyway.

When it came to TV comedies in the early 2000s, the networks had a tried-and-true formula that brought in big audiences during prime time and tons of advertising dollars with them. It was all about *Friends*.

BEN SILVERMAN: Not just *Friends*, it was *Friends* and *Baywatch*. It was *Friends* and *Friends in Bathing Suits*. That was like the landscape of TV at that moment, a downward spiral of beauty and superficiality.

EMILY VANDERWERFF (TV CRITIC FOR VOX): The 2000s are often called the golden age of television, but that's mostly because of dramas like *Sopranos, Deadwood, The Wire, The Shield,* all those great dark dramas with smart adult storytelling about complicated figures. That didn't really spread over to comedy. There are certainly good comedies in that era. *Everybody Loves Raymond* is a fantastic comedy. *Arrested Development* came out in 2003 and really changed everything. But it was not an era with a lot of great TV comedy.

BEN SILVERMAN: There were no single-camera comedies on broadcast television, no faux documentaries on television other than maybe *Reno 911!* So it was easy for people to pass. I understand why the head of CBS would have passed. I didn't feel it should be on CBS at that time. Like, I think it would have died there, frankly.

But Ben kept calling around, and finally he found one network—well, one person, really—who got it.

BEN SILVERMAN: A guy named Nick Grad who worked at FX. He knew what the show was and he loved it.

So Nick brought it to his boss, Kevin Reilly.

KEVIN REILLY (TELEVISION EXECUTIVE): Nick always had a good nose for sort of what's next. He was the guy I always looked to like, "Is this song cool? Yeah? Okay, great. I think it's cool too." This was one of those things where I'd heard of heard about it, and Nick was like, "If you can get it, we've got to have it." It was a perfect FX show.

FX was known for giving airtime to daring, experimental shows like *The Shield, Nip/Tuck,* and *Rescue Me. The Office,* with its unconventional format and dark sensibilities, would have fit right in. Ben and Kevin had several meetings to discuss the possibilities, and it appeared *The Office* had found its perfect home in the U.S. There was just one snag.

KEVIN REILLY: My contract was up at FX. I was in the middle of a lot of negotiations and it looked like I was going back to NBC. I talked to Ben and told him, "Listen, I'd like to take this with me." I think Ben smelled the opportunity. It would've made a great FX show, but I think he was like, "NBC? Well, that could be better."

Ben had Kevin's enthusiasm and support, but Jeff Zucker, the then president of NBC Entertainment, wasn't so sure.

BEN SILVERMAN: Kevin was like, "I may be the only person in the building who likes this, but I'll give you the pilot commitment." Little did he know, he was actually my *only* buyer at the time. He was the only one.

BRIAN BAUMGARTNER: Nobody was even considering it?

BEN SILVERMAN: No one! In all of television. Everyone else had passed.

HUMAN RESOURCES FILE

Kevin Reilly

Job Title: President of entertainment at FX (2000–2003); president of primetime entertainment (2003), then president of the entertainment division at NBC (2004–2007)

Hometown: Port Washington, New York

Training: Cornell University (ever heard of it?), Class of 1984, communications art major

Previous Employment: Manager of creative affairs at NBC; president of television at Brillstein-Grey Entertainment; helped develop shows like *Law & Order, NewsRadio, Just Shoot Me!, The Sopranos,* and *Saved by the Bell*

Post-Office Credits: Chief content officer, HBO Max (2018–2020); president of TNT, TBS, and chief creative officer for Turner Entertainment (2014 to 2020); president of entertainment at Fox Broadcasting Company (2007–2012) and chairman of entertainment (2012–2014)

Tech Support: Kevin the robot, Screech's sassy AI sidekick on *Saved by the Bell,* was named after him

Special Skills: Completely mute job interviews (as demonstrated in his season three *Office* cameo in "The Return")

BRIAN BAUMGARTNER: He had no idea?

BEN SILVERMAN: None.

We couldn't live with this terrible secret without sharing it with Kevin.

BRIAN BAUMGARTNER: Were you aware that when you discussed *The Office* with Ben, you were his only buyer?

KEVIN REILLY: [*Laughs.*] I am not surprised. Ben, in his way, always had me believe it was a long shot. "I think I can get it for you. I'll do my best, buddy." Anyone else in the broadcast networks at that time would've said, "No way." There really weren't a lot of buyers.

If Kevin Reilly had come to his senses, changed his mind, and said, "Nope, sorry, it's too big a risk for broadcast," our version of *The Office* might never have existed at all. But instead . . .

BEN SILVERMAN: Kevin's like, "Let's do it. Let's make it." I felt very good about it being there. NBC had a tradition of smart adult comedies. They're the highest aspiration in broadcast comedy in terms of quality. I loved *Cheers*, and *Family Ties*. And [former NBC president] Brandon Tartikoff was my role model and mentor. That's partially why I wanted to take *The Office* to NBC. Like I wanted to be part of that history of NBC comedies.

GREG DANIELS: It did not seem like a good idea to me. When I signed on to do the show, we were most likely going to sell it to HBO or FX. It was a big twist for me that after I agreed to do it, they switched it to NBC. I was also skeptical because everything on NBC was multicamera. *Will & Grace* was their number one show, which did not feel at all like *The Office*.

BRIAN BAUMGARTNER: How did you finally come around and decide to do it?

GREG DANIELS: I started to convince myself maybe the point of bringing *The Office* to a network like NBC was to move the ship of comedy in a different direction, towards something I liked more.

BRIAN BAUMGARTNER: So even if it failed miserably, you were doing your part?

GREG DANIELS: Yeah. Even if I just nudged it in that direction, maybe it would be valuable.

"Scraaaaan-ton"
The Office, **American Style**

By the summer of 2003, Ben and Greg were officially teamed up. They had their pilot commitment from NBC, and Greg began thinking, "What is the world of *The Office?*"

GREG DANIELS: I had this Margaret Mead metaphor that I liked to use. Mead was a cultural anthropologist who made her reputation going to some Samoan island and writing a book about the outlandish courting and mating rituals of the young people there.

Mead's 1928 book, *Coming of Age in Samoa*, documented the sexual habits of adolescent girls on the Samoan island of Ta'u.

GREG DANIELS: Somebody went back to the island thirty years later and the islanders were like, "Oh yeah, that old lady? We were telling her the craziest stuff." But I felt like the spirit of the show should be anthropology. An office is such a weird place that brings together all these different people and has its own unique culture. I thought it'd be interesting to approach the show like an anthropologist.

RICKY GERVAIS: I worked in an office for ten years, from 1989 to 1997, and that was the biggest influence on the show, the real life of being part of a working office. You're thrown together with random people and you have to get along. And David Brent, he was the Frankenstein's monster of those guys you knew growing up, like the teachers who sometimes embarrassed themselves, or your first boss who was an idiot. The people behaving in ways when they should know better.

Ricky had also observed a rising tide of corporate political correctness.

RICKY GERVAIS: People were being taught what to say and do, but they didn't really mean it. Guys like David Brent, they knew they couldn't be sexist upstairs because they'd get in trouble with HR. So they talked a good talk, lecturing about sexism, misogyny, and racism, but deep down they hadn't changed. They could get away with their bawdy jokes with the guys downstairs in the warehouse, who were untouched by this new PC culture. So Brent was caught between these two worlds.

If any of that sounds familiar, it's because David Brent was the model for Dunder Mifflin's boss, Michael Scott. Ben had developed ideas on how to connect the dots between Michael and other figures in American television history.

BEN SILVERMAN: The Michael Scott character was a version of Archie Bunker in *All in the Family*. He was similar to Homer Simpson as well, this political incorrectness married to the real world of the workplace. I felt the office itself as the location of the show was a very American conceit in a way. Office life and work life was really an American invention, and the shows and movies that informed Ricky's thinking came from a lot of what existed in America. I immediately saw the banality of the workplace and knew, having lived in those workplaces myself as an assistant and secretary when I was younger, that there's an underlying pathos there that hadn't yet been exploited in American television.

STEPHEN MERCHANT: I'm a big fan of American comedy. Like *Cheers*. The *Cheers* bar is this kind of surrogate family, which is very much what *The Office* is.

BRIAN BAUMGARTNER: It's funny that you bring up *Cheers*, because I always felt like our lineage in terms of American television was heavily weighted in *Cheers*. The difference with *Cheers* was these people had *chosen* to come to this place, day after day, and interact with each other. Whereas on *The Office*, they were forced into being together. But in both shows, the comedy came from a group of disparate people in the same place and how those relationships changed and evolved.

STEPHEN MERCHANT: We used to refer to Norm from *Cheers* a lot when developing the Tim character [who would become Jim in the American version]. If you remember, Norm had some sort of vague accountancy job that he didn't really like and was stuck in a rut. But he had a very dry sense of humor that he used to get through life. He was definitely an influence on the Tim character, as was Hawkeye from *M*A*S*H* [played by Alan Alda], which was another touchstone for us from American TV. Hawkeye used his wit in the face of, in his case, war. But it was the idea of using humor to get through the difficulties of life.

Ben and Greg set about creating their *Office*, deciding what to bring with them from the British version and what to leave behind. It remained a single-camera faux documentary, and like the British *Office*, they set it in a gloomy office park. They found a perfect backdrop in an old coal-mining city that was a little past its prime: Scranton, Pennsylvania.

GREG DANIELS: I wanted a place that was just outside of the city but nobody in New York ever visited. A place that was a little faded. There's something about the Northeast that feels like England to me in a lot of ways. With the weather, it's a little harder to live there. The people just seemed like they might be hiding their emotions somehow. I was reading John O'Hara, the short story writer, and he has a lot of stuff set in Scranton. I had a list of tons of cities that I thought would work, like Nashua [New Hampshire] and Yonkers [New York], but Scranton is a comedy word. It's got that hard K sound. *Scraaan-ton.*

But the key to the show's success, according to Stephen Merchant, had less to do with the specific location and more to do with the bittersweetness and melancholy of these characters.

STEPHEN MERCHANT: There was a show that was big in the UK when I was growing up in the seventies called *Whatever Happened to the Likely Lads?* The lyrics to the opening theme song was something like [sings], "Oh, what happened to you? / Whatever happened to me? / What became of the people we used to be?" I mean, it was all about failed opportunities and missed chances. So there's that sort of tradition in the UK, and I think traditionally in the U.S. that has not been so much the case in network TV. And when you think of *Friends,* it's very different.

BRIAN BAUMGARTNER: [*Sings.*] "I'll be there for you, you'll be there for me."

STEPHEN MERCHANT: So it seemed sensible to me that if they could rewire *The Office* at all, it would just be to maybe downplay some of those more cynical, sour British elements and dial up more of that American bright can-do optimism, without losing the fundamental DNA of what made the show work.

At the end of the day, Ricky and Stephen let Greg take the wheel.

STEPHEN MERCHANT: The one sensible advice I remember giving to Ricky was, from knowing a lot about American TV history and the attempts to translate British shows, they often failed when the original British people got involved. Because the British people came over and they thought, "Well, we're trying to do our thing here in America." And the truth is, they probably didn't know enough about America. They didn't know enough about the nuances or the subtleties of American culture. Or they were so busy trying to replicate the original that they couldn't find something fresh and new. Ricky and I, our biggest contribution initially was just taking a step back and trusting Greg to find the formula himself rather than meddling.

It may have been a gift that Ben and Greg didn't have to contend with too many cooks from the UK, but they still had a tough sell to make in the U.S.

BEN SILVERMAN: It was always like, "Okay, here's the pitch . . ."

GREG DANIELS: An unlikable lead.

BEN SILVERMAN: A single camera, and nobody in the cast is really attractive in a traditional television sense.

GREG DANIELS: Super awkward and slow.

BEN SILVERMAN: No laugh track, and a faux documentary. We know documentaries aren't popular. Now think about a *fake* documentary.

GREG DANIELS: The audience has to keep that in mind.

BEN SILVERMAN: And the camera is a character.

It was 2003, and two years had passed since Ben first fell in love with *The Office* on Henrietta's couch in London. Pressure was beginning to mount.

BEN SILVERMAN: I really thought, "Well, *Friends* is getting older. It's going to need a replacement." This is back when networks had lineups of shows that were similar. Like, you had a Friday night lineup with four family shows. *The Office* felt like it could be transformative. The British *Office* was critically beloved and BBC America had acquired it, so it was starting to get a little buzz within the United States.

But this was pre-Netflix, -Hulu, -YouTube, and -streaming in general. Not everyone was watching BBC America.

BEN SILVERMAN: I'm literally using my phone to tell people about the show. I'm calling them and sending them links and showing them [website] and pitching our take on it. I was telling people it will be the greatest show in the history of America. There was no comedy like this on in America today. And this hearkens back to the comedies of Norman Lear. We can do what those shows did. It's not just a *Baywatch* world, you know? It's not just a *Friends* world."

Not everyone shared his enthusiasm. Kevin Reilly may have greenlit the pilot, but he was still facing pushback from other executives at NBC.

KEVIN REILLY: There was still this thing that lived in the building post-*Friends* of "No, no, we want funny. But they're going to be sexy too, right? I mean, we need that." That had made its way into comedy, which had never been a part of comedy before. So I came in to NBC thinking, "*The Office* is exactly what we need to do." And a lot of people were like, "No, we need the next version of the next sexy single girl in New York living with some friends." And I was like, "No, we really don't." This was just the opposite of what everyone thought we needed, which was "Must See TV," which at that point had become almost a cliché.

So much about *The Office* was foreign to the upper echelon at NBC. They wanted a multicamera show about attractive urbanites dealing with minor obstacles. This most definitely wasn't that.

KEVIN REILLY: I had to listen to opinions about whether Americans associate documentaries with noncommercial heaviness. They're like, "It's just an obstructive format to most Americans." I'm just listening and thinking, "Oh my God, *really*?" Some of these people, they were professionals. They had their own lane of marketing or whatever they were in. But all I could think was, "Do you know what the F you're talking about?"

BRIAN BAUMGARTNER: But how confident were you that it could translate to a broadcast audience? At the time, a single-camera, mock-documentary, no-laugh-track sitcom just wasn't the norm on network television.

KEVIN REILLY: Yeah, but what I felt all along, from minute one, was that an office comedy is a staple of television. The tone is certainly different, and the lead's attitude is really different. But at the end of the day, you're not going to look at this and think, "I don't understand, what is it?"

BEN SILVERMAN: That is what the entertainment business is. You know, it's part of your life, every couple of months, you're basically playing the lottery. But the real lottery is the cultural lottery. The process, the production, the sales, the packaging, the negotiations, all that stuff aside, it's what the audience thinks that fucking matters. That's my scorecard in life. Everything else is irrelevant. My entire scorecard is based on cultural impact.

Despite the misgivings of basically everyone at NBC, except for Kevin Reilly, they had their pilot order. The news broke in January 2004, just as the UK *Office* won two Golden Globes for best TV comedy and best comedy actor (Ricky Gervais). But would the NBC remake ever make it on the air? Some critics were already recoiling at the idea. *San Francisco Chronicle* writer Tim Goodman predicted that "NBC will give us good-looking twentysomethings in Manhattan, chewing scenery to the deafening tune of a laugh track." We'd come this far despite improbable odds, but as Steve Carell noted . . .

STEVE CARELL ("MICHAEL SCOTT"): We were all hanging by a thread.

The entire history of *The Office*, summed up in one sentence.

How did this show that every reasonable person predicted wouldn't make it beyond a pilot somehow become one of the most iconic and beloved shows in modern TV? How did a show with so much against it—a history of American remakes of British shows sucking, a showrunner whose last hit was animated, a network that preferred comedy with chiseled chins and perky optimism—rise above all that to become . . . well, *The Office*?

Ben Silverman and Howard Klein, executive producers of *The Office*.

2

"Scranton Hot"

CASTING THE LOVABLE MISFITS OF DUNDER MIFFLIN

AN OPTIMISTIC SEASON ONE CAST.

BEN SILVERMAN: I just wanted to get this thing made. It's the summer of 2003 and I'm like eighteen months into this project and we haven't even shot a page of script yet. The show is getting bigger and bigger in the UK. It's been picked up for a second season. I've landed Greg Daniels to adapt it. I've gotten Ricky and Stephen and the BBC to sign off on it. I have one buyer who's shifted from one network to another with more authority and an ability to do it, and now I want to make it. So the next hurdle is casting.

BRIAN BAUMGARTNER: That's one hell of a hurdle.

BEN SILVERMAN: Casting was key to this show's architecture. I knew that the characters and who we cast had to be real and not too pretty. That was one thing we all agreed on and it was another leap of faith from the broadcast network. We were going to try and do something more experimental.

BRIAN BAUMGARTNER: So who was discussed in that first casting meeting? It was me, wasn't it?

BEN SILVERMAN: It was *all* about Brian Baumgartner. [*Laughs.*] Telling the story just reminds me of how many millions of elements had to come together to create anything meaningful or successful.

It's hard to imagine now, with *The Office* such a fixture in pop culture, but the actors didn't just walk into their roles and inhabit them. The process of finding the perfect mix of characters—the people you looked at and immediately thought, "Well, of course that's Dwight, of course that's Jim and Pam, who else could they be?"—was a long and sometimes nerve-racking road.

Before *The Office*, we were just a bunch of actors (and some nonactors) looking for our big break.

JENNA FISCHER ("PAM BEESLY"): Before *The Office*? I was a struggling actress. I was auditioning for anything and everything I could. I had done a pilot called *Rubbing Charlie*. That's real.

BRIAN BAUMGARTNER: Really? [*Laughs.*]

JENNA FISCHER: Starring Scott Wolf and myself.

BRIAN BAUMGARTNER: Were you . . . rubbing Scott Wolf?

JENNA FISCHER: Yeah, he was Charlie. And I rubbed him 'cause I was a masseuse.

BRIAN BAUMGARTNER: So it was really *your* pilot?

JENNA FISCHER: It was really about Charlie. The more accurate title might have been *Charlie Is Rubbed*. That was 2002, and at this point I was finally making a living as an actor for one year. I had been in Los Angeles over seven years, but I was finally earning all of my living from just acting. And then the pilot wasn't picked up.

RAINN WILSON ("DWIGHT SCHRUTE"): Before *The Office*—well, going way, way back—I did theater for about ten years in New York before I did any TV or film. So really, I was a theater actor. I came out to L.A.

Assistant (to the) Regional Manager Dwight Schrute (Rainn Wilson).

in '99, and through 2001 or 2003, it was a lot of struggling and toiling around, doing commercial auditions and voice-over auditions and little guest spots on TV shows. I was on *Charmed* and *CSI* and—

BRIAN BAUMGARTNER: I did *CSI*!

RAINN WILSON: You did *CSI* too?

BRIAN BAUMGARTNER: I was a "furry," a guy who gets sexual gratification out of wearing a big furry suit.

Brian appeared in the *CSI* season four episode "Fur and Loathing," first broadcast in October 2003.

RAINN WILSON: I was Creepy Guy in Supermarket. I'm not kidding. Creepy Guy in Supermarket.

Rainn appeared in the first season finale, "The Strip Strangler," which originally aired in May 2001.

OSCAR NUÑEZ ("OSCAR MARTINEZ"): I was auditioning stuff, but my day jobs were catering and babysitting.

ANGELA KINSEY ("ANGELA MARTIN"): I was working at the ImprovOlympic, iO West, an improv comedy theater in Los Angeles. I helped run the training center and performed there any time they'd give me stage time. So usually about three nights a week I did improv. I was in a show with Kate Flannery, who ended up playing Meredith on *The Office*. The name of our show was *Girl Team Balls*. It was Sunday night at like ten o'clock, which is *really* when you want to see comedy.

JENNA FISCHER: I was putting my heart out there and I just thought, "I'm going to become a vet technician." I was very sure. I was working with an animal rescue group and taking care of cats in my own home. I was learning how to do things like fluids and all kinds of medical things. Neutering and releasing cats in the wild.

CREED BRATTON (THE ONE AND THE SAME): I did a bunch of stuff before *The Office*. *Quincy* and *Eight Is Enough* and a bunch of TV movies and things. John Crosby, the famous agent, saw me in a play with Beau Bridges, and I had my hair and I was very, very confident. So he signed me and I didn't have to go out or anything. He just said, "You got a job over here." Back in those days, they would just say, "You got a job over here."

BRIAN BAUMGARTNER: You lived a rock star life.

CREED BRATTON: Oh God, yeah. For years. Lucky to be alive.

BRIAN BAUMGARTNER: John Krasinski and I talked about this all the time. You'd walk in and begin to tell a story, and it was so outlandish that it couldn't possibly be true. But maybe it is.

CREED BRATTON: I might have embellished it a little bit, Brian. Do you know what I mean? But I don't have to embellish much.

BRIAN BAUMGARTNER: You don't, bro. You partied with Jim Morrison.

CREED BRATTON: I hung out with that band all the time. John Densmore [the Doors' drummer] was the best man at my wedding. And that's all real.

JOHN KRASINSKI ("JIM HALPERT"): I'd just gotten a manager in New York. I'd gone out to L.A. to shoot this pilot and I thought that was the greatest thing in the world. And then they immediately didn't pick it up and I thought my life was over.

JENNA FISCHER: I made a grandiose announcement to my management and agents that I would be quitting acting. I couldn't take it anymore. I couldn't take the rejection. And my manager said to me, "Jenna, will you give us one more year? You're so close, you really are." My acting coach yelled at me and said, "Don't be stupid, you're doing great. This is what an actor's life is! It's a series of minor accomplishments and tons of rejection. This is being an actor, you're doing it!" So I said, "Okay, I'll do one more year."

JOHN KRASINSKI: Before I left L.A., my manager said, "You should meet this person, Allison Jones." So I went by and met her and wanted her to adopt me. And then she said, "You should pay attention to this thing coming out soon. It's called *The Office* and you should come in for it."

You may not recognize the name Allison Jones, but she's the reason you know any of the actors on *The Office.*

JENNA FISCHER: I'd been auditioning for Allison for years and gotten a few things. My very first speaking role on television was for *Spin City,* the Charlie Sheen years, which was cast by Allison. She called me in for a Steven Spielberg miniseries that I bombed. It went nowhere. I was horrible. And she said, "Maybe drama is not your thing." [*Laughs.*]

Even before signing on to populate the Scranton branch of Dunder Mifflin, Allison had already helped change the face of television, curating the unconventional casts for shows like *The Golden Girls, The Fresh Prince of Bel-Air,* and *Boy Meets World.* But by the late '90s, she was yearning for something different.

ALLISON JONES (CASTING DIRECTOR): I'd just finished a pilot called *Roswell High* for the WB [which eventually became *Roswell*]. Every actor had to look like the kids from *Dawson's Creek.* It was torture. Every kid had to be beautiful and blah blah blah blah. We tested

Heath Ledger and he wasn't even cute enough to be on the show. So all the rejects from that, I gladly brought in for *Freaks and Geeks*.

For the short-lived but beloved NBC dramedy about Michigan high schoolers, Allison assembled a motley crew of unknowns like Jason Segel, James Franco, Seth Rogen, Linda Cardellini, and Busy Philipps.

ALLISON JONES: They were so much more interesting and talented. And it was great that [creator] Paul [Feig] and [executive producer] Judd [Apatow] just wanted real kids. I think I love watching people. [Growing up], I hung out with nerds and sympathized with them and was one myself a little bit. *Freaks and Geeks* was kind of the first cool show I worked on, which is probably why it failed. [It] changed the whole scene of comedy. The writing, the reality rhythm, the non-beautiful people. [It was] the first time I'd ever done anything like that. 'Cause all the teen shows at the time, the kids had to be beautiful and twenty-five.

But it caught the eye of executive producer Greg Daniels.

GREG DANIELS: While I was at Fox, I did a pilot that was based on me growing up in New York [*Life's Too Short,* starring Michael McKean and Samm Levine]. It was like a *Seinfeld*-y family show. I was casting it right when *Freaks and Geeks* had been canceled [in 2000]. I saw all of the kids from the show, and a lot of them burst into tears in their audition 'cause they were so sad that their show got canceled. I ended up using Samm Levine. But anyway, I was really into *Freaks and Geeks*. I really liked Allison's choices. When I started thinking of all of the casting directors I could go to for *The Office,* I was like, "I want to work with *her.*"

Allison had a secret weapon, her casting associate Phyllis Smith.

Phyllis Smith

Occupation: Actress

Hometown: Lemay, Missouri

Training: University of Missouri–St. Louis, Class of 1972, B.A. in elementary education

Previous Employment: Cheerleader for the St. Louis Cardinals football team (1973), burlesque performer with Will B. Able and his Baggy Pants Revue (mid-'70s)

Post-Office Credits: Played "Sadness" in the movie *Inside Out* (2015); recurring role in Netflix drama *The OA* (2016–2019)

Special Skills: Tap dancing, ballet, basketball, doing her taxes while shooting *Office* B-roll scenes

Overtime Hours: Was cast as Steve Carell's mom in *The 40-Year-Old Virgin* but their scenes together were cut

Allison and Phyllis had worked together since the late '90s, and though Phyllis didn't have acting ambitions, she did have some experience in front of the camera.

PHYLLIS SMITH ("PHYLLIS VANCE"): I was working as a receptionist in an aerospace defense company in Sherman Oaks. A friend of mine who worked for Stu Billett Productions called and said, "Phyllis, they need a mousy woman for a court show." I really didn't want to, but I had one hour for lunch, so I drove over the hill [into the San Fernando Valley] to do this audition. This was in the olden days when we wore nylons, and I went to the bathroom, and as I was pulling them up, I ripped a huge hole. My entire knee was out.

ALLISON JONES: Who called you about it?

PHYLLIS SMITH: Oh, poop, I can't think of her name. We ended up in a conversation. I wasn't mousy enough to be the mousy woman, but in the course of the conversation, I said, "I think I might be good at casting." About a year later, she called me and that's how I ended up [in casting].

The bulk of TV pilots are cast in January and February, then rushed into filming in March. But Greg Daniels decided to take a different approach with *The Office*. He *started* the audition process in October 2003.

GREG DANIELS: We went into this really long casting process and for some reason we were off cycle. I was really happy, because there were so many aspects to factory television that reduced the quality. And one of them was trying to cast when every single other pilot was casting. So we were casting in the fall, which is not when they cast, and we had at least three months and we saw everybody.

ALLISON JONES: We did it the old-fashioned way, with headshots. People would send headshots physically in the mail and we would look at them.

GREG DANIELS: Allison is a huge student of comedy and knows everything. She sees every show, knows every person, goes to every improv group.

PHYLLIS SMITH: I'm not just saying this 'cause she's sitting here, but she can remember every actor that not only opened their mouth to her but just walked through a room. She just had an eye. She had an eye for somebody that was unique and different.

GREG DANIELS: We set up in one of those bungalows on the Universal lot. It was pretty much me and Allison and Phyllis and Teri Weinberg and Howard Klein. That was the general crew for all the casting. It was kind of funny because the bungalow was in earshot of the tram, the Universal Studios tour. The tram would go by, and they used to say something like, "In these bungalows, the television shows of the future are being made." [*Laughs.*] We had to hear it over and over again.

ALLISON JONES: I always liked to cast non-star people. I think it pays off the most in the end. Getting the people that I've known for years, who I know can step it up and be really interesting and funny. People from the Groundlings and the UCB [Upright Citizens Brigade] that just did not get a break. It was really fun to put them together with terrifically beautiful, subtle writing.

"Too Weird for TV"
Assembling the Cast

BRIAN BAUMGARTNER: Were you aware of the British version of *The Office*?

RAINN WILSON: I was. My college friend Sam Catlin [a writer on *Breaking Bad* and showrunner for the AMC series *Preacher*] had somehow gotten an advance DVD of the first episode, and he even had a British DVD player. So I was truly one of the first people to see it in the United States. We loved it, we were blown away. And then he got his hands on a couple more episodes and we'd have dinner and watch two or three more episodes.

JOHN KRASINSKI: I'd seen and fallen in love with the British show. I was down at Virgin Records—remember that store?—I went to the Virgin Records in Union Square and bought the special edition in the black DVD case. I binge-watched the whole thing.

ANGELA KINSEY: I was a huge fan. Huge fan. I thought it was amazing. I grew up with a lot of British television 'cause I grew up overseas. [Her family moved to Indonesia when she was two years old.] I grew up on *Fawlty Towers* and *Good Neighbors,* so that kind of sense of humor really appealed to me.

KEN KWAPIS (DIRECTOR OF *THE OFFICE* PILOT): I hadn't seen much of it. I think I may have only seen the pilot episode of the British show, so I quickly watched as much as I could. I'm not even sure if the Christmas special was out yet.

BRIAN BAUMGARTNER: I was a nerd and a theater actor and I wasn't making any money, but I was one of the first people, at least at my level, who owned a TiVo. And I TiVo'd everything. I watched everything. I watched it on BBC America, but maybe it was just the first season that we were able to get over here. I can't remember. So when I heard they were doing an American version, I went to my agent at the time and said, "*This* is the show. This is the show that I must be on. They've gotta be looking for unknown people." My agent said to me, and this is a direct quote, "They're looking for unknown people, but not like you. Unknown, but not *totally* unknown."

JENNA FISCHER: In the breakdown for the casting call, it said "Unknown Actors Only." This was why I'd been so frustrated and wanted to give up. I would go through these long audition processes for television shows and I would get as far as the on-camera test part, and then they would give it to Alyson Hannigan [Willow from *Buffy the Vampire Slayer*]. I could not break through Alyson Hannigan.

ALLISON JONES: The unknown thing was not a mandate, but it was understood. It was the same with *Freaks and Geeks*. It wasn't articulated much; it was just sort of obvious that you needed new faces.

Angela Kinsey and Jenna Fischer:
Two unknown actors in an unknown office.

JENNA FISCHER: I was this unknown actor and I had absolutely nothing to offer a billboard on Sunset Boulevard. I had no name recognition. So I couldn't get these big lead parts until *The Office,* when finally the thing that had been working against me was my gift, which was that I was unknown.

BRIAN BAUMGARTNER: Was there pushback from the network about that?

ALLISON JONES: Some pushback, but the network then was not as intrusive as they are now. They don't see every single goddamn audition before they approve who we tested. We just told them who we're testing.

KEN KWAPIS: There probably were a few contenders who had a higher profile. But I think at the end of the day, Greg's instincts were right. That it should be a show where you're not only discovering a group of actors, but it really does fool you into thinking you're eavesdropping on a real office.

BRIAN BAUMGARTNER: I remember hearing the phrase "Scranton hot" used at some point. Do you remember those conversations?

ALLISON JONES: "Scranton hot" sounds familiar. It's like when we did *Veep,* they had to be Washington, D.C., attractive, not *real* attractive. They had to look basically dumpy. "Scranton hot" was definitely a thing.

GREG DANIELS: Because it's a documentary at an ordinary paper company, the people do not have to be incredibly good-looking. No disrespect to anyone. But if you picture a show like *Friends,* they're all hot. I think that the mockumentary thing allows you to cast for comedy and charisma above all other things.

ALLISON JONES: Greg had us bring in a lot of his friends who wrote for *The Simpsons,* who were awesomely weird and great.

GREG DANIELS: I brought in Mike Reiss, one of the original head writers of *The Simpsons,* and this writer I knew named Chuck Tatham.

ALLISON JONES: It was the first time I realized writers were just as funny as actors when it came to this kind of comedy, if not more so. Some of those people, God bless them, were too weird for TV.

GREG DANIELS: The first person I hired for anything on *The Office* was B. J. Novak. He was a writer-performer hire. Writer-performers were great on *SNL* when I was a writer [between 1987 and 1990]. And also, one of my favorite shows growing up was *Monty Python's Flying Circus,* and they're all writer-performers.

ALLISON JONES: B.J. came in and gave a little speech saying how he would just love to be in this project blah blah blah. I don't want to say groveling, but that comes to mind. A lot of people did that. It was cute.

GREG DANIELS: I saw B.J. do stand-up, and he made a joke about not learning much in college 'cause he had a double major: psychology, reverse psychology. I was like, "Wow, that's a damn good joke."

"Dare to Bore Me"
The Auditions

KEN KWAPIS: I remember when Jenna came in for the screen tests. She was sitting a little bit apart from other people, and all the other candidates were being super chatty and friendly and gregarious. And Jenna was very quiet. She put out such a wallflower vibe that I actually started wondering if she was there by mistake, that she was actually there to interview for a receptionist job.

JENNA FISCHER: I had a monologue that was scripted, and I did the scene where Michael fires Pam and she calls him a jerk, where he fake fires her as a joke. Greg was there at my first audition. I remember Greg wringing his hands, like he couldn't believe he's going to start this project and he's so excited. The way he was looking at me, he seemed very curious, kind of like, "She's not doing much."

GREG DANIELS: Jenna came in and kind of blew my mind, because I didn't understand it. I was like, she doesn't appear to be acting. She appears to simply *be* Pam.

KEN KWAPIS: Of course, she was completely in it. She was *in* it. But I was so thrown. I thought, "Maybe she misread the notice."

JENNA FISCHER: I improvised an interview with Greg.

GREG DANIELS: I had all these weird questions for her that were like, well, you wouldn't ask an actor. I was like, "Where have you worked?" It was like a real interview for a receptionist.

JENNA FISCHER: My take on it was this girl Pam was being forced by her insane boss, Michael, to be part of a documentary that she cared nothing about. And Pam has had no media training whatsoever. So I thought, okay, if that is my circumstance, what would I do in this real situation? So Greg starts this interview with me and he says, "Pam, do you like being a receptionist here at Dunder Mifflin?" And I just said, "No." That's it. That's all I said. I sort of thought about the question. And then I said no. He waited for me to say more and I didn't and I just sat there, and then he started laughing and then he kept asking me more questions. I thought, "He's either going to love this or hate it, right?"

ALLISON JONES: We used to tell the actors, "If you think you're doing too little, you're still doing too much." Right? We gave the "less is more" direction to everybody.

JENNA FISCHER: Allison told me, "Please do not come in and do a bunch of comedy shtick. A portion of the audition is going to be improvisation, but we're not looking for slick and clever, in your face. Just play it real." And then she told me, "Jenna, dare to bore me." I'll never forget those four words. "Dare to bore me."

ALLISON JONES: We tested other Pams, but I think Jenna was sort of the high bar. Kristen Wiig auditioned for the part and she was terrific. But for some reason I didn't bring her back for Greg. I usually bring back anybody who's good and I'm embarrassed I didn't bring back Kristen.

JENNA FISCHER: I believed with my whole heart that this was the part for me. I believed I was the one who should play it. And I thought, "If they don't pick me, then they're not doing the show I think they're doing."

RAINN WILSON: It was one of those rare times where I was like, "This part is mine."

JENNA FISCHER: I am literally the only person who should play this part. This is mine.

RAINN WILSON: No one knows this world of total white trash nerd-dom. This is my thing.

HUMAN RESOURCES FILE

Jenna Fischer

Occupation: Actress

Hometown: St. Louis, Missouri

Training: Truman State University, Class of 1995, B.A. in theater and journalism

Previous Employment: Waitress at Long John Silver's; telephone psychic (though never collected a paycheck because it felt like "dirty money"); performer in a sex-ed video for psychiatric patients; cameos in *Spin City* (2001), *Undeclared* (2001), *That '70s Show* (2005), *Six Feet Under* (2005)

Post-Office Credits: Starring roles on ABC series *Splitting Up Together* (2018–2019) and NBC miniseries *You, Me and the Apocalypse* (2015)

Special Skills: Types eighty-five words per minute with 90 percent accuracy

Emergency Contact: Jim (her father, not her fictional boyfriend/fiancé/husband on *The Office*); Dwight (her brother-in-law, not her fictional nemesis on *The Office*)

Possible Disciplinary Action: Stole prop engagement ring given to her by fictional boyfriend/fiancé/husband Jim

John Krasinski

Occupation: Actor, director, producer

Hometown: Boston, Massachusetts

Training: Brown University, Class of 2001, B.A. in English

Previous Employment: Daddy Warbucks in a sixth grade school production of *Annie* (1991); writing intern on *Late Night with Conan O'Brien* (2000); small roles in *Ed* (2003) and *Law & Order: Criminal Intent* (2004)

Post-*Office* Credits: Director, star, and cowriter of horror film *A Quiet Place* (2018), nominated for Critics Choice and Writers Guild screenwriting awards; plays titular character in Amazon spy thriller series *Jack Ryan* (2018–present)

Office Friendships: On the same high school Little League baseball team with B. J. Novak

Special Skills: Taught English as a foreign language in Costa Rica

JOHN KRASINSKI: My manager called and said, "They want you to come in for the show called *The Office*." I was still waiting tables, and I don't know where I got the confidence to go, "I don't want to go in for Dwight. Let me know when they're doing the Jim character." And they basically said, like, "How dare you?" They were very upset. My manager said, "Wow, that didn't go great." But then very luckily for me, four weeks later they still hadn't found a Jim, and they were like, "Now you can come in for Jim."

JENNA FISCHER: I remember the three other Pams so vividly. There was this one Pam who had on knee-high leather boots and I was so judgmental. I was like, "Oh, honey, Pam would never wear boots like that."

JOHN KRASINSKI: We were all in this room doing auditions, and I remember I got really nervous. Man, this is like a flashback. I'm having like an acid flashback. B. J. Novak walked in, who I hadn't seen really since high school. We went to high school together [Newton South High School in Massachusetts]. That really blew my brain out. I mean, imagine somebody from your high school walking into a scenario that's already bizarro. I was so nervous, and then I got more nervous because B.J. had acted and directed everything at high school, and I was barely an actor. I mean, I wasn't an actor, I was a waiter. I was like, "Ooh, what part are you going out for?" And he was like, "I'm doing this part called Ryan." And I was like, "You're not going for Jim? Cool, man, that's awesome."

ALLISON JONES: John was effortless. Effortless. I'd seen him in a [Kodak] commercial where he got his head shaved or something. And I remember a casting director in New York saying, "This kid John Krasinski is effortlessly funny. You won't believe how he's funny. He just talks and he's funny." I put him on tape in New York. We were wearing the same man's J.Crew sweater. I remember thinking, "Oh, shit, I hope he doesn't notice." His was brown, mine was green.

JOHN KRASINSKI: While I was in the waiting room at 30 Rock, six Jims that looked identical to me went in and did their auditions, and when they left they were high-fiving each other. I was the last one. Right at that exact moment, they were like, "We're going to take a lunch break for an hour." And I was like, "Ooh, maybe see one more? Can we get one more in?" Someone sat down across from me with a salad and said, "You nervous?" And I said, "No, you know, you either get these things or you don't. But I'm terrified for the person creating the show because, I mean, I just feel like Americans have such a track record of taking brilliant shows and ruining them." And he goes, "I'll try not to. My name's Greg Daniels. I'm the executive producer." I definitely did that green vomit face. I swear to God. I went out in the hallway and threw up in my mouth. And then I called my manager and said, "I'm going to leave now. There's no way I can go into this room." And he was like, "You have to." I remember opening the door to uproarious laughter and it was not laughter with me. It was definitely laughter *at* me. I remember Greg telling me later, "I'll never forget that you told me that. It really helped your audition, 'cause you were really honest. That's a vibe I want on this show. Someone who will be honest and make sure that we're all doing good work." Now I go into every audition for anything with an attitude of "So this movie sucks." [*Laughs.*] Hasn't worked since, but . . .

"It Sounds Like a Fairy Tale"
Finding the Perfect Jim, Pam, and Dwight

GREG DANIELS: When I started to adapt the show, I tried to take it apart like a watchmaker and see how it was constructed and then put it back together. And I thought it was really brilliantly constructed for those four characters because they each are connected to each other in different ways. Pam and Michael have a relationship, so when you're doing all the Pams, you've got to test them against the Michaels, see how they work. And Dwight has to be tested against the Jims and the Michaels.

ALLISON JONES: He used to graph the qualities of actors. He'd put down what he needed and what he saw in each of them. He had a very scientific mind when it came to things like that. And of course that drove me nuts.

GREG DANIELS: Yeah, I'm super methodical. I feel like if I have time to make a decision, I'm going to chase down every option.

ALLISON JONES: We were in a casting session once. Do you remember this, Phyllis? We were all sitting at a conference table in this room. There was a lull and all of a sudden Greg just gets up and jumps out of the window.

PHYLLIS SMITH: Fortunately the window was close to the ground. It was in a Universal bungalow. But we were all like, "What just happened?"

ALLISON JONES: And then [casting director] Nancy Perkins said in a thick Boston accent, "My God, I've heard of producers wanting to jump out the window before, but he *just did it!*"

PHYLLIS SMITH: I don't know why he did it, but it was funny.

ALLISON JONES: He needed to get a sweater in his car or something.

KEN KWAPIS: There were a lot of people saying, "This is going to fail because no network will allow you to do what they did in the UK version." But Greg was leading the charge that it wouldn't work unless it had the same offbeat quality of the original. That affected every decision, including not bringing the finalists for a role in front of a bunch of really humorless network executives.

JENNA FISCHER: Normally when you test for a show, you perform your scenes live in front of a conference room full of executives. You do a live audition for them.

ALLISON JONES: You'd tell the actors, "Okay, be funny." That was the sitcom way to do it. And it didn't matter the level of subtlety.

TERI WEINBERG (CO-EXECUTIVE PRODUCER): We thought, if we go into a room, they'll never make this show. They'll just say, "Oh, well, that's a huge mistake. *Huge.*" We wanted to give the actors an opportunity to really create the chemistry, and you could feel the unusual kind of rhythms and the beats that the actors would take depending on what the scene was.

GREG DANIELS: We got this idea to do old-fashioned screen tests. We blocked off three days and took the different top three or four candidates for each role and we pitted them together in different improvs and filmed it.

JENNA FISCHER: We were told that because the camera was such an essential part of our show and relating to the camera was so important, that they wanted to do an on-camera series of test scenes with the final four actors for each part.

TERI WEINBERG: We were able to actually kind of produce them, 'cause Ken directed everybody. And we were able to take some time to make sure we got the best takes. I think we were the first of its kind. And I think because of that, it started to kind of shift the way people were auditioning.

JENNA FISCHER: They called us into an actual office building for two days and they mixed and matched us and they taped us doing scenes.

KEN KWAPIS: What was really unusual is that we actually shot those screen tests on the bullpen of what became Dunder Mifflin. We were actually shooting screen tests in the location. It just changed the whole tenor of how the cast played the scenes.

JENNA FISCHER: We were able to give those looks to the camera. We were able to react when we noticed the camera was there when we thought it wasn't. That was, it really was such a huge element of the show. Greg's other argument for doing it that way was that the show was small and the moments that played the biggest were small moments. He didn't really feel like auditioning in a conference room was going to give the executives the right feel for what he was going for, what the show was.

GREG DANIELS: It was great for Ken 'cause he worked out a lot about the shooting style doing this.

KEN KWAPIS: Greg asked the actors to do a lot of improvisation. And sometimes we were working on scenes that ended up being in the pilot.

RAINN WILSON: I just completely improvised off the top of my head. I said something that later ended up in an episode. I said, "Dwight Schrute, named after my father, Dwight Schrute, named after his father, Dwide Schrude. Amish." So somewhere in the back of Dwight's ancestry was someone named Dwide Schrude.

GREG DANIELS: It was fun for me too, because I came up with lots of little improv games.

TERI WEINBERG: I don't think any one of us had ever really kind of been through anything like that before. Actors would come in and read a scene, and then they would improv, and Greg would throw ridiculous little lines out or say things like, "Tell me how you got into your refrigerator this morning." Just these really kind of weird, random things.

JOHN KRASINSKI: They did one where I had to go to the bathroom and I asked Rainn to watch my phone. He did this thing where he pretended security doors were coming down. And he was so good. He was so infuriating in the best way, like as his character.

RAINN WILSON: That was not really my gig. I didn't do the Upright Citizens Brigade or the Groundlings. I wasn't really an improv guy, but I did improv pretty well.

JOHN KRASINSKI: It was so incredible. And by the end, I think I broke and laughed because he was so infuriating. I remember leaving the scene being like, "He might get it because I'm actually so annoyed being in this room with him." As John Krasinski rather than Jim Halpert. He was so good at what he was doing. He was making me physically angry.

RAINN WILSON: After I was cast, Greg came to me and said in a very diplomatic way, "You improvise better than you act when you're on script. When you're doing scripted stuff, it feels a little heavy and a little forced." This was before we were going to shoot the pilot. It kept me up at night. I was like, "Oh shit, what does that mean? I'm a good improviser and a terrible, terrible regular actor." So I begged my manager to see the audition tapes. And sure enough, he was right. When I improvised, it was a little looser, a little more off the cuff and weirder. When I was doing scripted stuff, I don't want to say it sounded like a theater actor, but it sounded scripted. It didn't have that documentary feel. It was a great learning experience for me as an actor.

JOHN KRASINSKI: I know it sounds like a fairy tale, but I remember Jenna Fischer walking in, and as soon as she crossed the threshold on the door, I was like, "Well, that's it. That is exactly who should play Pam. I hope she can put two words together because she has the part."

GREG DANIELS: There was one part of me, in trying to get an interesting love story with Pam and Jim, that thought maybe it should be an interracial love story. I had one version of it where Craig Robinson was Roy, not Darryl. There was a really likable actress, Erica Vittina Phillips, and I was like, "Well, could *she* be Pam?" But she was a pretty distant second to Jenna. She was the one where you're like, "Duh, this is Pam." I felt like that about John too. There were some other good guys for Jim, but not close to John.

JOHN KRASINSKI: What happened was I watched Jenna go in with all the other Jims and I was like, "She's the tipping point. She's it." I remember saying to myself, alone in a corner, "If I don't go in with her, I know I don't have it." Then I walked in and saw Jenna, and I was like, "I'm back! I have a shot."

JENNA FISCHER: It was very clear to me that John was Jim and I believed I was Pam. People ask a lot about chemistry. What is chemistry? Chemistry doesn't mean that John and I are in love in real life. Chemistry means that there was no other person who made me feel more like Pam than John Krasinski when he was being Jim. There was something completely effortless about being Pam when I was around him. He just locked me into the character.

JOHN KRASINSKI: I obviously had no filter as a child, because after the audition, I turned to her and was like, "You know you're going to get the part, right?" And she was like, "Oh my God, I said the same thing about you. As soon as I saw you, I was like, 'That's Jim.'" It was really weird.

JENNA FISCHER: Not only did I think he was the best Jim, I thought I can do the best job as Pam if he's Jim. So when they told me I was Pam, I had to know. Is John Krasinski Jim?

JOHN KRASINSKI: When I got the part, which was amazing, I legit jumped on a couch and probably twisted my ankle 'cause I think I went in the crack. The only question I asked my manager at the time was, "Did Jenna Fischer get it?" It was like I didn't even get fully happy until I knew that she was doing the part.

JENNA FISCHER: And they said yes. And I was like, "Okay, then we're going to be fine." 'Cause I was a little worried. If it's not him, I hope I can still do it.

A trio cast (or made?) in heaven: Jenna, John, and Rainn.

"Ten Percent More Hope"

THE SEARCH FOR MICHAEL SCOTT

GREG DANIELS: *Before we started casting anyone or hiring the casting director, Ben had the lead on Steve Carell from [Universal CEO] Stacey Snider.*

BEN SILVERMAN: *She calls me on the lot and says, "Ben, I love The Office. It's so brilliant. It's so awesome." She knew more about it than almost anyone else in television, because she was always looking overseas for content. And she had an idea for me. What about Steve Carell for the lead? She said, "Have you seen Bruce Almighty? He does this fifteen-minute thing and it's the most brilliant comedic tour de force I've seen. And we're developing a movie for him, 40-Year-Old Virgin, and I think he's going to be a major star."*

GREG DANIELS: *We watched his scene in Bruce Almighty and said he would be terrific, so we asked his managers to tell us if he got any other offers. But I've got a process. We started negotiating*

with Allison Jones to be the casting director. I didn't want to hire Allison and just tell her we already cast the lead. It took two weeks to do Allison's deal as a casting director. And in those two weeks, Steve took Come to Papa.*

BEN SILVERMAN: *It was a short-lived NBC sitcom and he was like the fourth lead.*

BEN SILVERMAN: *When we found Rainn Wilson, we really thought maybe he could be Michael Scott. We weren't positive if he could be, but we were gonna bring him into our casting world and see what role worked for him.*

RAINN WILSON: *On that first audition, I auditioned for both Michael and Dwight. And my Michael was just terrible.*

BEN SILVERMAN: *He went back and looked at his tape, and he was so embarrassed and horrified at his Michael Scott because he realized he was*

essentially doing an imitation of Ricky Gervais.

GREG DANIELS: I remember taping myself on a video camera late at night, doing the sides for Michael. 'Cause I was like, I don't even know what to tell them, you know? I did it a bunch of times, and I realized that one of the keys for people trying out for Michael was that he's thinking that if he does a good job on this documentary, maybe Jennifer Aniston will watch it. That's in the back of his head.

BEN SILVERMAN: We kept adding cast members, but no lead. I am panicking. We don't have Michael Scott. We've got a troupe of assembled talent on a clock, because you start assembling this cast and you don't get them forever. You basically have an option on them for a window of time and then you lose them. So we're dealing with all these extensions and expansions because we've now been casting for longer than you'd normally cast a show. We've been casting this thing for

months when normally you cast for weeks.

ALLISON JONES: Ben talked about Paul Giamatti and Philip Seymour Hoffman. At the time, movie stars wouldn't touch television. Wouldn't touch it. Bottom of the barrel. Giamatti just said no right off the bat. Then we went to Hoffman, the late great Philip Seymour Hoffman, and he said no as well. We rejected a lot of great people. I mean, Adam Scott right off the bat. Greg and I really liked Patton Oswalt for Michael Scott. He gave, of course, a fantastic reading and was a stand-up at the time. Louis C.K. wasn't available and he had a deal at CBS.

BEN SILVERMAN: Our immediate short list for the Michael Scott character was Bob Odenkirk.

ALLISON JONES: I wanted Bob for a long time. He was like the king of this kind of comedy. He sort of invented it with David Cross [on the HBO underground hit Mr. Show with Bob and David]. I couldn't believe he even came in for it.

Steve Carell

Occupation: Actor, writer, director

Hometown: Acton, Massachusetts

Training: Denison University, Class of 1984, B.A. in history

Previous Employment: Postal carrier in Littleton, Massachusetts (1984), Second City performer (1991–1994), *The Daily Show* correspondent (1999–2004)

Post-Office Credits: Starring roles in movies like *Foxcatcher* (2014), *The Big Short* (2015), *Battle of the Sexes* (2017), *Beautiful Boy* (2018), and *Irresistible* (2020); starring roles in TV series *The Morning Show* (Apple TV+, 2019–2020) and *Space Force* (Netflix, 2020)

Side Project: Owner and proprietor of the Marshfield Hills General Store in Marshfield Hills, Massachusetts

Sick Leave: Called in sick during the 2007 writers strike with a case of "enlarged balls"

Special Skills: Hockey; plays the fife

Emergency Contact: Nancy Carell (also known as Carol Stills, Scranton's leading real estate agent)

GREG DANIELS: We looked at everyone in town but Carell. But then at the end of the process, we still missed Carell.

BEN SILVERMAN: I call Kevin Reilly [a reminder: NBC's president of prime-time development] and I'm like, "You've got this guy in your show, but he has to be *our* guy." And he goes, "You didn't hear it from me, but I don't think *Come to Papa* will come back, but I can't tell anyone."

GREG DANIELS: Kevin shared that it might be safe to risk shooting with Carell because *Come to Papa* wasn't looking too strong.

BEN SILVERMAN: It was very stressful. We still had Bob as somebody we were in love with as a comedic performer. But Steve, even though he's from the Northeast, had such a midwestern-accessible, lovable comedic energy, like the great prime-time sitcom stars of the fifties and sixties. He had that thing. There was something about us that wanted to soften the character. Bob has hard edges, like he has angularity to him. He's brilliant, but he literally has angularity. Rainn does too, you know, and that edge made him perfect in his creation of Dwight.

ALLISON JONES: For me, it was a tough choice between Odenkirk and Carell, but my big worry is always that they're not going to pick the right person. They're going to pick somebody because a network person says they didn't do a good job in our pilot six years ago. That's the panic that I get when I'm casting a pilot.

BEN SILVERMAN: *Come to Papa* wasn't a giant success, but it also wasn't like a giant failure. So it was anxiety provoking. And we also had this ticking clock of losing actors every month. We only had the rights for a certain amount longer too. You have to start making this stuff or you lose the ability to get the right to make it. We weren't positive we had Steve because he was contractually obligated to *Come to Papa* for a longer time period. But luckily I think NBC might've owned that show also, and we basically haggled and negotiated our way to an audition with Steve.

STEVE CARELL: I remember, before I auditioned, I was talking to Paul Rudd. I'd never seen the original one and he asked what I was up to. This was right after *Anchorman*. I told him I was going to audition for the American version of *The Office* and he said, "Ugh, don't do it. Bad, bad move. I mean, it's never going to be as good." Like what everybody was saying.

ALLISON JONES: When I saw Steve Carell, and Phyllis may attest to this, I was on the floor laughing at how good he was.

KEN KWAPIS: One of the things that Steve did so well, he's the one character who's excited about a documentary crew being there. Because Michael Scott fancies himself a superstar. But he somehow both played to the camera and was also himself the subject of a documentary. It's one of the things I just marveled at. Michael Scott is grandstanding and making jokes and playing to the camera, but the character doesn't quite realize that he's under the microscope. Steve somehow found that weird duality.

"Stanley the Manly," played by Leslie David Baker.

ALLISON JONES: Bob could have been seen as less accessible, maybe a bit less . . . I don't want to say sympathetic 'cause he's sympathetic. But Steve's Michael Scott was simple, sweet and simple. Bob was a little more cerebral.

PHYLLIS SMITH: But it would have been a different story. A different Michael with Odenkirk.

ALLISON JONES: It would have been different, the other side of the coin to Steve Carell. But Steve was the choice. It had to be Steve Carell. I was watching the monitor, watching Steve's test, and I was doubled over with laughter. Greg noticed that.

KEVIN REILLY: When you look at Steve, you kind of know at his core, he's a good guy. Even playing an asshole. You just know that he's really not that bad a guy. He's a more benign version. And the line that I will always remember is, I said, "Greg, what's your take on the show?" Early on. And he said, "It's the original show with ten percent more hope." And that, I think, is what Steve embodied.

"I Didn't Know He Was Auditioning Me"

FILLING OUT *THE OFFICE*

BRIAN BAUMGARTNER: I don't know if you and I ever talked about this, but do you know that I pulled one over on you guys? I outsmarted all of you.

KEN KWAPIS: I don't doubt that you're smarter than me, but how?

BRIAN BAUMGARTNER: I met with Phyllis and Allison Jones. I didn't know them, and they said, "Okay, we want you to audition for the role of Stanley." I went home and thought, "That's not the part that I should be auditioning for." So when I went in, I read for Stanley as though it were Kevin. Then I left the room and was walking out the door. And Allison or Phyllis, I forget who, ran after me and said, "Brian, wait, wait, wait. They want you to read for this other role." So I went back and read for Kevin.

KEN KWAPIS: I think that's fantastic. I think that actors could follow your lead and go to an audition and play the part they have in front of them as if they were the other character.

BRIAN BAUMGARTNER: It'll probably work out way better, people.

Brian Baumgartner

Occupation: Actor, director

Hometown: Atlanta, Georgia

Training: Southern Methodist University, Class of 1995, B.F.A. in theater

Previous Employment: Artistic director of the Hidden Theatre in Minneapolis (1995–1999), cameos in *Arrested Development* (2005) and *Everwood* (2005)

Post-*Office* Credits: Roles in Amazon's *Hand of God* (2017) and *Hot in Cleveland* (2013–2015); the voice of a sleepy black bear in the Netflix original *Trash Truck*

Extracurricular: Lead singer/drummer for Scrantonicity

Special Skills: Making chili, sinking three-pointers

Dream Job: First base for the Atlanta Braves

PHYLLIS SMITH: I remember when Leslie [David Baker, who was eventually cast as Stanley,] came in, he had another audition to go to. So we said, "Go do your other audition and come back." When he came back, he'd fought the traffic and was in a real crummy mood when he came in. It must've worked. [*Laughs.*]

OSCAR NUÑEZ: They probably gave me the sides for Stanley, 'cause there was no other character to do. And then they're like, "Let's have him back again." They asked me to improvise and that's where I get really happy.

BRIAN BAUMGARTNER: You knew Angela before the show, right?

OSCAR NUÑEZ: I did. I believe from the Groundlings or ImprovOlympic.

ANGELA KINSEY: We had done a sketch comedy show called *Hot Towel*.

BRIAN BAUMGARTNER: *Hot Towel*? Why do sketch comedy shows all have weird names?

ANGELA KINSEY: 'Cause you're in your twenties and you think you're hilarious.

BRIAN BAUMGARTNER: *Hot Towel* is hilarious?

ANGELA KINSEY: Like the hot towel they hand you on a plane? We were like, "Oh, let's be a hot towel." Well, I don't know. So I knew Oscar, and Kate Flannery and I had done improv together. I knew Dave Koechner [who played Todd Packer]. I used to call lights for his show *Beer Shark Mice*. I knew all the improv circles. Who else? I'm trying to think . . .

BRIAN BAUMGARTNER: Greg Daniels?

ANGELA KINSEY: I was related to Greg by marriage. You guys know that, right? I just loved Greg. He was so supportive of my career. He would come to my improv shows. I look back on it now, they probably had to get a babysitter. When you're in your twenties, you don't think of that. You're like, "I have an improv show at ten o'clock." So he was going to be doing the remake and he said, "This is kind of in your wheelhouse."

BRIAN BAUMGARTNER: Is there anything specifically you remember about the day you went in to audition?

HUMAN RESOURCES FILE

Oscar Nuñez

Occupation: Actor

Hometown: Colón, Cuba (till age two), then Boston and Union City, New Jersey

Family History: Parents went to school with Fidel Castro at the University of Havana

Training: Fashion Institute of Technology (for fashion), the Parsons School of Design (for writing); 1997 graduate of the Warner Bros. Comedy Writers' Workshop

Previous Employment: Performer at the Groundlings improv theater (1998); cameos in *Curb Your Enthusiasm* (2000), *Malcolm in the Middle* (2002–2003), *Reno 911!* (2003), and *24* (2003)

Post-Office Credits: Played Desi Arnaz in world premiere stage production of *I Love Lucy: A Funny Thing Happened on the Way to the Sitcom* (2018); roles in TV series *Benched* (2014), *People of Earth* (2016), and *Mr. Iglesias* (2019–present)

Special Skills: Certified dental technician (with a degree from Magna Institute of Dental Technology)

Disciplinary Action: Reprimanded for making a blow job joke in a 1998 episode of the game show *Match Game*

Angela Kinsey

Occupation: Actress

Hometown: Born in Lafayette, Louisiana, raised in Jakarta, Indonesia

Training: Baylor University, Class of 1994, B.A. in English

College Nickname: Junior Mint

Previous Employment: Intern on *Late Night with Conan O'Brien* (1993–1994); operator for 1-800-DENTIST; performer with Los Angeles improv groups the Groundlings and iO West

Post-Office Credits: Starred in Netflix series *Haters Back Off* (2016–2017); starred in movies *Half Magic* (2018) and *Tall Girl* (2019)

Overtime Hours: Played "Angela," who works at the children's gun section at the Mega Lo Market, on two episodes of *King of the Hill* (1997–1998)

Emergency Contact: Her two cats (Snickers and Oreo) and two dogs (Biscuit and Buster)

ANGELA KINSEY: I was auditioning for Pam. I remember it very, very well, because before I went in, Greg said, "Angela, that sounds kind of funny saying this, but I am not going to acknowledge you. Okay? Like we don't know each other." He said, "Trust me on this. If they think you're there just like anyone else, it's going to serve you better. I know you can do this." So I was like, okay, got it. And you know my poker faces. Horrible. But I'm like, okay, I won't make eye contact.

ALLISON JONES: I remember Phyllis and I saying to Greg, "We should pretend we don't know she's related to you."

ANGELA KINSEY: I walked in and there was a room full of people. I had really worked hard on the scene. I was reading with Phyllis, 'cause we all read with Phyllis. There's a moment when Michael fake fires Pam in front of Ryan, and it's such a jerk move. And Pam calls him a jerk and starts to cry. When Phyllis as Michael fake fired me, I called her a jerk and everyone started laughing. I remember in my mind thinking, "I don't think I was supposed to get a laugh there."

BRIAN BAUMGARTNER: You got a laugh on the jerk line.

ANGELA KINSEY: Then two months went by. I was waiting to hear and I got a call from my agent saying, "You know that show *The Office*? They really liked you. But they just thought you were a little too feisty for Pam." Shocker. Shocker. And they were like, "There's another character, she works in accounting and she's sort of stuffy, she doesn't really have anything nice to say about anybody." I went in and read with Ken Kwapis and it was like one line. I'll never forget it because he said, "Well, Angela, you made a real meal out of that line." I was like, wait, is that good? I don't know.

ALLISON JONES: We had a little plan with Greg. We're going to push for Angela because we know she's right, but we're going to pretend we don't know she's related to him. When we were in the room saying we should hire Angela, Greg for some reason objected. Phyllis and I were like kicking each other under the table. But somehow, I don't know what happened there, but we got Angela. Maybe that was his reverse psychology or something.

OSCAR NUÑEZ: I didn't know she got the job. I showed up for work and she was there in the accountants' [corner], and that's like an actor's dream come true. I'm like, "What are you doing here?" She's like, "What are *you* doing here?" I'm like, "Oh my God, Angela, we're on this show. We're on this bloody show!"

All eyes (and cameras) on Oscar Nuñez.

BRIAN BAUMGARTNER: What did you think of me? 'Cause then it was just you and Angela and then I was like the new guy.

OSCAR NUÑEZ: Weren't you there already? Weren't you there for the pilot?

BRIAN BAUMGARTNER: You clearly don't have any recollection about meeting me.

OSCAR NUÑEZ: No, I knew you were funny from commercials. You had that Jack in the Box commercial out, which was brilliant.

BRIAN BAUMGARTNER: Thank you. That's the nicest thing you've ever said about me.

KATE FLANNERY ("MEREDITH PALMER"): I remember they said no makeup. Like, *really* no makeup. Usually when they say no makeup, they mean lip gloss and some mascara. But it was like, "No, no, no, take it off, take it off, take off the lashes."

BRIAN BAUMGARTNER: Do you remember what they told you about Meredith?

The elusive Creed Bratton.

KATE FLANNERY: They just said she was lactose intolerant, divorced, and had a hysterectomy. Go!

KEN KWAPIS: I feel also responsible for Creed.

BRIAN BAUMGARTNER: How did you know Creed?

KEN KWAPIS: When I was on *The Bernie Mac Show,* Creed was a stand-in. I remember one day, Creed and another stand-in were having a conversation while we were lighting and I kept eavesdropping on them.

At one point I heard Creed say something like, "And then Hendrix taught me this lick that one night." Then I turned back over my shoulder and he was doing some air guitar for his fellow stand-in. So I went up to him and introduced myself, and he introduced himself as "Creed Bratton, formerly of the Grass Roots," which was a Bay Area pop band in the mid-sixties that opened for people like Janis Joplin and the Doors. So we became pals. And then I went off to do other things and lost touch with him for a while. But then I heard through a mutual friend that he was looking for work and he'd heard that I was directing the pilot of *The Office* and did they need stand-ins?

CREED BRATTON: I said, "Look, I love the Ricky Gervais show so much. Is there any way I could come and read for something over there?" Ken calls me back and says, "I told Greg that you were a very interesting guy. He said, 'Well, if he's that interesting, let's see if we can work him into the mix.'"

KEN KWAPIS: I told him, "There's no guarantee of anything, but if you want to be an extra in the

Creed Bratton

Occupation: Actor, musician

Hometown: Coarsegold, California

Training: Bought a guitar from a Sears mail-order catalog at age thirteen

Previous Employment: Lead guitarist for the psychedelic pop/rock band the Grass Roots (1966–1969); cameo appearances in *Playboy After Dark* (1969), *Quincy M.E.* (1977), and *The Magical World of Disney* (1986)

Post-Office Credits: Performances at the SXSW festival (2010 and 2012); released two albums, *While the Young Punks Dance* (2018) and *Slightly Altered* (2020); film roles in *The Ghastly Love of Johnny X* (2012), *Saving Lincoln* (2013), and *Band of Robbers* (2015)

Disciplinary Action: Fired (or possibly quit) his band at the Fillmore West

Special Skills: Spider solitaire; hitchhiking across Europe, Africa, and the Middle East

background of this paper company for a week, you're welcome to take a seat at this desk."

Most of the cast were unknowns, but none more so than Phyllis. Prior to *The Office*, she was not an aspiring actress. She was a casting associate, doing jobs like making lists of people who might audition for roles, contacting their agents, and then reading lines with the actors. She had been doing all of that for almost two decades.

ALLISON JONES: But then Ken Kwapis came up to me and said, "Could you let Phyllis read? Because I think she'd be good in the show."

GREG DANIELS: My understanding is that Ken is the one who suggested casting Phyllis, but I hopped on that fast. I thought that was great.

KEN KWAPIS: I'll tell you what happened. It was Greg, myself, Phyllis, and Allison. Phyllis was reading lines with the actors, and some of them were playing it to the hilt and working a little too hard. Phyllis, meanwhile, was reading her lines in this kind of a monotone way, sometimes not even looking up at the actors, just looking down at the sheet of paper. I just became fascinated with her. There were a couple of actors whose auditions I kind of missed because I kept throwing Phyllis these glances. During a break, I took Greg aside and I said, "This woman really belongs in a paper company."

PHYLLIS SMITH: I was frightened because I wanted to do a good job for the actors. I didn't want to screw it up for them. I didn't know he was auditioning *me*.

ALLISON JONES: I wasn't allowed to tell you. You read with everybody.

PHYLLIS SMITH: I read with Krasinski and I remember thinking, "Oh, he's the one." Yeah. It just felt right.

JOHN KRASINSKI: Before I had that audition with Jenna, I went into a room with Phyllis and she played Pam, she played Dwight. I was doing these scenes with her and she was incredible. And when I left, I joked to Greg, "Man, you should hire *her*." And then supposedly Rainn said the exact same thing. And Jenna said the exact same thing.

TERI WEINBERG: I remember us asking, "Allison, how would you feel if we steal Phyllis and cast her in the show?" It was pretty amazing. It was amazing to see her life changed.

KEN KWAPIS: I asked Phyllis if she would be willing to basically quit her day job to sit at a desk behind Rainn with no dialogue and no guarantee that this show is going anywhere. And she said yes.

PHYLLIS SMITH: No one really ever came to me. Wardrobe was actually the first one who called and said, "I understand you're playing the character of Phyllis."

KEN KWAPIS: There's one additional detail that's so wonderful. After Greg said sure, let's ask her to be in the bullpen, and she agreed to do it, Greg and I had a discussion and he asked, "Do you know if she can act?" I took Phyllis aside and I said, "Do you have a lot of acting experience?" And she said no, not really, but some years earlier she had worked in burlesque in Branson, Missouri. And I said, "Stop it!" Then later that week, she brought in a photo of herself in a wonderfully old-fashioned burlesque outfit.

PHYLLIS SMITH: I'd never had training. So I bought books on comedy and improv in particular, because you guys were so great at it. It kinda helped me to feel a little more secure about it. I just felt insecure about the whole thing.

STEVE CARELL: She did? I never knew that.

BRIAN BAUMGARTNER: I never knew that either.

STEVE CARELL: It's shocking to me because I always thought she was one of the best improvisers of any of us. Everything was completely honest and she just listened and responded within character. That's what it is. That's the crux of it.

PHYLLIS SMITH: Because I'd done that other [acting] job nineteen years prior. I kept my [Screen Actors Guild] dues up. My dues were completely paid. But it wasn't because I thought I was going to be an actor. My contribution was because I like actors, you know?

ALLISON JONES: What was the first job nineteen years ago? Was it the mousy [girl on the court show]?

PHYLLIS SMITH: No, I didn't get that job. It was a documentary that was actually shot in Illinois for women's right to vote. It was a period thing.

BRIAN BAUMGARTNER: Everything just felt right. Whether the actors were super confident, like Rainn and Jenna, or totally nervous, like

Phyllis Smith and Allison Jones: The casting duo that made Phyllis a star.

John and Phyllis. When we came together, we knew in our heart that this ensemble was going to work.

TERI WEINBERG: We knew it was all of you because everybody didn't fit a mold that we were looking for, but they brought something special and beautiful. It was like making a puzzle. Everybody just fit in so beautifully.

And now that the puzzle was complete, the hard work was behind us. We just had to make a pilot, get it picked up by NBC, and then build a loyal audience that would watch us, week after week, and slowly fall in love with these characters until they felt like members of their own family. Okay, so it wasn't quite that easy. But as we'd soon learn on day one of shooting the pilot, everything that made it harder was also making it better.

That's what she said.

STEVE CARELL AND GREG DANIELS DEBATE
WHO TRULY IS THE WORLD'S BEST BOSS.

3

"Everything That Makes It Harder Makes It Better"

FILMING THE PILOT

RANDALL EINHORN (DIRECTOR OF PHOTOGRAPHY): I think what I loved so much about the show was that it was just so collaborative. It wasn't always easy to find a way to do something, but we always figured it out.

Though Peter Smokler was the original DP for the pilot, Randall Einhorn was brought in for the first season and became the guy responsible for how *The Office* was shot. He picked the cameras, the lenses, even the filters. A DP decides how the cameras move, how each scene should be lit, and how to frame what you see at home on your TV.

RANDALL EINHORN: One of the things that Greg used to say was "Everything that makes it harder makes it better." Which I think is kind of a metaphor for life.

Metaphor or not, Greg Daniels was entirely correct, at least on *The Office*: everything that made it harder really did make it better. And not in a glass-half-full kind of way. It wasn't like if the roof of your house collapsed and you said, "It's not the end of the world." This wasn't about overcoming; it was about looking at the things that made our job more difficult as tools.

RANDALL EINHORN: I think it comes from Albert Einstein. He said, "In the middle of difficulty lies opportunity."

BRIAN BAUMGARTNER: That's brilliant.

RANDALL EINHORN: He said it in German, which sounds much more lyrical. "*In der mitte . . .*" I don't know what it is.

BRIAN BAUMGARTNER: Oh, so you're bringing out your German now?

RANDALL EINHORN: That's all the German I know.

Much like German, Greg's maxim isn't an easy lesson to learn. It's not as if Greg said, "Everything that makes it harder makes it better," and we were all like, "Oh yeah, I totally get it!" It took time to sink in, for us to see the method in his madness. But it eventually became our mantra, which we applied to every aspect of the show.

It was especially helpful in creating the world for *The Office*, both at the fictional Dunder Mifflin and at the very real, very small actual office where we shot the series.

It was early 2004 and we were all excited to start making the pilot, even though we realized our show was going to be very different from what was currently on TV. The most popular shows of 2004 were about hot people having hot problems—*Desperate Housewives, Lost, ER, Grey's Anatomy, House,* and *Boston Legal.* Or they were gritty crime dramas with lots of violence and tough guys, shows like *The Sopranos, The Wire, The Shield, NYPD Blue, Deadwood,* and more than a few *CSI* spin-offs.

We were none of those things. So how would we stand apart in that TV landscape?

RANDALL EINHORN: I used to refer to *The Office* as a tofu hot dog. Greg kind of latched on to that idea.

BRIAN BAUMGARTNER: What does it mean?

RANDALL EINHORN: It's good food wrapped like junk food.

Greg wanted the show to reflect reality. And not the reality of reality shows like *Survivor* and *The Real Housewives of Wherever,* which pretended to reflect reality. He wanted *The Office* to be about real reality, with characters who seemed like they'd lived in this office long before the cameras showed up.

GREG DANIELS: When I did *King of the Hill,* we were in an office building and surrounded by office culture. At the time, I was regretful that we weren't on a cool entertainment lot, just the eighth floor of some Century City office building. But I'd hear stuff on the elevators all the time. Like once, I heard this woman in the elevator say something like, "I don't want to be a bitch, but . . ." I thought, well, that's a good character. And that became Angela. [*Laughs.*]

BRIAN BAUMGARTNER: Oh my God.

GREG DANIELS: There was a guy who always said things like, "Got to go back to the orifice." He was the kind of guy who calls Target "Tarjay."

Greg's original idea for the pilot involved the Dundies, an annual awards ceremony that Michael Scott throws for his staff as a way of boosting morale but also showing off his comedic gifts. It was also an homage to Greg's dad.

GREG DANIELS: That was actually based on my dad giving out awards comically at his annual chili party.

Greg's dad, Aaron Daniels, was president of ABC Radio Network in New York (before retiring in the early '90s). He competed as a frontenis player in the 1968 Olympics in Mexico City, not because he was a professional athlete but because he learned that the U.S. didn't have an official team for the little-known racquet sport. His team, which started training just weeks before the Olympics, lost every match.

GREG DANIELS: He used to do a managers' meeting every year at his company where he'd wear a Carnac hat—you know, the turban—and his name is Aaron, so he'd be "Aaronac."

If you didn't grow up watching *The Tonight Show Starring Johnny Carson,* one of his most popular characters was Carnac the Magnificent, in which Johnny wore a turban and cape and predicted the answers to questions that were sealed in an envelope.

GREG DANIELS: My first joke-writing experience was writing jokes for Aaronac. As I became a comedy writer, some very good people like Conan O'Brien and [*Simpsons* writer] Mike Reiss wrote for him. A lot of good comedy writers wrote for Aaronac. We used that in the Dundies. Michael has a Carnac turban and he does the exact same joke that was the first joke I wrote for my dad. The answer was something like, "The PLO, the IRA, and a hot dog stand," and he takes out the envelope and the question is "Name three businesses with better health care plans than Capital Cities Communications." Anyway, I used to do an actual awards show for the *King of the Hill* staff called the Swampies, named after Jeff "Swampy" Marsh, who was one of our designers who went on to create [the 2007–2015 Disney Channel animated series] *Phineas and Ferb.* He had a big personality, so we called it the Swampies and I got those little plastic salesman trophies that are not too hard to find.

BRIAN BAUMGARTNER: And that inspired the Dundies?

GREG DANIELS: Yeah. 'Cause I thought with the Dundies, by giving awards to everybody, you could introduce all these different characters.

But then Greg decided to do something untraditional, maybe even a little crazy. Instead of writing an original script, creating his own version of *The Office,* he decided that the pilot would stay intentionally close to the British script.

The show's fearless leader, Greg Daniels.

GREG DANIELS: I realized that I would be getting notes from mid-level NBC executives if I did a brand-new script, but if I rewrote the original script we could go into production sooner with almost no notes. I decided to rewrite the original. I remember saying to myself, "Kevin Reilly says he likes the original show, let's see if he really does." Because, at that point, my biggest worry was changing it too much. Later, we realized we needed to change it more, but I stand by the decision that the strategic thing to do was start with the original.

RAINN WILSON: Networks are notorious for stepping in and being like, "I don't like that person's haircut," and "Why don't you say something different here?" and "That's not funny," and "Why don't we reshoot this?" Greg said to NBC, "You guys love the British pilot, right? It's pretty brilliant, right? Well, here's the script."

That didn't mean Greg was just piggybacking on the success of the British *Office*. He had a vision for our show beyond just the pilot. And to get there, it meant creating a unique sitcom world unlike anything else on television at the time.

GREG DANIELS: One of my theories was that the show had to be handmade. It couldn't be a factory product. What I didn't like about network television was how much of a factory it was. The writers wrote jokes and the jokes got passed down to the actors and they didn't overlap much.

BRIAN BAUMGARTNER: So you wanted to focus on making the *world* of *The Office*.

GREG DANIELS: That's right, exactly.

BRIAN BAUMGARTNER: Finding the rhythms and realities of that office world without necessarily making it a joke factory?

GREG DANIELS: Right, yeah. I really felt like the challenge of the pilot was: Can we do something that feels like *The Office* and not like *Will & Grace* and not blow it?

To create that world, Greg brought in Ken Kwapis as the director. Ken was also super focused on heightening the realism.

KEN KWAPIS: I have a very, very specific memory of our meeting, because it went very well. And at a certain point I felt so comfortable with Greg—we were talking about the British show—and I said, "One of the things that confuses me about the British show is that I can't quite understand visually the layout of the office." I was taking a chance, because as a director you want to demonstrate that you're a person who can think visually. And here I was basically saying, "I can't figure it out at all!" And happily, Greg said, "Neither can I!" So we sat on the floor next to a coffee table with pieces of paper and pens and tried to draw the layout of Wernham Hogg.

BRIAN BAUMGARTNER: Did that help you make sense of Dunder Mifflin?

Ken Kwapis

Occupation: Director

Hometown: Belleville, Illinois

Training: Northwestern University, University of Southern California

Previous Employment: Directing *The Larry Sanders Show* (1992–1993), *Freaks and Geeks* (1999–2000), *Malcolm in the Middle* (2000–2004), *The Bernie Mac Show* (2001–2006)

Post-Office Credits: Director of films like *Big Miracle* (2012) and *A Walk in the Woods* (2015); directing TV shows like *Happyish* (2015), *One Mississippi* (2016–2017), *Santa Clarita Diet* (2017–2019), and *#BlackAF* (2020)

Performance Reviews: Comes highly recommended by Robert Redford (for directing *A Walk in the Woods* in 2015) and Big Bird (for directing Sesame Street's *Follow That Bird* in 1985)

Special Skills: Compulsive list making, creating confession scenes

Emergency Contact: Captain Kangaroo (who produced Ken's directorial debut, "Revenge of the Nerd" [1983], an episode of *CBS Afternoon Playhouse*)

KEN KWAPIS: We talked a lot about where people were, how the desks faced each other. That was actually a big part of my work in prepping the pilot. I had to figure out where different characters lived.

They wanted to make sure their version felt true to life. So they decided to film it in an actual office instead of on a set, which is way harder.

KEN KWAPIS: But that was definitely something Greg and I spoke about. How do you create an atmosphere of—what's the right way to put it?—an atmosphere that's *not* a show? How do we create a real workplace, where people feel a little bit trapped?

How did we create a real workplace? Well, obviously, we did it by making everything harder.

"The More Specific, the More Universal"
Creating the World of *The Office*

John Krasinski, upon learning he was cast in *The Office*, immediately drove to Scranton, Pennsylvania.

MATT SOHN (DIRECTOR OF PHOTOGRAPHY): It was one of my favorite things. John did a road trip and went through Scranton and took his Handycam and shot stuff in Scranton because he was so excited that he was a part of it. And it ended up making the show. How funny is that?

That's all true. John Krasinski was living in New York City, and the trip to Scranton was just a two-hour road trip. There was no reason for him to visit Scranton, other than just—

JOHN KRASINSKI: Pure nerd-dom. It was just me being super nerdy. When Greg contacted me to say, "Congrats, you have the part," I was so excited. I was twenty-three, and at that time in my life, my only experiences were being in college and just sorta letting life happen. So I was excitable like a puppy. I said to Greg, "I'm going to Scranton to do research. There's actually a paper company there." And he was like, "Okay, cool." I went with my friend Kevin Connors.

Kevin Connors, the son of Jack Connors, the founder of Boston ad agency Hill Holliday (which did the Dunkin' Donuts ad "America Runs on Dunkin"), was Krasinski's dorm roommate at Brown University and executive produced John's 2009 directorial debut *Brief Interviews with Hideous Men.*

JOHN KRASINSKI: I had a tiny little camera, like one of those early digital HD things. Not even HD. It was just like a digital camera. And I shot the Scranton sign out of the sunroof of Kevin's Jeep, with us driving at the full speed limit. I should've stopped but I didn't. I just popped out of the sunroof and was like, "Wait, wait, wait!" I was filming as we drove by.

And that blurry footage, taken from a Jeep sunroof in very unsafe conditions, was used in the opening credits of *The Office.*

JOHN KRASINSKI: And then Greg goes, "Can I have that footage?" And I said sure. And then he said, "I might use it for the opening of their show." And I went, "What?" And he was like, "So I have to buy it from you. Can I buy your footage?" And I was like, "Oh no, no, no. You can just have it." Again, super young. He was like, "No, we've got to buy it." I think he bought it for a thousand dollars.

BRIAN BAUMGARTNER: Dumb decision.

JOHN KRASINSKI: So dumb, so dumb. That could have been the greatest investment of my life.

BRIAN BAUMGARTNER: That sign doesn't exist anymore. Did you know that?

MATT SOHN: No!

BRIAN BAUMGARTNER: Well, it exists. It's now in the mall [the Marketplace at Steamtown in downtown Scranton].

MATT SOHN: Oh gosh. Why'd they move it? Was it causing accidents?

BRIAN BAUMGARTNER: Probably. So why'd you go to Scranton at all? Was it for research?

JOHN KRASINSKI: I just wanted to immerse myself in Scranton. I didn't know what I was doing. I wasn't a trained actor. I was like, "This is probably what people do, right? This must be what actors do to really get into a role." And then I went to a local paper company and interviewed the boss.

The Pennsylvania Paper and Supply Company, founded in 1922, is a third-generation business in downtown Scranton.

JOHN KRASINSKI: I interviewed people. I don't know if this footage has ever been seen, but I did real interviews. Greg loved it and I think he got a couple ideas from some of it. The boss [of Pennsylvania Paper and Supply] found out [that our TV show] was based on the English one and realized that the boss is the boob. He reached out and was like, "I don't want [your interviews with us] to ever air! Don't make me look bad!" It was not great.

This real-life paper company boss wasn't the only one apprehensive about being the subject of a TV comedy. The city of Scranton was still licking its wounds from a 1974 Harry Chapin song called "30,000 Pounds of Bananas," about an infamous banana truck accident in Scranton during the mid-'60s. It wasn't exactly fodder for tourism.

STEVE CARELL: Scranton didn't want to be the butt of a joke. I remember initially they balked at the idea. Greg assured them that this wasn't what that was. It was about an honest, hardworking small town. It wasn't a joke.

RAINN WILSON: I remember Greg saying that he wanted it to be on the East Coast, so there could be other branches. It's close to New York or Philly if you need to go there, but it's just one of those cities that time has forgotten.

KATE FLANNERY: It goes along with Slough, England [where the British *Office* is based], which is a forgettable town long past its glory days. Growing up in Philadelphia, Scranton was always the butt of many jokes. I went there to underage drink as a teenager.

GREG DANIELS: When I picked it, I talked to people in Scranton, like journalists, and there's this guy, Josh McAuliffe, who worked at the Scranton newspaper. [McAuliffe has been a staff writer at the *Scranton Times-Tribune* since 1999.] He was really skeptical that we were going to be nice to Scranton. I had to say to him, "Look, *King of the Hill* was set in Texas and I didn't make fun of them. I understood them. I did the work to figure out what life was like for people in Texas." The point is not to do cheap jokes, making fun of the environment. Be specific and find a world and you'll be okay.

There was beauty in the mundane. Scranton might not have a reputation as a place where people come to chase after their dreams, but Greg found something to love in this former coal-mining town.

GREG DANIELS: The city is so much more beautiful than our corner of Van Nuys [in Los Angeles] that we were shooting in, next to the granite cutter, you know? I feel like we did a little bit of an injustice to how pretty Scranton is.

BRIAN BAUMGARTNER: It's very green and has that wonderful lake.

GREG DANIELS: It's got a lot of natural beauty, which is very hard to re-create in Van Nuys.

What was easier to re-create was the Scranton office itself. All you needed were the right props, things that most casual viewers wouldn't have noticed. The vending machine, for example, is filled with locally produced snacks like Herr's potato chips, Crystal soda, and Gertrude Hawk chocolates. The bumper sticker on Dwight's filing cabinet advertises Froggy 101, a local country music radio station. The break-room fridge has magnets featuring local businesses like Sheetz, a chain of gas station convenience stores, and the Wilkes-Barre/Scranton Penguins hockey team.

Scranton Office decor.

ANGELA KINSEY: Every menu on the refrigerator [in *The Office* set] is from a local Scranton restaurant. They reached out to the Scranton city council and said, "Send us all of your businesses! Send us your maps and just anything happening in Scranton!" That was on the walls all around us. All of those places were real places.

GREG DANIELS: [Our prop master] Phil Shea used to go to Scranton, and he had all these deals with different businesses and radio stations, and he'd come back with props for the set. They were all super authentic.

MATT SOHN: Anybody who knows Scranton recognizes something from our set.

GREG DANIELS: It was something I took from *King of the Hill*. *The Simpsons* was supposed to be set in generic America, and I really didn't want to imitate *The Simpsons* at all with *King of the Hill*. So we got really specific. There's an artistic theory, I forget who said it, but it's something like "The more specific you get, the more universal it becomes."

"What Am I Supposed to Do?"
Breaking in *The Office*

The quest for authenticity didn't end with props. We were trying to re-create a mundane reality, and both Greg and director Ken Kwapis wanted us to look like people who actually lived in that world.

GREG DANIELS: Ken said to all the department heads, "We're not going to be making everything perfect. No one will be yelled at if a hair is out of place or a boom mic gets in the shot. We're going to flip that." Ken wanted everybody to believe they worked at a paper company by taking the Hollywood out of it so that it would feel realistic.

KEN KWAPIS: The wardrobe choices, the makeup and hair choices, it was all designed to make it feel like these are people who don't belong on television, let alone on a prime-time half-hour comedy.

JENNA FISCHER: Ken Kwapis insisted that we clear the set of all crew members. That's very rare. Usually there are all kinds of people standing around, watching you act and they're being quiet, particularly hair and makeup. Ken wouldn't let [them] come in and touch us up.

KEN KWAPIS: As I recall, we kind of gave everyone a little compact mirror.

JENNA FISCHER: I would powder myself at my desk [between takes].

BRIAN BAUMGARTNER: My compact mirror got lost in the mail, by the way.

JENNA FISCHER: [Ken] just thought, if my hair moved or there was something wonky about the collar on my shirt, that's reality. We're making a documentary here. Nothing should be too polished.

LAVERNE CARACUZZI-MILAZZO (MAKEUP ARTIST): They're supposed to look natural.

That's Laverne Caracuzzi-Milazzo, the head of our makeup department. She'd worked on shows as diverse as *Malcolm in the Middle, Monk,* and *The West Wing.* But this was the first time she'd been tasked with making actors look . . . unremarkable.

LAVERNE CARACUZZI-MILAZZO: There's a very different everyday look in Scranton as there would be to an everyday look in L.A. or New York or Dallas or wherever. Ken kind of left it up to us. We never got any notes saying, "Oh, it's too much."

Another of Ken's ideas was for the cast to bring in objects to personalize our desks and make them our own. Phyllis had a photo from her burlesque days in the '70s. Brian brought in a football, because he's a sports nut so why shouldn't Kevin share that passion? Angela chose a picture with her grandma . . .

ANGELA KINSEY: It was me and my grandmother Lena Mae Kinsey. It's a black-and-white picture and my eyes are closed. I just thought it was really funny that she would frame it.

BRIAN BAUMGARTNER: So she's got a sentimental side?

ANGELA KINSEY: Yeah. I saw her as this sort of stuffy gal, but she wasn't malicious. She just took work very seriously. She wasn't there for shenanigans, you know. And that's sort of how I approached her. The one line Greg told me is she probably doesn't have a lot of nice things to say about everyone.

BRIAN BAUMGARTNER: Was her grandma her best friend?

ANGELA KINSEY: I don't know. I also had a prop on my desk from Phil Shea, a paper clip holder that's shaped like a big cat, a big chubby cat, lying on its side, and one of its ears was chipped. I still have that to this day. That's one of the things I took with me. So I have this cat paper clip holder and a photo of me and my grandmother, and that kinda informed the character.

OSCAR NUÑEZ: They didn't pay me enough for that. I was just an extra when I first got there. You want me to bring something from my own life? Make me a regular, then we'll talk.

BRIAN BAUMGARTNER: You must have brought something.

OSCAR NUÑEZ: You know what I brought? I brought in a picture of me and my dog, a mini schnauzer named Lila.

RAINN WILSON: I brought a bunch of family photos [of] my uncles driving Trans Ams from the seventies. And a lot of my nerdiness, of me playing Dungeons and Dragons and being in marching band and

Character building through set design.
Phyllis Smith, Angela Kinsey, and Leslie David Baker
show off their personalized desk decor.

on the chess team. I brought pictures of my relatives and ancestors in Wisconsin and Minnesota, who are farmers.

BRIAN BAUMGARTNER: Beet farmers?

RAINN WILSON: No. But Greg Daniels always said that the beet farmer thing was his grandparents. I think they were literally beet farmers.

GREG DANIELS: My grandfather came from Russia and had a beet farm. That always struck me as really weird. It's not very American, you know what I mean? It's not like we would grow corn. Beets just seemed like such a weird thing.

RAINN WILSON: When people ask me about playing Dwight, I always say that I think my goal was to make Dwight very specific. I do think this is true as an actor, that the more specific you make your character, the more relatable your character is. Having Dwight stand a certain way, drive a certain way, sit in his chair a certain way, have certain attitudes about certain things that are very specific, it made him more human and therefore more relatable.

Another way Ken immersed us in the world of selling paper was by having us do real work in the office, long before we started shooting.

JENNA FISCHER: Everyone in the cast had to be hair and makeup ready and at their desks starting at 7:30 A.M., and we would "work" for thirty minutes. Ken would walk around with just a camera operator and a boom and record us, just B-roll of us at our desks.

KEN KWAPIS: We started each day shooting basically documentary footage of the whole cast, the entire ensemble, just pretending to work.

JENNA FISCHER: I remember sitting there that first day and thinking, "What am I supposed to do?"

KEN KWAPIS: What was great about it was there was no story going on. It was just everyone at their desks. You and Angela and Oscar doing accounting work, or Phyllis making an imaginary sales call.

RAINN WILSON: The copy machine worked and the phones worked. We had to call each other and just be working in the office. I mean *every* day. We shot it over five days. For about a half an hour every morning we were just improvising, just being in the space.

BRIAN BAUMGARTNER: Ken and Greg had devised a little scheme. For many pilots, everything feels very new because it *is* new. You're starting a new show and you're in a new environment. Greg wanted the office to feel lived in.

OSCAR NUÑEZ: It wasn't a pilot for us. We're office workers. It's a documentary. We were boring before the cameras showed up. [*Laughs.*]

ANGELA KINSEY: It didn't feel like any other set I'd been on. It was almost like I was on a reality TV show, and I'd been mic'd and told to go work in an office somewhere.

BRIAN BAUMGARTNER: We didn't have any marks like you do on a normal television show, where they show you exactly where you're supposed to stand so the camera can capture you perfectly in your scene.

ANGELA KINSEY: That's right. Where the focus is on walking up to a certain spot and delivering your lines. We didn't have that.

BRIAN BAUMGARTNER: They just let us wander and do whatever. Do you remember what you did when we were supposed to be doing fake work?

OSCAR NUÑEZ: Gosh, I don't know. I would doodle. Did I bring a book in?

BRIAN BAUMGARTNER: The computers didn't work yet. I don't think we got internet until season two.

JENNA FISCHER: I'd actually been a secretary. That was how I made my living when I wasn't acting. So I started doing some highlighting and using the Wite-Out. I heard Phyllis and Leslie make fake sales calls.

RAINN WILSON: I'm doing sales calls like, "Hello, Mr. Schwartz. I'd love to sell you some paper today." I didn't even know anything about the paper industry.

JENNA FISCHER: The whole room just started to feel like a real office. It was Ken's idea to get us into a headspace and it worked.

KEN KWAPIS: I think everyone sort of just figured out what their jobs are at a paper company. It started to create a sense of what their normal day is like.

MIKE SCHUR (WRITER AND "MOSE SCHRUTE"): Ken essentially eliminated the artificial membrane between "this is reality" and "this is fiction." Even if you're in the deep background, you've got to be at your desk and it's a pain, right? You guys could have all been in your trailers, playing video games or calling your children or whatever. It's asking a tremendous

Rainn Wilson

Job Title: Actor, blogger

Hometown: Seattle, Washington; briefly lived in a "haunted" Victorian mansion in Nicaragua as a child

Training: University of Washington, Class of 1986, B.A. in drama; Tisch School of the Arts, MFA in acting

Previous Employment: New Bozena clowning troupe, "slacker vaudeville on acid" (mid-'90s); Lahnk the alien in the movie *Galaxy Quest* (1999); reserved mortician Arthur on HBO's *Six Feet Under* (2003–2005)

Post-Office Credits: Movie roles in *Cooties* (2014), *The Boy* (2015, nominated for Fangoria Chainsaw Award for Best Supporting Actor), and *Blackbird* (2019); voice of super-villain Lex Luther in animated features *The Death of Superman* (2018), *Reign of the Supermen* (2019), and *Justice League Dark: Apokolips War* (2020)

Office-Related Accident: During "Beach Games" episode, accidentally kicked sand into the eyes of Leslie David Baker (Stanley), scratching his cornea and resulting in emergency hospital visit

Dependents: A pet zonkey (a zebra crossbred with a donkey) named Derek

Political Ambitions: Picked as running mate (purportedly in jest) by Republican presidential candidate Senator John McCain in 2008

Kate Flannery

Job Title: Actress

Hometown: Born in Philadelphia, raised in Ardmore, Pennsylvania

Training: University of the Arts, Class of 1987, BFA in acting

Previous Employment: Played Alice in 1993 touring production of *The Real Live Brady Bunch*, reenacting Brady Bunch episodes in thirty cities; small roles in *Curb Your Enthusiasm* (2002), *Boomtown* (2005), and *The Bernie Mac Show* (2004)

Post-Office Credits: Appearances on *Brooklyn Nine-Nine* (2016), *New Girl* (2016), *Young Sheldon* (2019), and *Dancing with the Stars* (2019); regularly tours and sings with Jane Lynch (since 2013)

Special Skills: Did most of her own stunts, including getting hit by a car (was so bruised from the scene, she had to wear body makeup for the Emmys the following week)

Extracurricular: Member of Mono Puff, a singing "supergroup" formed by They Might Be Giants cofounder John Flansburgh

Sales Experience: Was the voice of Wendy in several Wendy's restaurant commercials

amount of the actors to sit at your desk for as long as you did. But there is a theory behind it. From the first frame, it felt like everyone was really working in that place. Nothing about it felt fake.

KATE FLANNERY: I feel like everyone had a focus immediately. You weren't looking for someone to throw you the ball. You were busy doing your work. I remember Jenna and I had a whole dance, we had these clearance papers that we would sign for each other. It was so bizarre, but it was fantastic. We had all that weird medical paperwork that the prop department had found. Remember that?

BRIAN BAUMGARTNER: That's right! Our prop papers were essentially old expired medical documents from people's procedures.

KATE FLANNERY: A ton of them. They lasted for years.

BRIAN BAUMGARTNER: They were covered in numbers so it looked like something you'd find in an actual paper company, but it was like, I don't know, the red blood cell count numbers for Jason Alexander from 1976. It was all about recycling.

KATE FLANNERY: There you go. We were doing some green work. Repurposing.

MATT SOHN: You guys didn't have the internet, right?

BRIAN BAUMGARTNER: No internet. We were doing Post-it Note communication back then.

The internet definitely existed back in 2004, but it wasn't the sublime time waster it is today. Facebook had just launched in February, but it was still solely for Harvard students. YouTube wouldn't be around until 2005, and Twitter a year after that. Google introduced Gmail on April 1, 2004, and most people thought it was a joke. According to a *New York Times* story from that year, the "majority of Americans who surf the Internet still do so by dialing in on regular telephone lines." So office employees looking to avoid doing actual work had to find other distractions.

OSCAR NUÑEZ: We used to pass notes back to each other. Angela still has some doodles that I did back in the day. It was very exciting to be there.

RAINN WILSON: We were literally doing expense reports and calling clients. It was like performance art.

JOHN KRASINSKI: It was like an acting exercise. I remember being like, "Oh, this is so nerdy." But by the end of it, we were all kinda into it. We were dialed in.

KEN KWAPIS: One of the things that really strikes me when I look at the pilot now, it feels like they've been working there for years. It doesn't feel like, "Oh, here's a new show." It feels like we've wandered into a place that's been going about its dreary way the same way it has been for the past couple of years or more.

OSCAR NUÑEZ: It had to be a boring workplace. The camera would scan the room and some people knew they were being filmed and some just ignored it, like nothing was happening. People didn't try to do bits. It's funny enough just to see someone looking over and rolling their eyes. Like they're thinking, "What do you want from me? I'm trying to work here."

KEN KWAPIS: It gave a voice to a lot of actors who didn't have a speaking role in the pilot. Some of the things we shot on the B-roll that were so mundane got into the credit roll at the beginning, during the title sequence. Like Rainn sticking things into the paper shredder.

BRIAN BAUMGARTNER: Or me with the adding machine.

KEN KWAPIS: The adding machine, right. I think Steve Carell adjusting the Dundie trophy on his desk was from one of those B-rolls. I remember getting a comment from some executive who didn't understand why we had these long, lengthy shots of like the water cooler. "Why is there a ten-minute shot of Rainn sharpening pencils? What is the purpose of this?"

BRIAN BAUMGARTNER: "We're *paying* you for this?"

KEN KWAPIS: [*Laughs.*] Right, right. You can shoot a lot of footage in a half hour. One of the things that I discovered in this process is that the cast, they knew they were being observed, they knew they were the subject of a documentary. So when we then moved into a scene, a proper scene, the actors kept that same attitude. They were still the subjects of a documentary. It wasn't like we now shifted into "show mode." We were still in documentary mode. So it helped set the tone for everyone in terms of the performance style.

It wasn't just the actors who got to spend time in the office. The writers were also encouraged to explore Dunder Mifflin and make it their own.

MIKE SCHUR: When we were writing the first season, Greg would tell everyone to spend half an hour and just mill around the set. We would sit at different desks and notice things like, "Oh, from Pam's desk, she can't quite see Angela. That's interesting," or "Creed's got his back to the door so he's always going to be surprised when anyone comes in." These tiny observations didn't feel like anything, but the whole show was about these tiny little observations and tiny

The camera catches a moment between Krasinski (Jim Halpert) and Jenna Fischer (Pam Beesly) on set of "The Fire."

moments. When you've actually lived inside them as an actor or a writer, they become more meaningful and you understand them at a deeper level, you know?

"We Tried to Make the Office a Prison"

BRIAN BAUMGARTNER: We shot the pilot and the first season in the production offices above the soundstage in Culver City. You didn't make any changes to the production office, right? The walls were where they were.

KEN KWAPIS: That's right. When we built the Dunder Mifflin set, one of the things that Greg and I discussed was not making any of the walls movable.

GREG DANIELS: On a Hollywood set, they make the walls "wildable," which means any room you're in, you can pull the wall off so that the camera can get back and get a great shot.

RANDALL EINHORN: We didn't do any of that. It was a real office—it was J. J. Abrams's office at one point, I think—with real doors and real low ceilings and real everything.

GREG DANIELS: Our aesthetic on *The Office* was nothing should be wildable. The obstacle of a column in the way is subconsciously interpreted by the audience as another piece of evidence that this is actually happening. This is real, which makes it much more intense, right?

KEN KWAPIS: It was Greg's choice to find this warehouse in this scrubby section of the Valley so that even if it wasn't in actual Scranton, it was definitely not Hollywood.

GREG DANIELS: We moved to a different lot between season one and season two. I wanted to get a lot that was closer to where Steve lived, to make his commute a little easier. I drove all around the San Fernando Valley, looking for the right place. I wanted us to be off by ourselves, so I was looking for small, independent lots. And almost all of the ones I visited did a lot of porno. [*Laughs.*] I remember one that was like, "Oh this is nice." It appeared to be child-friendly because it had like a storybook tree with a swing. And then I realized, oh wait, it's a sex swing. I didn't want to go to a lot that had porn connections.

KEN KWAPIS: It definitely felt like, where are we? Why are we coming all the way out here to shoot this show in a warehouse? Greg really wanted to give us every opportunity to *not* feel like we were on a show.

GREG DANIELS: The lot that we ended up in, it was a new lot that had only done commercials. When we landed there, it was very remote. It was in Panorama City. I remember going online and going to Yahoo restaurant recommendations or whatever. You type in your address, and then you're supposed to type in what type of food you're looking for. So I typed in the address of our lot, and then I typed in "healthy eating," which is one of the food choices. Then it popped up "There is no healthy eating in Panorama City, California."

KEN KWAPIS: The idea was that since this was a "documentary," directors had to respect the physical limitations of the space. If you couldn't get an angle, you couldn't get an angle. It was a way to signal to directors coming down the line that, you know, you had to honor the space.

GREG DANIELS: Because subconsciously, you're like, "Oh my God, they can't quite see what's happening." So they have to lean forward. You're going through the blinds and around the side. There was always a debate about how much to lean into that device, and the writers often would want to do it more than the rest of the crew.

KEN KWAPIS: One of the things I loved—not just in the pilot but in, you know, episodes in the second season in particular—was creating a sense that we were blocked from seeing the action properly. Whether it was a pillar or a file cabinet, something was in our way and we couldn't quite get a good angle on things.

BRIAN BAUMGARTNER: And that increased the realism.

KEN KWAPIS: Yeah. So much of what Greg and I discussed in terms of the camera style was how to create a sense that we were observing people, observing characters. Obviously it's not a secret that the staff of Dunder Mifflin knows they're being observed. They know they're being filmed. But most of the staff members don't want to be filmed except for Michael Scott. So it was trying to come up with visual ideas like, if I'm shooting you and I'm this far away from you, you'd know I was there. But if we hide behind a shrub or a file cabinet and eavesdrop on the action a little bit, we could sort of observe without characters knowing we were there looking at them.

ANGELA KINSEY: They had to truly work in the space they were in, because it is a documentary. They can't fudge it by moving a wall because it's messing up [their] shot. You had to work around it. The camera was trying to find you and if they missed you it could get blurry. They didn't want it to feel like a polished network television show.

RANDALL EINHORN: Everything was difficult. And every single thing that made it more difficult made it better.

There's that mantra again.

RANDALL EINHORN: Because you had to work for it. It made it seem more real. So we were always putting stuff in the way and, you know, making it more inconvenient. The more real and crowded it felt, it allowed the comedy to go a little bit further. We tried to make the bullpen environment of the office seem like a prison, which I think we did. Then outside could be the liberation. Like when Dwight takes [Ryan] to his beet farm, and B.J. is on his knees in the field, planting the seeds, and we backed the camera way off and just let the sun play and it was gorgeous. We tried to make the outside a break from the monotony of fluorescent tubes.

"Go Ahead"
The Genius of Ken Kwapis

Ken found other subtle ways to keep us homed in on that reality, including one memorable phrase.

GREG DANIELS: He would never say "Action."

BRIAN BAUMGARTNER: That's right. He was always, "Go ahead."

ANGELA KINSEY: "Go ahead." And then you do your scene.

JOHN KRASINSKI: Yeah, "go ahead." It was my favorite thing.

STEVE CARELL: "Go ahead." In the most calm, inviting way.

KATE FLANNERY: It was an understanding that you're not just suddenly turning on, you're already in. So just continue. Go ahead. It's perfect. It's like the perfect direction.

BRIAN BAUMGARTNER: It's very hard to describe. He'd act as though he was about to tell you something, and then he'd say, almost like an afterthought, "Go ahead." Like he had a thought that he was about to tell you but then he forgot what he was going to say, so he just brushed it aside and said, "Yeah, forget it, go ahead."

KEN KWAPIS: It's not something I've always done, but I can tell you exactly when I started doing it. I directed the pilot episode of *The Larry Sanders Show,* Garry Shandling's show. When Garry and I were prepping the pilot, he very much wanted a sense of verisimilitude. He came up to me and he said, "Is there any way that you can develop a shooting style so that the actors actually don't know when the camera is on?" And I didn't know how to do that. I mean, it was kind of a brilliant idea, but I didn't know what to do with it. I finally came up with the idea that we would start each scene without the usual announcements, without a first AD saying, "Rolling speed." We didn't give anybody the signal to start. I told Garry, "I'll just say, I don't know, 'go ahead' or something like that." Garry would take the signal and he'd chat with the cast for a while and then, at some arbitrary point, he'd just launch into the scene. So there was this sense that the line between acting and not acting got very blurry.

BRIAN BAUMGARTNER: So it's like tricking actors into not acting?

KEN KWAPIS: In a way. It takes some of the onus off of it. This sounds kind of pretentious to say, but there's real life and then there's the scene. And so if you can erase the line between real life and the scene, I think that helps.

THE ACCOUNTANTS' CORNER

BRIAN BAUMGARTNER: *Remember that time we were almost fired?*

ANGELA KINSEY: *Which time? When we made Oscar tell a story really loud under the window?*

BRIAN BAUMGARTNER: *That's the one. It was during the first season. They were shooting in the offices upstairs, and you and me and Oscar were down in the parking lot . . .*

ANGELA KINSEY: *And Oscar got really animated and worked up. He's kind of a very passionate storyteller.*

BRIAN BAUMGARTNER: *What were we even talking about?*

ANGELA KINSEY: *I really can't even remember.*

BRIAN BAUMGARTNER: *The show was brand-new. They hadn't aired an episode yet.*

ANGELA KINSEY: *We were the supporting cast. We weren't a big-ticket item on the show. We were easily replaceable.*

BRIAN BAUMGARTNER: *So we were out in the parking lot killing time, and Oscar started telling this story very loudly.*

ANGELA KINSEY: *Very loudly. This is when he kind of blames me. We were standing over in the sun and I was like, "Guys, let's go stand in the shade." I scooted up against the wall of the building, apparently right under a window where they were filming. And then Oscar continued his story.*

BRIAN BAUMGARTNER: *He was doing the accents and the gestures and I was roaring with laughter and Angela was like, "Stop it, stop it!" You were screaming. And then—*

ANGELA KINSEY: *Ken Kwapis himself leaned out the window, our director, and said, "Hey, guys, can you keep it down? We're trying to film here." We were like, "Oh my God!"*

BRIAN BAUMGARTNER: *My face turned white. I was petrified.*

ANGELA KINSEY: *Oscar pretty much hugged the wall. I made myself so small that I turned into a shadow. I don't think Ken saw me. I think he just saw Oscar. You went flat up against a dumpster, remember that?*

BRIAN BAUMGARTNER: *He was so mad.*

ANGELA KINSEY: *Oscar still says, "Kinsey almost got me fired."*

BRIAN BAUMGARTNER: *It felt like we might be. We walked away going, "We're fired, we're done. We're done." Like, they have no use for us. They haven't found a way for us to be funny yet. We are done.*

THE ACCOUNTANTS WHO ALMOST GOT FIRED.

We were having a blast. But honestly, none of us really believed that this little world we were creating would last.

> **JENNA FISCHER:** We shot the pilot in March 2004 and my thirtieth birthday was March 7, 2004, and I did not invite any of you to my thirtieth birthday party because I assumed I would never see you again. I was so sure that making the pilot was the end of our show, that it would never get picked up. Not because it wasn't good, but because it was so good and so weird and so special that no one would give us a chance. There was just this feeling of "Have fun making your pilot. That's all it'll ever be."

Even Greg Daniels, their leader, wasn't certain the show had a future.

> **GREG DANIELS:** I remember saying to everybody after we wrapped the pilot—I had such a great time working with all these guys, it was like a dream—I remember saying to everybody, "If this is all we get, I'm happy. It was great fun." In the beginning it didn't look like we were going to be on for very long. So you took what joy you had.

Everyone felt that way, except for apparently one person, according to Rainn Wilson.

> **RAINN WILSON:** After shooting the pilot, John, Jenna, Steve, and I went out for a sandwich, down the road in Culver City from that crappy little studio we were at, to this crappy little sandwich shop. I had a tuna sandwich. Steve was like, "I think this thing could be really special and I'm betting that these are the roles that will define us for the rest of our lives. No matter what we do for the rest of our lives, this is what we'll be known for."

STEVE CARELL: I think we all sensed it. We all knew.

Okay fine, maybe we didn't all know. But we *wanted* to believe. Like those kids in *The Polar Express* on the fence about Santa Claus, we wanted to believe. We knew we had something special, but would the rest of the world agree?

Or, more important for us to make even one more episode, would the network agree?

JUST A GROUP OF ORDINARY-LOOKING LOSERS:
THE OFFICE CAST IN SEASON ONE.

4

"Let Me Tell You Why This Isn't Going to Work"

On March 24, 2005—a couple of months after George W. Bush was inaugurated for his second term as U.S. president and just days before the premiere of *Grey's Anatomy* (a show that, as of this writing, is still making new episodes)—*The Office* pilot was finally unleashed on the world. It was a Thursday, and our little show was sandwiched between ratings juggernauts *The Apprentice* and *ER*.

JENNA FISCHER: Brian, do you remember coming to my house and watching the pilot?

BRIAN BAUMGARTNER: Yes, I do.

JENNA FISCHER: Most of us were there, I think. Greg said maybe we should all watch it together. I've got a big living room, so I said, "Why don't we all come to my house?" It was the beginning of us all gathering together to watch the show every week.

Hold on, we're getting ahead of ourselves.

Before we got the DVD of our pilot so we could watch it on Jenna Fischer's floor, Greg Daniels and Ken Kwapis actually had to edit and deliver the episode to NBC. How hard could that be?

If you thought the "everything that makes it harder makes it better" credo ended when the cameras stopped filming, you're kidding yourself.

KEVIN REILLY: You guys just went off and made the pilot, and the dailies were looking great. There were no issues. And then the edited episode was delivered.

BRIAN BAUMGARTNER: What did you think?

KEVIN REILLY: It was very . . . slow. I could see the show in there, but it needed a lot of sculpting. You could see the comedy, you could see the characters. That was not a concern. But man, we sure were defying people's patience.

TERI WEINBERG: The rhythms were not like any kind of comedy on TV at the time. We took pride in those super long pauses, where nobody was talking and the fourth wall wasn't being broken. We were defying the conventional broadcast comedy rhythms and tropes by just being a fly on the wall in one of the most boring places on earth, a paper company.

GREG DANIELS: Pretty much everything I like or have worked on is character comedy. If you're going to go with character comedy, the audience has to learn who these characters are, right? And that takes time. They don't start with a bang usually. So I wasn't thrown or worried when we started slow.

KEVIN REILLY: This is where Greg and I forged our relationship, because it could have been brutal. At least I thought it was a creatively fun thing. Many of these pilots are screened after two cuts. If we had done that, it would've been dead, just dead. But I think he did fourteen cuts of the pilot, right? It may have been sixteen. You'd have to ask Greg, but it was definitely double digits.

GREG DANIELS: Ultimately, in the edit room, which lasted forever, we did twenty-three cuts.

KEVIN REILLY: Really? Wow, okay. I think that's where I saw his true gift. With each edit, it just got sharper and sharper. He was hunting for the essence of it in every scene.

GREG DANIELS: I ended up losing a bunch of stuff, like the thing with [Michael's] testicles . . .

In a deleted scene, Michael tells Pam that he thought he found a lump in his testicles that morning but it turned out to be nothing, and then he awkwardly changes the subject to Pam's smoked turkey sandwich.

GREG DANIELS: But there were some good things that got added, like Michael's WORLD'S GREATEST BOSS mug that he bought from Spencer's Gifts.

KEN KWAPIS: One of the reasons I was so happy with how Greg cut the pilot is he didn't cut it for tempo. Or in other words, he didn't make it more up-tempo. It still had weird pauses, where if it was any other television show, they'd either add canned laughter or three more jokes in that space. Or music. There's nothing, no music or anything. If it ever aired, it'd be the driest show on a broadcast network.

"If it ever aired." That was a big if. And before that decision would be made, there were test audiences who had to see it. Test screenings are rather common in Hollywood, for both movies and TV shows. Audiences from both coasts are selected for an advance screening, and they share their thoughts on comment cards.

BRIAN BAUMGARTNER: Do you remember how the pilot tested?

GREG DANIELS: Um . . . I'm guessing not good.

The test screenings in early May 2004 were so awful that the media reported on it. "America Remakes *The Office*, but No One's Laughing," announced a *Guardian* headline.

TERI WEINBERG: The pilot tested worse than I think any other pilot had ever tested on NBC besides *Seinfeld*. Typically, if something tests really bad, it's DOA. And if it's not DOA, good luck trying to convince your network that it's a pilot that they should bet on.

GREG DANIELS: What they told me about the testing was: "We're going out to a mall and grabbing a bunch of people. You can have one question to disqualify people." I really thought about this, and the disqualifying question I picked was "Are you a fan of [the ABC Jim Belushi sitcom] *According to Jim*?" [*Laughs.*]

BRIAN BAUMGARTNER: Oh, that's so mean!

GREG DANIELS: I know it's mean. But I didn't want *The Office* to be a conventional sitcom, so I had to pick something.

"*Office* Gossip: It's a Downer," wrote the *New York Post*.

GREG DANIELS: I had prepared Kevin for this. I knew we weren't going to test well. Everything that I liked never tested well. *Seinfeld* didn't test well. *The Mary Tyler Moore Show* didn't test well. *Cheers* didn't test well.

A review of the screening on Ain't It Cool News—which, in 2004, was a go-to website for entertainment news—was especially harsh, remarking that "the lady next to me said she found it 'depressing'" and "a guy from *The Daily Show* tries to fill Ricky [Gervais]'s shoes and can't."

MIKE SCHUR: In the history of television, the same story gets repeated over and over and over again. A pilot airs and it's the lowest-rated pilot in the history of TV, blah blah blah. It's true. Jerry Seinfeld has a letter with the ratings for *Seinfeld*'s test screening framed and hung on his wall.

Jerry Seinfeld and cocreator Larry David actually had the framed test-screening letter hung above a toilet. "We thought if someone goes in to use this bathroom, this is something they should see," Jerry told *TV Guide*. "It fits that moment."

MIKE SCHUR: *Cheers* was the lowest-rated pilot that NBC had ever aired to that point.

During its first season in 1982, *Cheers* was at the bottom of the Nielsen ratings, just barely beating out soon-to-be-canceled shows like *Zorro and Son* and *Ace Crawford, Private Eye*.

MIKE SCHUR: Greg warned NBC that it was going to test terribly. He was like, "It's a mockumentary. People aren't used to that. It's washed-out colors and fluorescent lighting. The boss's unlikable. It's going to test terribly, and you have to ignore it."

GREG DANIELS: It is firmly in the pattern of *Mary Tyler Moore* and *Cheers* and *Seinfeld*. I told them, "It's classic NBC comedy, and it's gonna work, but don't worry about the testing."

MIKE SCHUR: And then it tested terribly, and they didn't quite ignore it, but he had primed them to look at the results in a different way. It's very gutsy to tell a network that the thing they've spent millions of dollars on is going to bomb.

TERI WEINBERG: I think part of the reason it tested so poorly is it was something people had never seen before. They come to this testing, they get paid seventy-five or fifty dollars or whatever, and they judge your material based on twenty minutes and tell you if it's good or bad. We didn't care so much about testing.

BEN SILVERMAN: I get a call from NBC that the testing came in and it's horrible. And I'm like, "You're testing this next to old *Friends* episodes." I said to Greg, "I told you. I knew no one would like it." I'm depressed, you know, but challenged.

KEVIN REILLY: When things are going well and you have a hot hand, the network either doesn't push back or you have the ability to go, "Well, that's great, Brian. That's fantastic input," and then just ignore it, right? But I had not established credibility with NBC yet. People knew me, they liked me, they had recruited me for the job. But at this point, I was advocating for things that don't look like what they're supposed to look like. So that gave other players more power to come in and say, "Let me tell you why this isn't going to work."

The pilot was screened for NBC employees, who gave it a score between 0 and 10.

> **KEVIN REILLY:** Every room was giving it a 1 or a 0.5. Nobody liked it. Except one room.

A special screening room was set up just for the assistants and associates. In other words, the young people.

> **KEVIN REILLY:** It was the only room I was interested in. There were like forty people in there. I went in and said, "What do you guys think?" And they told me, "Not only is this the best thing we've done, it's the only thing we'd watch that's currently on the air." That's all I needed to know.

> **TERI WEINBERG:** If it wasn't for Kevin Reilly, *The Office* would not have had a life. I really do believe he put his career on the line for us.

Thanks to Kevin Reilly and a roomful of NBC assistants, our show had a glimmer of hope of surviving. But it was far from a done deal. On May 16, NBC was set to announce the new lineup.

> **BRIAN BAUMGARTNER:** When did you find out we'd been picked up?

> **JENNA FISCHER:** May 13 came and no one said anything. There's this thing called upfronts in New York in mid-May, where they announce to all the advertisers what their new season is going to be. They weren't telling us if we'd been picked up and I had to go to a friend's wedding in San Diego that weekend. Then I got the call on May 15 that we were picked up but only for five more episodes, and NBC would love me to be in New York for the announcement the next day.

> **BRIAN BAUMGARTNER:** The next *day*?

JENNA FISCHER: Right? They weren't going to provide me with an airline ticket or a hotel room, but if I could get there, they'd love for me to be there. So I was like, "Fuck yeah, let's go to New York!" I drove to the Long Beach Airport in my wedding outfit and booked my own flight, found my own hotel. Same thing with John, Rainn, Steve, and B.J. We were all there for the big announcement.

A typical season for a network show is twenty-two episodes, though sometimes a new and unproven show will get thirteen episodes at first. We got six total (the pilot plus the five-episode pickup) for our entire season.

JENNA FISCHER: The message was pretty clear. "We're only picking you up for five more because we don't totally believe in this show or you. So we're gonna do it very reluctantly, if we ever air them, 'cause we're not even sure." It was such a hesitant pickup. But we were celebrating like we'd gotten five seasons.

BRIAN BAUMGARTNER: We didn't even have a date for the premiere yet.

JENNA FISCHER: That's right. It was maybe midseason, maybe never. We're not sure. We'll see how it goes.

KEVIN REILLY: Greg had made some money on *King of the Hill,* so he was willing to cut his rate and take the shorter order. He could have stood on principle and said, "I'm not doing it. I'm not doing six," and the show would have been dead.

BEN SILVERMAN: I felt like NBC didn't give a shit enough to even pay attention to it. It was kind of like, "Oh, that thing will run itself out. Let them keep playing in their sandbox for a little longer."

RAINN WILSON: No one does six episodes for a first season, especially back in those days of network television. Network television only makes money when they have over a hundred episodes and they can syndicate it. They want to shoot as many as possible. So it was really weird that they found some money in the budget to shoot six under-the-radar episodes of *The Office*.

BEN SILVERMAN: And they put us on after *The Apprentice,* which was very strange at the time. We aired later than normal because they thought *The Apprentice* being set in a workplace environment was the right match for the show.

It wasn't the best news, but it wasn't like NBC had passed. We were making more episodes of this show we loved, and as Greg reminded us . . .

GREG DANIELS: Let's make these five count. If this is all we get, let's say what we can say with this show.

Others were even more optimistic.

SEASON ONE
Episode Guide

TITLE	DIRECTED BY	WRITTEN BY	ORIGINAL AIR DATE
Pilot	Ken Kwapis	Ricky Gervais & Stephen Merchant and Greg Daniels	March 24, 2005
"Diversity Day"	Ken Kwapis	B. J. Novak	March 29, 2005
"Health Care"	Ken Whittingham	Paul Lieberstein	April 5, 2005
"The Alliance"	Bryan Gordon	Michael Schur	April 12, 2005
"Basketball"	Greg Daniels	Greg Daniels	April 19, 2005
"Hot Girl"	Amy Heckerling	Mindy Kaling	April 26, 2005

KEVIN REILLY: At that point I was thinking, "The rebuild of NBC is going to happen and this is going to be one of those pieces." I looked at the rest of the stuff on our plate, and it was all shit.

The *New York Times*, for one, agreed. In TV critic Alessandra Stanley's review of our pilot in March 2005, she noted that while she thought it "pale[d] in comparison" to the British *Office*, it was "still funnier than any other new network sitcom."

KEVIN REILLY: It's not like I could go, "Wow, I've got ten other great shows to choose from." It was just, "Look, this is going to be a slog, but it's going to be worth it."

TERI WEINBERG: Every single one of us who was involved in the first season, we came to work each day and said, "If we're only making six total episodes, let's make the best episodes that we know how to make. Let's come in here and do the work and do it with love and do it with everything that we have and do it for ourselves." We all showed up on that lot every single day—I'm getting emotional about this—and made an incredibly beautiful show. It was for all of us, whether you were in the cast, whether you were in the crew, whether you were in accounting, whether you were in props, catering, whatever. Everybody came and it was like we were on our own island.

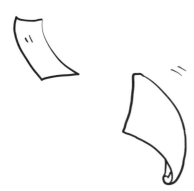

"Serial Killer–Level Writing"
The Writing Staff Convenes

Greg decided the time was right to bring in new writers—specifically writers willing to do double duty as writer-actors.

GREG DANIELS: I spent my small writing budget beautifully. For upper level, I brought on Paul Lieberstein, who had written some of the best *King of the Hill*s; Larry Wilmore, creator of *The Bernie Mac Show*; and Lester Lewis, from *The Larry Sanders Show*, who was brilliant with story and character. I snagged Mindy Kaling as a staff writer, whom I had seen on stage in her play *Matt and Ben* while talent scouting with my wife. And for mid-level, I hired Mike Schur, who was coming from *SNL* and had married a fellow *SNL* staffer like I had. Mike's brain felt like a slightly better-oiled version of my own.

BRIAN BAUMGARTNER: What was it like meeting Greg?

MIKE SCHUR: We had a shocking amount in common. We both went to Harvard for the *Lampoon,* both wrote at *SNL* and met our girlfriends and then later wives there.

Greg's wife, Susanne—who's also Paul Lieberstein's sister and currently the global head of original content for YouTube—was answering phones for Lorne Michaels. Schur met his wife, Jennifer, the daughter of Regis Philbin, in January 1998, when she was a writers' assistant on the show.

MIKE SCHUR: My son was born with red hair and Greg's son, Owen, also has red hair.

BRIAN BAUMGARTNER: That's just eerie.

MIKE SCHUR: So instantly, I was in love with Greg. I wrote to my agent and said he was going to teach me how to write. I deeply and truly believed that was the case. During that first season, the only permanent writers on the staff were me, Mindy, and B.J. And none of us had ever written a sitcom. I think B.J. maybe had written a few episodes of a Bob Saget sitcom or something.

Novak penned two episodes of the short-lived WB series *Raising Dad* (2001–2002).

MIKE SCHUR: I had only written at *SNL,* and Mindy was a playwright and sketch performer. So Greg essentially led a graduate-level class on sitcom writing.

GREG DANIELS: As a showrunner, the faster you can train writers to write like you, the faster you have some valuable help. I would download as much of my beliefs about writing as I could, and try to counter the aesthetics of most sitcoms with other artistic ideas, like how a cracked pot is more valued in Japan than a perfect pot because the crack gives it character and backstory. I invented terms to make the ideas memorable. It was probably an awful lot of pontificating.

MIKE SCHUR: I had a notebook and was like jotting things down. Greg would say things like, "Well, what makes a good story?" And then he'd start talking about the basic building blocks of storytelling: motivation, stakes, twists and turns, escalations, stuff like that. I realized, "Oh, this is a class. I'm in a class now." And I remember turning the page in my notebook that I was sketching dumb pitches on and starting to take notes like I was in college.

BRIAN BAUMGARTNER: You were thinking this subconsciously?

MIKE SCHUR: No, no, I was writing as if Greg were the professor in a biochemistry class. This is not a joke. I still have my notes and I still go back and look at them to this day. That was probably August of 2004, and I still have moments trying to write something where

I'm like, "Why doesn't this make sense?" And I'll go back and look at what Greg said off the top of his head. That's one of ten thousand examples of why the show worked, because Greg was that thoughtful and thorough about everything.

Schur remembers one brainstorming session in the writers' room where he suggested an episode involving a stray dog wandering into the Dunder Mifflin parking lot and getting adopted as the office pet.

MIKE SCHUR: Greg got really excited and was like, "Oh, I had a similar idea!" And he brought out a spiral notebook and he flipped through it. Flip, flip, flip, page after page of like serial killer–level writing.

BRIAN BAUMGARTNER: Like really tiny and neat handwriting?

MIKE SCHUR: Yeah. Filling the entire page, margin to margin, things underlined. And he goes, "Here it is." His idea was about a stray dog that gets adopted by the office, and they're all caring for it. He was like, "Dwight could have this relationship

HUMAN RESOURCES FILE

Mike Schur

Occupation: Writer, producer, actor

Pseudonym: Ken Tremendous

Hometown: Ann Arbor, Michigan

First Script: "The Robbery," a collection of (in his words) "nonsense and Monty Python ripped-off non sequiturs," written when he was ten

Training: Harvard University, Class of 1997, English major and president of the *Harvard Lampoon*

Previous Employment: Writer/producer *at Saturday Night Live* (1998–2004)

Post-Office Credits: cocreator of *Parks and Recreation, Brooklyn Nine-Nine,* and *The Good Place*

Special Skills: Making obscure references to the 1996 David Foster Wallace novel *Infinite Jest* (a "dizzying Connecticut intellect," according to office coworker Mindy Kaling)

Dislikes: Chin beards, wearing heavy denim on beet farms

with the dog, and Michael would be really sad 'cause the dog didn't seem to like him. And then Jim and Pam would kind of take over care of the dog, feeding it or whatever, and then at night there was a question of who would take the dog home.

And Pam would take it home one night and Jim would take it home another night, and the dog would sort of become almost a surrogate domestic animal for Jim and Pam. And then Roy would come in and Roy would bond with the dog and then the dog would go home." He laid out an entire story from beginning to end, where this plot device of a dog just related to every single character in the office. He got to the end of his eight-minute-long pitch and there was a beat and I remember going, "I feel like we should do your version. [*Laughs.*] It seems like maybe you've thought this out."

Armed with these little details and Greg's magical notebook, the writers embarked on creating script number two, our first original episode.

"Asleep in a Woke World"
The Making of "Diversity Day"

The second episode of our first season, "Diversity Day," was written by none other than B. J. Novak.

OSCAR NUÑEZ: It was an excellent script from a very young seventeen-year-old. B. J. Novak used to come to the set on his skateboard.

BRIAN BAUMGARTNER: Wait, he was seventeen at the time? Are you sure?

OSCAR NUÑEZ: No, I'm just saying that for comedic effect. But he was young.

He was twenty-five years old.

OSCAR NUÑEZ: So young. How much did I hate him? I hate him so much, and still do. I'm kidding, of course. B.J. is so talented and it was a really, really good script.

BRIAN BAUMGARTNER: I remember reading the script for "Diversity Day" and thinking, "Boy, I don't know if audiences are going to give our show a chance, but I hope they do because we're doing something really cool and risky."

"Diversity Day" was our first episode not based on something written by Ricky Gervais and Stephen Merchant. We were looking to make *The Office* uniquely our own, and uniquely American.

GREG DANIELS: In England, for whatever reason, ambition is looked at very poorly. So to make the Tim character likable—

Tim was the Jim equivalent in the British *Office*, played by Martin Freeman.

GREG DANIELS: —they made sure he didn't seem too ambitious. That was a way they signaled to an English audience that he was super likable. But it's different in America.

BRIAN BAUMGARTNER: We like ambition.

GREG DANIELS: Exactly. A lot of times, people were like, "If he doesn't like his job so much, why doesn't he just quit or get his shit together, right?" It was something we had to adjust for.

What set "Diversity Day" apart, however, was how it took on a lighthearted, comedic topic, one devoid of any controversy or potential landmines whatsoever: race in America.

What were we thinking?

RAINN WILSON: If there was a new show coming out today and they had a "Diversity Day" episode, with characters saying things like "try my googi, googi" to an Indian person and jokes about Asian drivers and Arabs being too "explosive," there would be a lot of angry people on social media saying it was inappropriate. There would be a huge backlash against it.

BEN SILVERMAN: "Diversity Day" is still one of my favorite episodes of TV, let alone on *The Office*. It is so funny and dangerous and different in a real and non-PC way. I don't know if you could even say any of the things we said in that episode anymore.

The plot, in a nutshell: After Michael Scott tries to entertain his coworkers by retelling a racially charged Chris Rock stand-up routine— "N—s vs. Black People" from Rock's 1996 HBO special *Bring the Pain*— Dunder Mifflin corporate mandates a sensitivity-training course. Michael sabotages it with his own group exercise, in which the entire staff wears forehead flash cards listing different races, like Italian, Jamaican, and . . . Martin Luther King Jr.?

GREG DANIELS: Tom Wong, our writers' assistant, was the one who suggested the thing with the cards. He had that exact thing happen to him in some workplace training. We were like, yep, we'll take that. That's great.

It goes from bad to worse when Michael instructs them to try guessing the races listed on each other's heads by using only stereotypes.

ANGELA KINSEY: I think my card said "Jamaica," right? When we shot that scene, I remember looking around and thinking, "I'm not seeing this on TV right now."

BRIAN BAUMGARTNER: That episode has one of my favorite jokes in the entire show. When Michael asks Oscar if he prefers a term that's less offensive than "Mexican."

OSCAR NUÑEZ: And he was so serious about it. Everyone just had to bite their tongues so they wouldn't laugh, because Steve was being so earnest.

GREG DANIELS: I'm fascinated with the idea of an Ur story, like the most representative story to explain a character. Ur was the biblical town that Abraham was born in, and I use the term in writing to mean the one episode that is the most foundational and representative of all the themes that the show is using. On *King of the Hill,* it was Hank's unmentionable problem, where he's constipated and he has to have a colonoscopy. The fact that people were talking about his constipation was the worst thing that could happen to Hank. "Diversity Day" was an attempt to find that super representative story of Michael. How is he going to respond when the worst happens to him?

Michael may have been a very different character from David Brent, his British doppelgänger played by Ricky Gervais. But they had a similar cultural blind spot in common.

RICKY GERVAIS: David Brent was fascinated with difference, and he had that terrible white middle-class angst about anyone thinking he was sexist or racist. So he overcompensated. He was basically a good person, but he panicked around difference, around disability or color or anything like that. We're laughing at that white angst and people getting it wrong. He's trying to do the right thing but he's not equipped to do it.

Paul Lieberstein

Occupation: Writer, executive producer, played Toby Flenderson

Hometown: Westport, Connecticut

Training: Hamilton College in Clinton, New York, Class of 1989, economics major

First Job: Father's law firm

Previous Employment: Writer and co-executive producer for *The Bernie Mac Show, Greg the Bunny, The Drew Carey Show,* and *King of the Hill*

Post-Office Credits: Executive producer and writer on TV series *Space Force* (2020) and *Ghosted* (2018); writer, director, and star of 2018 feature *Song of Back and Neck*

Office-Related Accident: B. J. Novak "almost killed him" with a surfboard in 2007 during a vacation in Costa Rica

Special Skills: Playing the vibraphone; forlorn expressions

So "Diversity Day" wasn't about racism, necessarily. It was about one very misguided man trying not to be racist and getting it very, very, very wrong.

STEVE CARELL: But he's trying.

BRIAN BAUMGARTNER: He's trying really hard.

STEVE CARELL: It's why I bristle a little when people try to compartmentalize Michael as a racist. He's a person with an enormously good, kind heart who lacked a great deal of information about the world around him. He was as asleep in a woke world as you could be. [*Laughs.*]

BRIAN BAUMGARTNER: But trying his best.

STEVE CARELL: Trying his best! There's a difference between being intolerant and being ignorant. Sometimes intolerance and ignorance go hand in hand, for sure. But I think he was a very earnest and decent human being. He just didn't . . . *get* it all the time, you know?

BRIAN BAUMGARTNER: Do you always search for the good in any character you're portraying?

STEVE CARELL: I think you have to, because otherwise you're just demonizing or judging them. And if you're doing that, you'll play it differently. You don't want to editorialize about them.

OSCAR NUÑEZ: I think Michael Scott got away with so much stuff because he was genuinely coming from a place of innocence. He would say these ignorant things and you would hate him. And then something horrible would happen to him, and you'd feel sorry for him and be like, "Oh, he's not such a bad guy." Then he'd do something horrible again, and again, and again. That was the cycle of the show. It's a wonderful formula.

"Diversity Day" didn't just clarify Michael Scott's personality. It was when the entire cast became more than just background players.

BRIAN BAUMGARTNER: Pretty much everybody had a moment or a joke in "Diversity Day." And it's also when they started the rivalry between Michael and Dunder Mifflin's HR rep Toby Flenderson, played by the newest staff writer to join the show, Paul Lieberstein.

PAUL LIEBERSTEIN ("TOBY FLENDERSON," WRITER, DIRECTOR, PRODUCER): We needed someone to come in and do one line, and Greg had this idea that he wanted to break down the wall between the writers and actors.

BRIAN BAUMGARTNER: Were you excited?

PAUL LIEBERSTEIN: I was such a writer in my head and I was really focused on the script. We were up all night writing until four in the morning. I stumbled onto the set the next day, and I didn't really know my line very well.

> TOBY: Hey, we're not all going to sit
> in a circle Indian style, are we?

PAUL LIEBERSTEIN: I didn't know Steve was going to improvise at all. I didn't know he would make more of it than it was. He came back with—

MICHAEL: Get out.

PAUL LIEBERSTEIN: I was so tired, I didn't even know how to respond.

TOBY: I'm sorry?

PAUL LIEBERSTEIN: And, you know, he took it from there.

MICHAEL: No, this is not a joke. Okay? That was offensive and lame. So double offensive.

It laid the groundwork for their relationship and inexplicable rivalry.

PAUL LIEBERSTEIN: We've talked about Michael not being mean on purpose. I guess we have to exclude Toby from that. 'Cause he did

The Office rivals: Michael and Toby.

not have that relationship with anybody else. Yeah, he *hated* me. [*Laughs.*]

BRIAN BAUMGARTNER: Steve's face any time he was looking at you, he almost looked like a different person.

PAUL LIEBERSTEIN: It was like I'm a Nazi, and he thought he was doing a service to the world by hating me.

Throughout the episode, Jim tries in vain to close a big sale, which would've been worth 25 percent of his commission. He loses it to Dwight, and just as he's poised to wallow in self-pity, something happens.

GREG DANIELS: I said to B.J., "Here's what I want, something *like* this. Something like Jim's had a terrible day, and they're in this horrible, boring meeting. Pam falls asleep and her head falls on his shoulder and it's this precious memory for him. It totally turns his day around. Try to find something *like* that."

BRIAN BAUMGARTNER: He took you literally?

GREG DANIELS: Well, he came back and was like, "I tried. I couldn't find anything better than that." It just felt very relatable. We did 201 episodes, but the second one might've been the best.

"The Least Flattering Haircut for His Head"
The Actors Find Their Characters

For the rest of season one, despite thinking that we only had four more episodes left, we kept on working, building our world and fleshing out our characters.

JENNA FISCHER: As a theater geek, this was a dream job for me. I wrote a three-page essay of Pam's backstory, some of which I got from the script or from the British show and some that I made up myself. I had a whole backstory written, explaining why Pam is with Roy and how they met, all of which I just invented.

BRIAN BAUMGARTNER: How was Pam similar to Jenna?

JENNA FISCHER: Well, like Pam, it took me a long time to figure out how to speak up for myself. I spent many years sitting at a receptionist desk wishing that I was doing something else, daydreaming about becoming an actor. I could really relate to that feeling of wanting something more. But unlike Pam, it would not have taken me three years to tell Jim that I had feelings for him. [*Laughs.*] I'd have dumped Roy much quicker.

BRIAN BAUMGARTNER: Why did it take her and Jim so long to get together?

JENNA FISCHER: Well, when we meet Pam and Jim, they've already been working together for a couple of years and then it's still three more years after that before they figure some stuff out. But in my backstory for Pam, her parents were so enthusiastic about Roy. He'd been in their family for a long time. Pam's parents owned an appliance store in town and Roy worked there in high school, and that's how this weird, mismatched couple met.

In the "Sexual Harassment" episode, Roy comes in wearing a sweater and he does a little dance and he's joking with Pam's mom. That's the guy we don't see too often, but Pam's family sees him that way, and their families are very meshed. So it's not easy for her to get out of that relationship and just go to Jim. There's a lot to untangle.

Angela Kinsey created a backstory for her character, head of accounting Angela Martin, simply based on the layout of *The Office.*

ANGELA KINSEY: Of all the desk pods in the main bullpen, there's only one that has a glass partition. Do you realize that? It's Kevin and me, and in my backstory, Angela probably requested it. [*Laughs.*] Like, "Kevin, I need a partition."

BRIAN BAUMGARTNER: But you could see through it. Why wouldn't she request a partition where we couldn't see each other?

ANGELA KINSEY: I needed to be able to see you for work, but I didn't want to breathe in your air. [*Laughs.*]

Rainn drew some inspiration from Mackenzie Crook, who played Gareth Keenan (Dwight's British equivalent) in the original BBC show.

RAINN WILSON: I got to steal all of his best stuff. Like how Dwight always says the most ludicrous, preposterous stuff with a total deadpan straight face. I frankly stole that from Mackenzie. Another thing I stole from him was the haircut. I read an interview with Mackenzie where he said he'd gone to a local barbershop out in Slough or some suburb of London, and he got the least flattering haircut for his head.

Brian Baumgartner in character as Kevin Malone . . . the smartest, most handsome man in *The Office.*

Rainn Wilson in character as Dwight Schrute.

I spent a lot of time looking in the mirror, figuring out the most ridiculous haircut I could get.

BRIAN BAUMGARTNER: I think you found it.

RAINN WILSON: I have a huge forehead, so I wanted to frame my forehead perfectly with these little Venetian blinds, these draperies of hair, to highlight the enormity of my carapace. So the combination of the haircut with those glasses—which, by the way, I really do think Dwight has influenced popular culture, because now all the hipsters wear Dwight glasses.

BRIAN BAUMGARTNER: You were the first hipster.

RAINN WILSON: Yeah, I really was. I was a hipster nerd in those glasses, and now everyone who goes to Intelligentsia Coffee in Silver Lake is wearing the same glasses.

"Like a Raccoon in the Light Next to a Garbage Can"
The Dance Between the Cameras and the Actors

The "Diversity Day" episode was also when we started to realize that the limitations of our physical space might be a productive constraint, creatively. Ken Kwapis set up the episode so that everyone was kind of cornered into the conference room, even though that made it way harder to shoot.

KEN KWAPIS: There was a lot of discussion about whether or not we should move the training session out into the bullpen, because otherwise the whole episode was going to be stuck in the conference

Randall Einhron (*left*) and director Charles McDougall (*right*) blocking a scene.

room. We're trying to prove to the network that this is a viable show, and we're going to set our second episode inside a small room? But I remember having a strong gut feeling that it would be funnier if everyone was trapped in a small space, because it made it more challenging to shoot. Sometimes the cameras were in people's faces a bit too much.

RANDALL EINHORN: We tried to shoot *The Office* as truthfully as possible, but there were rules that some directors found inhibiting.

Randall Einhorn, as our director of photography, was the one who made sure our show looked like a real documentary.

RANDALL EINHORN: One of the rules was, if we were doing a scene and we needed to shoot it from multiple takes, we would never show a place where a camera should have been to get the rest of the coverage.

Randall Einhorn

Occupation: Director of photography

Hometown: Cincinnati, Ohio

Previous Employment: Shooting rafting videos on the Tully River in Queensland, Australia; worked on *Eco-Challenge* (1998–2004), *Survivor* (2000–2002), and *Fear Factor* (2001)

Post-Office Credits: Director for TV shows *The Kids Are Alright* (2018–2019), *The Mick* (2017), *The Muppets* (2015–2016), and *Fargo* (2014–2015)

Overtime Hours: Directed ten-part webisode spin-off *The Accountants*

Special Citations: Two-time Emmy nominee (for his cinematography work on *Survivor*)

Special Skills: Underwater camera work, not realizing that he has an Australian accent

BRIAN BAUMGARTNER: If it's a documentary, if Steve is standing in his office and someone is filming Steve and then we cut, we can go back and then we have a camera that's shooting over Steve to the people in the bullpen watching. You should see a camera man standing behind them. So when we did that shot, what you're saying is we had to purposefully make sure that we didn't show the spot where the camera should be.

Another rule was that they couldn't include any complicated shots that only a highly skilled cinéma vérité cameraperson could have pulled off.

RANDALL EINHORN: Find another way. It made everything so much more challenging and interesting and cool.

BRIAN BAUMGARTNER: This wasn't entirely new territory for you, right? You'd been doing mostly reality shows at that point?

RANDALL EINHORN: I came from outdoor adventure and then ended up in a fluorescent office. [*Laughs.*]

Rainn used to make fun of my Australian accent, which I don't hear. Do I really have an accent?

BRIAN BAUMGARTNER: You do. I'm sorry but it's true.

RANDALL EINHORN: Rainn would be like [*in a thick Australian accent*], "Mate, there I was in the outback. It was beeeeeautiful. I caught a wild boar, mate."

His mysterious Australian accent by way of midwestern upbringing aside, Randall had something that *The Office* desperately needed, and executive producer Ben Silverman was the first to realize it.

RANDALL EINHORN: I was DPing some extreme sports stuff with snowboarders Shaun White and Jeremy Jones in Jackson Hole, Wyoming. Ben came to Jackson Hole and decided I was the guy to shoot *The Office* because I can shoot outdoor, extreme sports.

BEN SILVERMAN: I knew we needed somebody from that world to shoot in that stylistic way, but also so that we wouldn't set everything up as slowly as a traditional scripted comedy.

RANDALL EINHORN: It always feels false to me when I see a camera right next to people who are having a very intimate conversation. I told Greg, "I think the camera should be a very, very long way away so that the audience has to lean in to get what's going on. They feel privileged by it. And it reads as more honest."

BRIAN BAUMGARTNER: I remember you shooting a scene and being like, "The shot is too pretty." And you would pull a plant over, so there were leaves in the corner of the screen. Like you were trying to block it.

RANDALL EINHORN: We were trying to be hidden as if we were, you know, gleaning something that we were privileged to see. We did it all the time on *Survivor*. If people were having a conversation, we'd stay way back on the beach. It makes it feel more real.

GREG DANIELS: One thing that I noticed was half of the time when it wasn't funny it was because we'd gotten the camera awareness wrong. We were in a situation where we should have been spying on them through the window blinds, but the cameras were right up in everybody's face.

BRIAN BAUMGARTNER: So the comedy came from these characters forgetting that the cameras were there?

GREG DANIELS: Or being embarrassed that the cameras kept catching them in the act.

RANDALL EINHORN: If Michael wanted to close his office door, the camera would look through the blinds. If he closed the blinds, okay, we'll come around to another window and find you. The camera was nosy and unrelenting. It wasn't going to give you the space. It might let you think you have the space to go have a private moment, but it probably had another angle on you.

KEN KWAPIS: In the pilot, there's a wonderful scene towards the end. Pam leaves the reception desk and there's this long moment where Roy and Jim are just leaning, neither one of them saying anything. Then Jim finally says something innocuous and Roy just bolts out of there. It's very weird, and it's a scene where both characters are not aware they're being filmed. It's just delicious, especially for a character like Jim, who's always so hyperaware of the camera, to catch him in an unguarded moment.

The camera even managed to catch characters at their most vulnerable when they were well aware they were being filmed.

KEN KWAPIS: That climactic scene when Michael Scott is trying to impress Ryan and he plays a prank on Pam and it backfires. We're kind of spying on them but we're in the same room with them. That is one of the most uncomfortable scenes to watch. I watched it not too long ago with some filmmaking students, and they were all marveling at the fact that the scene is so upsetting but also so funny.

STEVE CARELL: I remember when Amy Adams came in. [She first appeared as Katy, a handbag saleswoman, in the season one episode "Hot Girl."] It's sort of a tricky thing to figure out how to play to the camera. But she had it down. She was aware of the camera, but she played it very differently, because she was an outsider. She didn't know. "What are you doing there?" Like, "Were you recording what I just said?"

KEN KWAPIS: That was one of the key strategies in how we shot. If we could land on you and you're suddenly aware of the camera but you have nothing to say, right? You get these wonderfully long, weird pauses.

STEVE CARELL: You're either being caught or you're performing for the camera. For Michael, when the camera was documenting things that were more vulnerable, that he didn't want the camera to see, you could show his fragility. I think the camera added a depth to all of these characters, because it's a reflection, I think, of that public perception, what you want the public to see as opposed to what is the reality of the situation or the reality of the person, the character.

GREG DANIELS: I remember one episode where Michael was bragging to the camera, and then he got this horrible call, and he had to actually hide under his desk. The camera came around and caught him there, like a raccoon in the light next to a garbage can.

KEN KWAPIS: When Greg and I held the production meeting for the crew, we announced that the things that would get them fired on any other show, like a camera operator panning past the subject and then sloppily backtracking, wasn't just acceptable but encouraged.

GREG DANIELS: I would sometimes say, "Okay, the problem with this scene is you know what you're looking for." And I would have the camera operator close his eyes and I'd spin him around and say, "All right, find it on action." The scene would start and the camera guy would open his eyes and he'd be pointing the wrong way and he'd have to find what was interesting.

The result of those spins, when a cameraperson tries to figure out where he or she should be shooting, is called a "swish pan." Or at least that's what we called it. A typical TV show wouldn't have allowed something so jarring in a final cut. But on *The Office*, they were commonplace.

RANDALL EINHORN: The reason we did so many of those swish pans is we were telling a story of Jim looking at Pam, but then we see Dwight looking at Jim looking at Pam, and then we catch Kevin looking at Jim looking at Pam. It just keeps adding up, all that math.

BRIAN BAUMGARTNER: As an actor, the lack of marks was discombobulating. Traditionally, there are marks on the floor that tell actors where to go. But on *The Office*, there were no marks.

KEN KWAPIS: There was also no regard for whether you were actually facing the camera at certain times. In a multicamera comedy, everyone is presented in a very frontal view. But for us, the idea was "Don't worry about hitting that mark, we'll find you. Wherever you go, we'll figure out how to find you or we won't."

JOHN KRASINSKI: On episode two, I remember saying to Matt [Sohn, the cinematographer], "Just let me know where you want me to be." And he was like, "No, no, that's my job. Don't tell me where you're going to be. It will make it feel more alive." I think it might've been our weird secret. We had camera people trained in the art of instinctively moving the camera to the point where people don't realize. Randall and Matt would dive across a table, knowing full well that not only was injury imminent, but the take would only be maybe two and a half seconds before they smashed to the ground. I remember Randall would sometimes say, "I will not reposition myself for a better shot because then it will show that we were aware of what you guys were doing." And I was like, "Wow, that is so next level."

GREG DANIELS: I'd give notes very differently to camera operators than I would on most shows. On any other show, it'd be, "Okay, I want you to pan over here and then on this line I want you to push in," blah blah blah, whatever. But on *The Office,* I'd give notes to them like they were actors. I'd say, "You've been following this story and you know that this person, who's never expressed any interest in that person before, but you've suddenly noticed that they're eyeing them differently. Go for that."

RANDALL EINHORN: Yeah, I definitely feel like the camera was a character on the show, and some of the best direction I ever got from directors was the type of direction you'd give an actor. "You feel this, you're worried about this, you're curious about that, but you know this." The camera always had a point of view. It had an agenda. It had its own stories it wanted to tell. The attitude of the camera was, if it had a personality, "You're not going to hide from me. I'm going to follow you. I'm going to use my zoom lens or I'm going to look at you through the window and I'm just not going to relent, because I'm a curious being."

KEN KWAPIS: Every actor developed his or her own relationship with the camera, and some were more eager to acknowledge it. There are moments where it feels like Jenna wants to crawl under the reception desk. And John's character, I think pretty quickly it's clear that he wants to make a friend of the camera.

GREG DANIELS: Brian used to do something that was so useful. I don't know if I've mentioned this to you before, but we would have these scenes and they'd be funny scenes, but there was no point to edit. So we were like, "How do we get out of the scene?" We needed a button. And then we'd be like, "Kevin! Kevin's done something. Yep, there he is."

It could have been a glance to the camera or physical comedy like walking into a wall.

BRIAN BAUMGARTNER: I'm very proud of that. I would give Matt Sohn a little nod at the end, like a wide receiver to a quarterback, and he would whip the camera over to me.

JOHN KRASINSKI: Wow. Let's think back to what you just said. When the scene was going great, Matt would give you a nod and you'd think, "I'll make it better." You also said "like a receiver to a quarterback."

BRIAN BAUMGARTNER: Yeah? And?

JOHN KRASINSKI: A lot of people tuned out on that one.

But Jim Halpert, played by the just-as-conceited John Krasinski, could always be counted on for the perfect double-take expression to the camera, breaking the fourth wall, to punctuate any scene.

Jim Halpert revealing his true feelings to the camera.

MATT SOHN: I had this running joke that we'd throw to John and he'd give us the number four, which was a particular look he'd give us.

BRIAN BAUMGARTNER: You called it the number four?

MATT SOHN: We had it numbered. There were a couple of looks that were John looks, depending on the scene. "I'm throwing to John right here for a number four." Jim had the biggest relationship with the camera, because Jim played the everyday man. He was the one truly grounded, relatable person on the show. You could always find Jim for a look or a nod.

JOHN KRASINSKI: I remember Greg and I talked about this. I was the window to the audience. I was the character who, right when you were thinking, "This is getting ridiculous," I'd look at the camera and go, "You're right, this *is* ridiculous."

We were all lucky to be making something we loved. There was just one problem. Nobody was watching. It wasn't just that we weren't a top-rated prime-time show. We weren't even in the top one hundred.

JOHN KRASINSKI: I asked . . . um, what's his name? The NBC executive that came every Friday and he was a super-handsome dude. I'm going to remember his name. He was so nice, and handsome as well. Jeff?

BRIAN BAUMGARTNER: Jeff sounds right.

JOHN KRASINSKI: Jeff was the nicest guy. He would come down to the writers' room, and he was a super-nice-dressed, handsome-ass guy. And I'd be like, "What's up, Jeff?" And he was like, "I love this episode. This will be the last one." [*Laughs.*] And I was like, "Oh." And he was like, "Yeah, it's just not getting the ratings and the network doesn't get it. I love it, but this is going to be the last one." He said that every week of the first season. And in the fifth week I said to him, "Can you make me a DVD so I can give it to my mom? So she at least knows that what I was doing out here was real and that I wasn't living under a bridge somewhere?"

Like we did with the pilot, the cast still got together every week to watch the episodes live. It became a comforting ritual, a way to celebrate together what we'd accomplished. Maybe it wouldn't get any further than this, we thought, but at least we'd have these memories of laughing together in Jenna's living room and remembering to keep the front door closed so her dog didn't escape again.

As it turns out, the handsome NBC executive who may or may not have been named Jeff wasn't entirely correct about the future of *The Office*. We just didn't know it yet.

5

"The Office Needed a Billion Things to Go Right"

THE EMOTIONAL ROLLER COASTER OF SEASON TWO

THE OFFICE CAST, 2005.

MIKE SCHUR: I have what amounts to like a ten-minute-long explanation of why *The Office* survived. In order for any show to work, a million things have to go right, from casting decisions to who's in charge to hiring the right writers. *The Office* needed a *billion* things to go right.

Mike Schur knows what he's talking about. Not only was he writing for *The Office* from the very beginning, but he went on to cocreate shows like *Parks and Recreation* and *The Good Place*. If anybody has cracked the formula for a successful TV show, it's him.

But a billion things needing to go right? If you were a betting man or woman back in April 2005, no one could've blamed you for not wagering on *The Office* to make it.

JENNA FISCHER: We were a ratings disaster.

It didn't seem to matter how different or smart or specific our show was, people weren't watching. 11.2 million viewers tuned in for the pilot, but by the end of our six-episode first season, that number dropped by more than half, to just 4.8 million, according to Nielsen. The conventional wisdom was that we wouldn't be back for a second season.

BEN SILVERMAN: Part of what's great about the new wave of television is that a series has a chance to breathe and be discovered. At that time [2005], you didn't have that luxury. This was a day and time when the heads of the networks read the ratings at four in the morning of what happened the night before.

Among those executives was NBC Entertainment president Kevin Reilly, one of the only people at the network who believed in *The Office*.

KEVIN REILLY: [The ratings] went down every week. I remember having to go to this affiliate where all of the station heads come in for this yearly meeting. I had really talked *The Office* up in our last meeting. That morning I remember thinking, "Please just stabilize. Let me wake up and please show me the rating that holds week to week." And I wake up and of course it's hit a new low. And I've got to go out and do the presentation. All they're talking about is how they're losing money and what's going on with the network. It's not good.

MIKE SCHUR: For you youngsters out there, you used to have to call a number and there was a "Here are the fast national ratings for Thursday, October 13, 1997." And then they would read out the data, which is lunacy. It's like driving a horse and buggy to the saloon, getting them that way.

BRIAN BAUMGARTNER: I had that number. So every Friday morning, I'd call in from the makeup trailer and announce our ratings for the week to the rest of the cast. "Okay, guys, we got a 4.7." We knew our show would live or die by those numbers.

BEN SILVERMAN: Exactly. That process and those reactive programming decisions were definitely fear invoking.

BRIAN BAUMGARTNER: I had sheets from week to week so I could see what was happening. I'd be like, "Well, we were down a little bit last night, but March Madness is going on. So that accounts for why ratings should be a little lower."

MIKE SCHUR: [*Laughs.*] Big AFC Championship Game or whatever.

JOHN KRASINSKI: The ratings were so foreign to me. I had no idea. So when they were like, "You got a one," I was like, "One million people are watching!" And they're like, "No, that's not how it works." Brian, you were one of the people who really guided me through this.

BRIAN BAUMGARTNER: I loved interpreting the numbers for the rest of the cast.

JOHN KRASINSKI: I was like, "What is a one?" And you were like, "Let me tell you something. The lowest-rated *ER* ever was a seventeen." And I was like, "Oof, that can't be good."

And the reviews, well . . .

STEVE CARELL: It was a remake of a very heralded show, and it did not get good reviews out of the blocks.

BRIAN BAUMGARTNER: My favorite review is from a gentleman by the name of David Bianculli [a TV critic on NPR's *Fresh Air*]. The way he took us down, it was like dark poetry.

David Bianculli (from 2005): "As fights for independence from England go, it hardly ranks up there with the American Revolution . . . Where

Ricky Gervais let the boss's insecurities show through, Steve Carell is all noise and stupidity. He's like a sketch comedy character, not a real person. Not just foolish but a fool."

STEVE CARELL: Across the board, there was not a lot of critical love for the show.

Washington Post: "The quality of the original show causes the remake to look dim, like when the copying machine is just about to give out."

Slate: "The harder it tries (and even, at times, succeeds) in amusing us, the more melancholic we'll feel, remembering how magical things used to be."

STEVE CARELL: I think we all just disagreed. We felt like we were onto something, and it wasn't the British version. It was something unto itself. People have their own opinions and they're entitled to them.

New York Daily News: "So diluted there's little left but muddy water."

USA Today: "A passable imitation of a miles-better BBC original."

STEVE CARELL: You can't take any of that too seriously.

New York Times: "*The Office* has the potential to be a hit, though perhaps not overnight. It remains to be seen whether NBC finds the nerve to keep it on the air long enough to build an audience, the way *Seinfeld* did."

GREG DANIELS: I made a lot of *Seinfeld* comparisons in the beginning. I was like, "Look how small that started. It's something new, it's something unique, it's funny, let it grow." But it turns out every single producer made *Seinfeld* comparisons if you had a show that was struggling. No matter how good it was or how close it was to *Seinfeld,* they'd heard that argument before. They were like, "Well, if it's really like *Seinfeld, Seinfeld* only had four episodes or whatever in the first season." [*Laughs.*]

The debut season of *Seinfeld,* which aired in June 1990, was the smallest sitcom order in television history.

GREG DANIELS: So we get this little skinny pickup, and now I have the ability to hire writers. In the meetings [with writers], I'd describe the show, and the more you describe it, the more your thoughts started to coalesce. I realized, as I was trying to pitch the show over and over again to different writers, that this was the first comedy version of a reality show.

Greg wasn't looking for direction from the critics or anybody who wasn't coming to work every day at our cramped office set. Instead, he turned to the people who were already there, witnessing firsthand what we were trying to make.

GREG DANIELS: Phil Shea, the prop master, I would ask for his opinion all the time. And Dave Rogers, the editor. I completely relied on and cared about their opinion as much as any of the writers.

Meanwhile, over at NBC . . .

MIKE SCHUR: Kevin Reilly basically staked his entire professional reputation on *The Office.* He does a thing that executives very rarely do. He says, "I believe in the show, the show can work."

KEVIN REILLY: Picking it up the first year took some finesse, but nothing like the challenge of bringing it back. I think everyone thought, "Okay, you had your shot with this little thing. We're moving on, aren't we?"

BRIAN BAUMGARTNER: How did you get it revived?

KEVIN REILLY: That was brutal. It was one of the toughest things in my career. I'd realized, at this point, odds are I'm going to get fired. You get to that thing where you say, "Let me go down [my way]." So I wasn't going to let it go. That second year of going through the screenings, they just couldn't believe it. I remember at one point, I got in this debate with [NBC executive] Dick Ebersol. He does know comedy [he helped cocreate *Saturday Night Live* with Lorne Michaels] and he's a legend in the sports world. He hated *The Office*. Despised it. And I remember at one point, he was literally pounding the table. [*Pounds table.*] "Hasn't . . . America . . . voted on . . . this . . . show? What more . . . evidence do you need . . . that they . . . don't like it?" And I said, "Dick, I don't think so. We buried it." I was clinging to my sales pitch. It almost became a screaming match at a certain point. Then he stood up and laughed, and I laughed, and he gave me a big hug. I think he would have loved to put the knife right in my back. It was like when a Mafia don gives you the hug. You don't really want the hug.

But some people didn't think Reilly was pushing hard enough.

BEN SILVERMAN: I was incredibly hopeful and obviously passionate about the prospects of the show. I felt we had overcome the initial hurdle of comparisons to the UK *Office* with our first season. But it was still not by any means a sure thing. If anything, there was a sense among the senior management at NBC that they didn't understand it.

BRIAN BAUMGARTNER: Meaning Jeff Zucker?

BEN SILVERMAN: It was more of an institutional rejection. There were people in the marketing department and the promo department who didn't understand it. "How do we market this? How do we sell it? Is it a documentary? Is it a reality show?" And no one was a star! There was no star at that point.

GREG DANIELS: The marketing department, all they knew was *Will & Grace*.

BEN SILVERMAN: And some *Friends*.

GREG DANIELS: So they took single lines out of context and that was the first ad. Out of context, none of the lines played like jokes. We didn't do setup–punch line jokes. It was all behavior and context and acting. It was horrifying. You'd look at these ads and go, "Oh my God, we have the stupidest, most unfunny show in the world." And they were like, "Yeah, God, you guys are going down." [*Laughs.*] I had to say, "Look, the frame has to be different. You have to blow up one moment and let it play. Otherwise we're doomed because it isn't a highlight reel."

BEN SILVERMAN: I got into a beyond fight with Jeff Zucker. I remember going into Jeff's office, talking to him about another project, and I used that meeting to also push for *The Office*. I was like, "You *have* to do this. It *has* to happen. It's too good. Please pick up the second season." And from that, I was thrown out of his office. [*Laughs.*] But in a joking way. He was like, "Get the fuck outta here. I know you want your show picked up!"

Finally, in May 2005, almost a month after the last episode of our first season aired, Ben received the news he'd been waiting for.

BEN SILVERMAN: I got a phone call. They said, "We're going to say that we're ordering thirteen episodes, but we're only picking up six."

MIKE SCHUR: Greg convinced them to lie because an episode order of six sounds like we're going to get canceled.

GREG DANIELS: What actually happened was, Kevin Reilly wanted to announce the pickup more strongly, but he could only get a few picked up, so he asked us if we would go along with the lie. And we agreed. So basically, it came from Kevin and I acquiesced.

BEN SILVERMAN: A normal pickup would've been twenty-two. And then they say, "You have to make it for half the price."

NBC was offering a budget for those six episodes that was roughly the same price to shoot one episode of *Lost* and a third of the price of any other sitcom currently on TV.

BRIAN BAUMGARTNER: How do you make that work?

BEN SILVERMAN: I needed everyone to take less money on these episodes. It was probably the lowest price in the history of modern TV. My first call was to Ricky and Stephen, because I thought they would say, "Fuck you." But I was like, "I know you've worked for two years now on a promise, but we have this opportunity. If we let the work speak for itself, we'll make more of them than you ever made in the UK. And we'll have a chance to be part of a big broadcast hit in America," which still meant a lot back then. And everyone said yes.

Money wasn't the only compromise that NBC requested.

GREG DANIELS: Kevin Reilly said to me, "Okay, Greg, you have to come in and pitch me how you're going to change it, 'cause it has to change. You can't do the same thing for season two as you did for season one."

KEVIN REILLY: If this was going to sustain and do more than six episodes, Michael Scott couldn't be an idiot all the time. He had to have some appeal. How did he become the boss, this fumbling guy who sucks up oxygen and can't read a room?

GREG DANIELS: I'm not sure exactly where—I feel I might've been on vacation—but I wrote on a napkin, trying to come up with things that would rehabilitate Michael and change his character.

Episode Guide

TITLE	DIRECTED BY	WRITTEN BY	ORIGINAL AIR DATE
"The Dundies"	Greg Daniels	Mindy Kaling	September 20, 2005
"Sexual Harassment"	Ken Kwapis	B. J. Novak	September 27, 2005
"Office Olympics"	Paul Feig	Michael Schur	October 4, 2005
"The Fire"	Ken Kwapis	B. J. Novak	October 11, 2005
"Halloween"	Paul Feig	Greg Daniels	October 18, 2005
"The Fight"	Ken Kwapis	Gene Stupnitsky & Lee Eisenberg	November 1, 2005
"The Client"	Greg Daniels	Paul Lieberstein	November 8, 2005
"Performance Review"	Paul Feig	Larry Wilmore	November 15, 2005
"E-mail Surveillance"	Paul Feig	Jennifer Celotta	November 22, 2005
"Christmas Party"	Charles McDougall	Michael Schur	December 6, 2005
"Booze Cruise"	Ken Kwapis	Greg Daniels	January 5, 2006
"The Injury"	Bryan Gordon	Mindy Kaling	January 12, 2006
"The Secret"	Dennie Gordon	Lee Eisenberg & Gene Stupnitsky	January 19, 2006
"The Carpet"	Victor Nelli Jr.	Paul Lieberstein	January 26, 2006
"Boys and Girls"	Dennie Gordon	B. J. Novak	February 2, 2006
"Valentine's Day"	Greg Daniels	Michael Schur	February 9, 2006
"Dwight's Speech"	Charles McDougall	Paul Lieberstein	March 2, 2006

"Take Your Daughter to Work Day"	Victor Nelli Jr.	Mindy Kaling	March 16, 2006
"Michael's Birthday"	Ken Whittingham	Gene Stupnitsky & Lee Eisenberg	March 30, 2006
"Drug Testing"	Greg Daniels	Jennifer Celotta	April 27, 2006
"Conflict Resolution"	Charles McDougall	Greg Daniels	May 4, 2006
"Casino Night"	Ken Kwapis	Steve Carell	May 11, 2006

"He May Be an Idiot, but He's *Our* Idiot"
Finding Michael Scott's Heart

While Greg was tinkering with Michael Scott, a little film called *The 40-Year-Old Virgin* was released. The comedy, directed by Judd Apatow and starring Steve Carell, was about a shy and genuinely sweet man who had somehow made it through four decades without losing his virginity. Opening in August 2005, the movie became a blockbuster, bringing in over $177 million at the box office worldwide. Carell's newfound stardom was the fortuitous break our show needed.

JENNA FISCHER: I can hear in my imagination a conference room filled with NBC executives, all saying, "We aren't going to be the assholes who let Steve Carell, the number one box office comedy star, out of his television contract."

MIKE SCHUR: NBC has a movie star under contract. Now every movie star is on a contract, but at the time it was a big deal.

JENNA FISCHER: *40-Year-Old Virgin* came out while we were shooting season two. We went to the premiere while we were shooting.

KATE FLANNERY: The billboards for *40-Year-Old Virgin* were *everywhere*. There was so much hype about that movie that I had a good feeling. I remember when we went to the premiere, the second season hadn't aired yet. We'd just started shooting for a couple of weeks. And I had this profound, intense feeling at that premiere. I got in my car and I literally burst into tears. I was like, "I feel like something big is happening." And it had everything to do with Steve.

BRIAN BAUMGARTNER: Almost overnight, it seemed like everyone wanted a piece of Steve. And we had him. All of us in the cast started to feel a tiny ray of hope. Like maybe this movie could save us.

ANGELA KINSEY: I really felt like they were banking on Steve. And I was like, "Okay, I will attach myself to the Steve wagon. [*Laughs.*] I'm banking on him too." I thought that that was a really good sign. But I still wasn't confident. When we finished those first six [episodes of season one], they printed our names on pieces of paper and then laminated them and put Velcro on the back, and that's what stuck to the door of your trailer. I went up to mine and ripped it off and said, "I'm going to save that." [*Laughs.*]

BRIAN BAUMGARTNER: Because you were sure it was done?

ANGELA KINSEY: I just didn't know.

For Greg Daniels, however, *The 40-Year-Old Virgin* wasn't just proof that Steve Carell was bankable. The character that Steve created on the big screen reminded Greg of what he'd been trying to do in TV comedy for years.

GREG DANIELS: I realized that I'd been treating *The Office* like everything I had learned on *King of the Hill* didn't count. When that show started, Hank wasn't very likable. I had to rewrite that show and create situations where Hank could be conservative but in a likable way. A lot of the other characters on *King of the Hill* are there to make him more likable and appropriate. For instance, he has his niece [Luanne] there so he can be very Boy Scout-y. You know what I mean? [*In a Hank Hill voice.*] "Don't show me your underthings!" You go, "Poor Hank, he's doing his best."

He brought his ideas to the writers, and it did not go over well.

MIKE SCHUR: We were in these crummy trailers on the very edge of the Universal lot. It was like the area where they put you before you're fired. No running water, it's terrible. Greg gives us a speech and he says, "The reason we're back is largely because of *The 40-Year-Old Virgin*. We need to change Michael Scott. We need to take 20 percent of what is so endearing and likable about that character and swirl it into Michael Scott. And we need to take 20 percent of the optimism. I want every episode to end with a little upswing. Michael can still be terrible and offensive and oblivious and everything. But at the end of every episode, we're going to have a little upswing, just a tiny, little positive thing."

BRIAN BAUMGARTNER: Were the writers upset? Were they like, "We're trying to do this really deliberate downbeat thing, and now you're telling us to make it *happier*?"

MIKE SCHUR: Most of the people on the staff were like, "He's ruining the show. We may get canceled, but at least we honored the British show with how downbeat and sad everything was. And he's blowing it. He's totally blowing it." I remember we took a walk around the disgusting abandoned parking lot where they'd put us and talking to Paul [Lieberstein] and Mindy [Kaling] and everyone and just being like, "This is terrible. At least we could hold our heads up high creatively and say we did something really cool. This is a disaster."

JEN CELOTTA (SEASON TWO WRITER; FUTURE CO-SHOWRUNNER): There's this thing on TV, especially then and even before then, where everybody has to be so likable. And sometimes likable and softening takes any kind of edge and any kind of comedy away. You're just softening them into this benign mush.

MIKE SCHUR: And of course Greg was 110 percent right. Once we got into the actual story-breaking, our fears were allayed.

JEN CELOTTA: Our mission with season two was to try and understand this character more, to see the underbelly of him. He could do crazy, ridiculous things, but you understood *why*.

JENNA FISCHER: They started to allow Steve to display vulnerability, which he's so good at. They would let him break our heart a little bit.

GREG DANIELS: Season two was gradually kinda putting in new coordinates for Michael. Part of the other thing was figuring him out and going, "Oh, okay, he's good at his job."

Written by Paul Lieberstein, "The Client" (season two, episode seven) followed Michael and his boss (and soon-to-be lover) Jan Levinson as they meet with a client (played by Tim Meadows) and attempt to win back his business.

JENNA FISCHER: You see Michael start out as what seems like a total buffoon and turn into a masterful salesperson.

```
MICHAEL: [Making his pitch.] I know
this place. I know how many hospitals
we have, I know how many schools
we have. It's home, you know? . . .
Here's the thing about those discount
suppliers. They don't care.
```

BRIAN BAUMGARTNER: You see the reason that he actually has this job.

If that sounds familiar, that's because it's the exact ingredient Kevin Reilly asked Greg to add to the show.

GREG DANIELS: Everything that makes him a bad manager—his caring what other people think and desperate need to be liked—it also makes him a really good salesperson. So it became more like the Peter Principle. He'd been promoted past his level of expertise.

The Peter Principle, a management theory first suggested by Canadian educator Laurence J. Peter in 1969, proposed that excellent employees will keep being promoted up the hierarchy until they reach their "level of incompetence."

The Dundies.

Dwight Schrute on the keys.

JENNA FISCHER: In the first season, we just really leaned into Michael's mean-spirited buffoonery and the ways he irritated us. But now in season two, we were bringing out sprinklings of these very redeeming qualities in him.

GREG DANIELS: His team feels oppressed by him and is always rolling their eyes, but if an outsider criticized him, they'd back him up.

The show explored this idea in the first episode of the second season, "The Dundies," based on an idea that Greg had originally envisioned for the pilot, in which Michael holds an award show for the office at a Chili's restaurant.

MIKE SCHUR: "The Dundies" is a story where Michael is a buffoon, and he thinks he's hilarious and he bombs terribly. The only difference between what it ended up being and what the version would've been in season one is, in the end, some ding-dongs at the Chili's start making fun of him.

> **GUY AT BAR:** Sing it, Elton.
>
> **MICHAEL:** Hey, thanks, guys. Where you guys from?
>
> **OTHER GUY AT BAR:** We just came from yo' mama's house.

GREG DANIELS: When people who don't work [at Dunder Mifflin] start heckling him and throwing stuff, the staff rallies around him.

> **PAM:** More Dundies!
>
> **PAM AND JIM:** [*Clapping.*] Dundies! Dundies! Dundies! Dundies!
>
> **MICHAEL:** [*Getting his spirit back.*] All right, we'll keep rolling.

MIKE SCHUR: Pam sticks up for him and is like, "Hey, we can make fun of him, but you guys can't! Screw you!" Ninety-two percent of the way through the episode, it could have aired in season one with its tone. And then at the very end, you're sent away with a little bit of happiness in your heart that things aren't so terrible.

BRIAN BAUMGARTNER: The Dundies showed that Michael may be an idiot, but he's *our* idiot. And he's an idiot with good qualities. Like how he acts around kids.

GREG DANIELS: In the ending of "Halloween" [season two, episode five], you see Michael desperately wants to have a friend at work, but he can't 'cause he's the boss and he has to fire somebody and he's just so bummed out. But then he lights up when the kids come trick-or-treating. It was a different show after that.

JENNA FISCHER: It makes me cry every time I watch it. Every time. Or the end of "Office Olympics" [season two, episode three], where Michael is crying because everyone is so genuinely applauding him for his purchase of a condo.

STEVE CARELL: He put his foot in his mouth all the time, saying inappropriate things, but I don't think he ever valued one type of person over any other. And in that way, I think he was a very pure character. He's very dumb in terms of political correctness and being appropriate in public. But at the same time, I just don't think there was hardness in his heart towards anyone.

GREG DANIELS: It's always about intention. If Michael has a purity of intention, he can do the worst things in the world for comedy. But as an audience, you sense that he didn't do it in order to be cruel or to be a jerk. He's trying, and he just has poor social skills.

MIKE SCHUR: The idea of shading and nuancing and layering the wacky boss was revolutionary. When Ricky and Stephen did it, it was revolutionary. And I think the American version did it even better. We got to invest the time in just getting into the psychology of Michael Scott. I remember Greg saying to the writers in that speech, "We can do what we did last time and get canceled, or we can change it and we can run for ten years."

"You're on My iPod, Dude"
The Office Hits the Much Smaller Screen

BRIAN BAUMGARTNER: Rainn, I'm hoping that you remember this conversation. After we shot the first six episodes of season two, you and Steve and I, for whatever reason, were sitting in Steve's trailer and Steve said something. Do you remember what it was?

RAINN WILSON: [*Pauses.*] "Take your pants off?"

BRIAN BAUMGARTNER: He said, "Well, at least we got to do twelve [episodes]." And we all kind of agreed. We thought we were done.

RAINN WILSON: And wasn't the next order for four episodes, and then like one, and then two? Just dribs and drabs. And this is just not done in that world of network television.

MIKE SCHUR: I remember the joke was that we were being picked up act by act. NBC would watch act one [of an episode] air and be like, "All right, go ahead and air act two."

Unbeknownst to us, behind the scenes, Kevin Reilly had been working hard to convince NBC that *The Office* was worth every episode.

KEVIN REILLY: I kept ordering it, and I had crazy meetings where the head of finance would come in and I'd go down the list of the things we're ordering. Here's how many hundreds of millions of dollars it's going to cost to order these shows, and I'd ask, "Where's *The Office*?" It was this woman, Diane. She said, "Oh, you should talk to Jeff." Meaning Jeff Zucker, who's running the network at the time. So I called him and said, "Jeff, where's *The Office*?" And he's like, "No, no, we're definitely ordering it." But it's not in the tally sheet, and we're locking the numbers. "Let me talk to Diane." I come back in and there's four. "Diane, why are there four episodes of *The Office*?" "Did you talk to Jeff?" I went through this nineteen times. Eventually, I don't know, we just got there.

This is how it went for the entire fall 2005 season, and then . . .

MIKE SCHUR: Five million other things happen. We were put on after *My Name Is Earl,* which becomes a huge hit. Everyone's watching *My Name Is Earl* and then watching us. We started at a 70 percent retention rate, and that went to 75 percent and then 80 percent and 85 percent.

My Name Is Earl may've brought us a larger audience, but it was up to us to keep them. One of the episodes that proved the ratings weren't a fluke was "Christmas Party," which aired in early December 2005. Mike Schur wrote it and structured it around a Secret Santa draw.

Christmas Party: Are fifteen bottles of vodka enough for twenty people?

MIKE SCHUR: We knew certain things. We knew that Jim had to have Pam and we knew that Michael had to have Ryan. But then I put everyone else's name in and just did a random draw. And Kevin got Kevin. That's where that came from.

BRIAN BAUMGARTNER: Really?

MIKE SCHUR: Yes. When that happened, I was like, oh my God, that's perfect. He just buys himself a gift. He doesn't tell anyone and buys himself a footbath.

The premise was simple: there's a twenty-five-dollar limit for Secret Santa gifts at the office Christmas party, but Michael, feeling flush after receiving a hefty bonus, spends $400 on a video iPod for Ryan. Tempers flare when people open their gifts and realize that nobody else got something as cool (or expensive). After Phyllis gives Michael an oven mitt, he ends up turning Secret Santa into a Yankee swap. And of course, everyone starts fighting over the iPod.

MIKE SCHUR: There was no deal with Apple. They didn't sponsor it or anything. But the whole episode is about a video iPod. That episode airs and—in my memory, I could be wrong—the next day Apple announces it has a deal for content, to have like an iTunes Store where you can buy TV shows and movies.

When Apple released its first-generation video iPod in October 2005, the iTunes Store included a few hit TV shows from ABC like *Desperate Housewives* and *Lost*. But in December, NBC joined the service, adding eleven shows from its catalog. For $1.99 per download, iPod owners could watch new episodes of *Law & Order* and *The Tonight Show with Jay Leno* and old classics like *Dragnet* and *Knight Rider*. *The Office* was part of that mix. Just a week after "Christmas Party" aired, iPod users could download it and watch the episode on the go.

"We think this is the start of something really big," announced Apple CEO Steve Jobs at the time. He was talking about the whole video iPod package, not just our little show. But it was the start of something big for us.

MIKE SCHUR: That year [2005], everyone got everyone a video iPod for Christmas. And when you got a video iPod and set it up and went to the iTunes Store, the first thing that you saw was *The Office* and the Christmas episode. It was the number one watched thing on iTunes for thirty consecutive days. So everyone spends the entire break watching that episode and then other episodes of the show.

KEVIN REILLY: It was the canary in the coal mine for where we are today. Generationally, there was a breakdown in the viewing of network television as the go-to, one-stop shopping. There were now other platforms and places that people could get it. There's always been a generational turning of the page where young people want the next thing.

ANGELA KINSEY: I remember getting an email that our first Christmas episode had become the number one download on iTunes. And I was like, "What? Oh, that's it. Momma's getting rid of her Chevy Blazer!" And then I got a Honda. [*Laughs.*]

JOHN KRASINSKI: I was going back and forth between L.A. and New York, and I was walking through New York and this guy put his hand up real fast in my face and I thought I was getting assaulted. He was like, "You're on my iPod, dude!" And I was like, "What is an iPod? What are you showing me? Are you beaming me up to space right now?" And there was my dumb face on his iPod, which was an inch by two inches or something. That was trippy for me.

BRIAN BAUMGARTNER: I remember walking into Apple Stores and seeing *The Office* advertised on their billboards before we were anywhere near a big hit and going, "Wow, this is awesome."

BEN SILVERMAN: Apple treated us better than our network.

BRIAN BAUMGARTNER: And maybe better than we deserved at that moment. But they saw something in the show too.

BEN SILVERMAN: They got behind the show and treated it as their own.

JOHN KRASINSKI: Remember when Fred Armisen did that Steve Jobs impression on *Saturday Night Live*? It was on Weekend Update and he was pitching the iPod and kept mentioning *The Office*. He was like, "You can film a movie while watching a movie and making a phone call, all while watching your favorite episode of . . . *The Office*." I was like, "Whoa, if we're being parodied on *SNL*, this is big."

BRIAN BAUMGARTNER: Apple didn't pay for product placement in the Christmas episode, right?

BEN SILVERMAN: Nothing, at least not initially. They ended up giving us all these computers for the set and kind of investing in the show as both an advertiser and supporter. But we were already naturally drawn to Apple, because the show always touched on things happening in the real world.

BRIAN BAUMGARTNER: It's funny. It's a show about a dying industry being taken over by technology, yet the show uses technology to its advantage every step of the way. We became a hit because of iTunes, and we're being discovered by a new generation today thanks to streaming services like Netflix.

JOHN KRASINSKI: A lot of people get to say, "We owe it all to our fans," but I think we might be the only show who *actually* owes it all to our fans. When people started paying for shows they could watch for free on TV, then NBC had to pick us up for another season. That was just so mind-blowing to me.

RAINN WILSON: It was young people with their iPods who knew how to set up an iTunes account because their parents didn't. I think that blindsided everybody, including NBC, that we would be so popular with young people. The fact that we're most popular with twenty-two- to twenty-five-year-olds is really astonishing. We didn't think that. We were like, "Oh, people who work in offices will like the show. And people who've had bad bosses before and have had to work with annoying coworkers, they're the ones who are going to really relate to this show." Why are fourteen-year-olds gobbling it up? It still doesn't really make sense to me.

The network was finally starting to pay attention. The downloads weren't being captured in the ratings, but for the first time people were paying to watch our show. And as cast members, we were also doing everything we could to reach viewers.

"We Broke the Record for Longest Moment Without Talking"
From MySpace to "Booze Cruise"

Some of the actors created MySpace pages for their characters and interacted with fans from their desks. Jenna's MySpace blog was often stamped "From the desk of Pam Beesly," and it wasn't false advertising. She often wrote it on the computer at her Dunder Mifflin reception desk. She shared fun behind-the-scenes tidbits with fans, like one entry from the summer of 2006, where she revealed that she sometimes dressed in character only from the waist up. Below the desk, "I'm wearing sweatpants and Ugg boots and it's awesome," Jenna wrote. "If only I could have done that when I was a real receptionist."

JENNA FISCHER: I think it connected people deeply to the show, to have the actors of the TV show that you really love interacting with you, answering your questions, caring as much as you do. It kind of makes you feel like you're part of it in a more real, intimate way. Also, it was real. That connection was real.

BRIAN BAUMGARTNER: You'd write back to fans on MySpace?

JENNA FISCHER: I would type things to people, like an instant message, like, "Hey, when you watch the such-and-such episode, in this scene, you'll know I was typing this to you." It was before Twitter, before Instagram, . . . before Facebook. MySpace was the place where there was this social interaction and we got all this feedback from fans. In that interaction, I would hear a lot about Jim and Pam. I would hear a lot of people say things to me like, "I have someone at work that I have a crush on. Do you have any advice?"

Angela Kinsey also had a MySpace account, as did Brian Baumgartner. B. J. Novak wrote a blog for *TV Guide*, where he revealed intimate details from the set that made readers feel like they were part of our inner circle. He shared in a September 20, 2005, entry, for instance, that the extras playing the waitstaff at Chili's in "The Dundies" episode were all "actual Chili's workers from around the state. One of them, a pretty, friendly blonde, appeared to have a crush on John [Krasinski]." She slipped a letter to John that contained the following poem: "Perhaps you'd join me for a night of romance? / A dinner, a movie . . . maybe a dance?" As Novak noted, "The whole thing rhymed . . . John was freaking out."

MATT SOHN: You guys got the internet at your desks during the second season. I recall everybody going to MySpace and talking about the show and what they're doing right now and what's coming up. It was this early groundswell of using the internet for good and for press for the show.

RAINN WILSON: We were trying to save the show. [*Laughs.*] And our jobs.

MATT SOHN: That helped build an audience.

RAINN WILSON: There's something else that you're leaving out, which was Dwight Schrute did a blog for NBC.com.

From September 2005—just in time for the season two premiere—to early 2009, Dwight had his own blog posted semiregularly on NBC's official site, called *Schrute Space*.

RAINN WILSON: This was also very new. Oh, a network has a website and you can watch clips of the show on that website and each show has a different web page? You can sign up and be a fan and talk on message boards on those pages? This was very new in 2004, 2005,

2006. I asked if I could write a blog in Dwight's voice. I don't know where those blogs are. I should have printed them out or something. I don't think they exist anymore.

Dwight's deep thoughts, all written by Rainn himself (often while he was killing time on the set, trying to look busy at his computer), touched on subjects ranging from salmon—"It's so pink. And it smells like fish. Salmon sucks! I hate Salmon. I hope they all die in those rivers"—to sleet—"It's not snow (wimpy) or rain (annoying). It's its own thing"—to whether coffee makers count as robots.

RAINN WILSON: I think it was the first time someone did a blog as a fictional character. It was just Dwight holding forth on whatever. That got a lot of press and attention, and fans really loved finding Dwight's blogs and getting to know the character that way too.

A screenshot of *Schrute Space.*

BRIAN BAUMGARTNER: The thought was: What are people across America doing when they're at the office? How are they killing time when they're not working? They were on MySpace and posting pictures and writing blogs. If Kevin Malone existed in Scranton, Pennsylvania, he'd have a MySpace account. When I started getting requests to send signed pictures, I was like, "This seems like a lot of work," but then I created an account just for Kevin Malone. And Kevin was just a guy with a dull day job. He didn't know how to react when people wrote to him. "I don't know why you want my picture, but if you send me a signed picture of yourself then I'll send you a signed picture of me." So I have boxes of photos in my closet, from people sending their signed photos to Kevin Malone.

The internet wasn't just a way for fans to interact with their favorite characters (and actors). It also allowed them to have, if not input on the show, at least a little influence.

JEN CELOTTA: I remember us going on [the *Office* fan site] OfficeTally at the end of every episode to see what the fans thought. It was like live-time reviews of the show by the people who watched it, and it was just fascinating.

LEE EISENBERG (WRITER, DIRECTOR, CO-EXECUTIVE PRODUCER): The entire writing staff just crowded around a computer, refreshing like crazy to see if [fans] liked the B story. It was like they had so much power.

BRIAN BAUMGARTNER: How much did that influence what you wrote in new episodes?

JEN CELOTTA: I don't remember it ever affecting any story lines. But it was a barometer for certain things. If we were slowing down Pam and Jim and everyone [on OfficeTally] was like, "I like the fact that it's slow," we might not feel the pressure of it as much. There were little things like that, but it was never like, "They want this so we have to give it to them." We would have little debates in the writers' room, and there was one debate, I can't remember what it was about, but it was small but passionate. Lee [Eisenberg] was on one side of the debate and I was on the other. After the episode aired, somebody on OfficeTally said something totally agreeing with how Lee felt. I was like, "Huh, that's a bummer." A few weeks or months later, I found out Lee was that person. [*Laughs.*] He wrote an OfficeTally comment under a fake name.

BRIAN BAUMGARTNER: So the original burner accounts existed in the *Office* writers' room.

Between that and the iTunes deal, our fan base was growing. When the show returned in early 2006, the first episode of the new year was "Booze Cruise."

MIKE SCHUR: It was the highest-rated show we'd ever done. We passed *My Name Is Earl* in the ratings. We actually beat our lead-in. And from there, the show was launched. That's just lunacy. You can only hope and dream that things go right. That's not things going right, that's like the universe conspiring to help us in some crazy way. Even though the show is serialized, Greg designed it so that you could enter it at any moment and understand the dynamics and get hooked.

"Booze Cruise," the eleventh episode of the second season, was written by Greg Daniels and directed by Ken Kwapis, and it was the first *Office* episode shot outside of the Dunder Mifflin office.

JENNA FISCHER: We did two days on the boat overnight and we were getting seasick. [*Laughs.*] It was really insane.

BRIAN BAUMGARTNER: B. J. Novak threw up over the side of the boat.

JOHN KRASINSKI: We had shot till the wee hours and the sun was cracking, and we were in pitch-black water, like terrifying, shark-infested water.

BRIAN BAUMGARTNER: It wasn't Lake Wallenpaupack in northeastern Pennsylvania. We were on Long Beach [Harbor, California]. It was essentially the ocean.

Huddled together behind the scenes of "Booze Cruise."

JOHN KRASINSKI: Hammerhead sharks are all over the place there. No, it's true. And we were on a tiny boat and we were all exhausted.

RANDALL EINHORN: It was the biggest swing by far, because we were shooting on a boat at nighttime, which everybody knows you don't do that. It's really hard. I mean, they learned that on [the 1995 Kevin Costner movie] *Waterworld*. But a boat at nighttime? It was a junky old boat and it was pretty hard to move around on it. It was rife with potential disaster.

BRIAN BAUMGARTNER: It was stuffy and confined. So in a way, it was the exact equivalent of the office bullpen, but on a boat.

JENNA FISCHER: We were like a bunch of kids on a camping trip. We were so excited. It was like, "Sleepover! We get hotel rooms! This is so fun!" [*Laughs.*]

RANDALL EINHORN: We couldn't move the boat because it would be different on every take. So instead of moving the boat, we would move the lights. There were a couple of barges that had lights on 'em that would go on action, so that the lights are in relatively the same place for each take. It was a pain in the neck.

"Booze Cruise" was also the episode with the infamous twenty-seven seconds of silence between Jim and Pam. When the two friends get a moment alone together on the boat, Pam offhandedly says of her fiancé, "Sometimes I just don't get Roy." Jim isn't quite sure how to respond, and the two stand there together, perfectly silent, for an uncomfortably long time.

KEN KWAPIS: The length of the silence was not something we'd planned to the second. But John and Jenna both knew there were no rules about pace. They're not doing a scene, we're observing them. We're observing two people having a moment. So it was not objectionable to let the moment linger. I don't remember, when we shot it, feeling like, "Oh my God, this is it. We've broken the record for longest moment of not talking."

JOHN KRASINSKI: It felt like a big deal when someone told me the number of seconds. If someone was counting, it surely wasn't Jenna or me.

KEN KWAPIS: But I do remember mostly that it felt very truthful. It could have been half that length, it didn't really matter. It just felt very truthful. I turned in my cut and probably worked with Greg on it, but it was Greg who ultimately fought to keep it in at that length. But for me, if you're involved, you don't feel the time passing. Those two actors were just so invested. I don't think they had a clue that they were stretching the limits of what's acceptable on a broadcast half hour of television.

BRIAN BAUMGARTNER: ["Booze Cruise"] was our seventeenth episode, but up until this point, I was on the show as a guest star. Meaning I was never a hundred percent sure that I would be invited back from week to week. The same went for Leslie, Kate, Oscar, Phyllis, and Angela.

ANGELA KINSEY: I found out I was going to be a series regular at like two in the morning, 'cause we were doing night shoots [for "Booze Cruise"]. There's a photo that I think Oscar took of Jenna and me when I found out, and we're jumping up in the air holding hands.

BRIAN BAUMGARTNER: Before that call, were you thinking you might be fired?

ANGELA KINSEY: I remember saying to my mom, "Pretty much anyone can go." And she was like [*in a Louisiana drawl*], "Well, every office needs a bitch." [*Laughs.*]

On January 6, the day after "Booze Cruise" aired, Kevin Reilly woke up at four in the morning and looked at the ratings.

KEVIN REILLY: And the show actually grew. It stabilized. It was a respectable rating. Honestly, I don't wanna admit it, but I might've teared up.

BRIAN BAUMGARTNER: You'd been fighting for this moment for so long.

KEVIN REILLY: The show went from good to great. Everybody was locking in and getting in the groove. The show truly became the American version of *The Office*. All of a sudden it was like, "Oh my God, this is now its own thing. And this thing could go a hundred episodes or more."

JOHN KRASINSKI: I used to go to this same diner every morning with my buddy Danny. We went every single morning and I got an iced coffee and started the day. On a Wednesday, because we used to air on Tuesdays at that time, I walk into the same diner, and the same people were now looking up and whispering, "That's the dude from that show." That was my moment that I really knew something had changed, people were watching. It was weird because I was really happy about it, obviously, but I was also a little freaked out because that sort of secret club that we had was no longer secret.

We were a little less than halfway through season two and finally gaining traction. And then, long shot of long shots, Steve was nominated for a Golden Globe in late 2005, in the Best Actor—Television Series Musical or Comedy category.

"Redneck Cousins at a Wedding"
The Office Crashes the Golden Globes

We were all beyond excited to be invited to a real awards ceremony. Except, well, we didn't exactly get into the ballroom of the Beverly Hilton Hotel, where the actual festivities take place. On January 16, 2006, the night of the awards, we were upstairs, on the hotel's rooftop.

BRIAN BAUMGARTNER: Or more specifically, the rooftop of their parking garage.

JENNA FISCHER: We were all invited to watch the Golden Globes at a viewing party, hosted by NBC Universal, with other executives. I believe we were like the only actors in the room.

ANGELA KINSEY: Oh my gosh, we were just like the farm mouse come to town. First of all, we had to go right from work. We had to get ready at the end of the day, and I had my hair in a ponytail 'cause I'd been playing Angela Martin all day, so guess what, I just wore a ponytail to the Golden Globes. I remember I got a spray tan 'cause I thought I was really white, like *too* white in my dress. Rainn made fun of me. [*As Rainn*] "So one day on *The Office*, Angela Martin is pale, and the next day you look orange? Angela!"

BRIAN BAUMGARTNER: I happened to live adjacent to the Beverly Hilton Hotel, so a bunch of us—David Denman [who played Roy], Oscar Nuñez, Angela Kinsey, and myself—we met at my house beforehand and drove to the Globes in Denman's Honda Civic. We had to park around the corner.

ANGELA KINSEY: We weren't allowed to sit in the main room. Only Steve got invited into the main room where the fancy people were.

JENNA FISCHER: They served sushi and lots of booze, and we all got shit-faced. We were super-duper drunk. Sort of because I think we felt like this might be the one and only swanky awards party any of us ever go to, and we were going to live it up like a bunch of redneck cousins at a wedding.

BRIAN BAUMGARTNER: We're surrounded by all these executives making deals in the corner. And we're being all rowdy in front of the big-screen TVs.

JENNA FISCHER: Then it came time for Steve's award and everyone knew that Jason Lee was going to win for *My Name Is Earl*. He was the odds-on favorite. And when they announced that Steve won for *The Office,* do you remember what happened?

ANGELA KINSEY: We about fell out of our chairs. Literally, we fell out of the sofa. We made such a scene.

JENNA FISCHER: We were like baseball players winning the World Series. We were leaping on one another.

BRIAN BAUMGARTNER: *Whooo!*

JENNA FISCHER: We piled on each other. It was such a display. The room was so confused by us.

ANGELA KINSEY: The fancy people were like, "Who are those guys?" We were screaming, we were so excited.

RAINN WILSON: Was that when he gave the really funny speech about Nancy?

Steve's acceptance speech was written by his wife, Nancy, or so he claimed. He thanked all the usual suspects, but kept coming back to Nancy, "who put her career on hold in support of mine, and who sometimes wishes that I would let her know when I am going to be home late so she can schedule her life, which is no less important than mine."

BEN SILVERMAN: I just remember the absolute joy we all felt in the affirmation that Steve got and the show got by association. I remember how fun it was to be young and part of something so successful, and we didn't even get hangovers then. You know what I mean? It was like you could do anything and be anyone.

JENNA FISCHER: When the awards were over, Steve came up into the party [on the rooftop] and we tackled him. We were passing the Golden Globe around. We piled into this little photo booth.

BRIAN BAUMGARTNER: Yes! That was one of my favorite moments. And you can still sort of see in that photo—because again, we were the redneck cousins of the Golden Globes—I had dipped something into the chocolate fondue, and it all went right down my white shirt. All the way, just straight down, all over it. Just because we were that classy.

JENNA FISCHER: That was when I thought, "Okay, they're not going to cancel us now. Steve just won a Golden Globe. [*Laughs.*] I have a job!"

BEN SILVERMAN: Later on, I remember having an intimate moment with my father on a plane, when I told him, "I think this is it. I think we're going to be okay. This show's going to survive. We'll be able to eat, and we don't need to worry about health insurance today as much as we did yesterday." It was that transformative.

BRIAN BAUMGARTNER: People were starting to pay attention to us now. Our show was getting recognized.

Steve's Golden Globe win was both a validation of what we were doing and also the spotlight we needed to keep doing it. At this point, NBC finally got behind the show. All the little things really did come together. We went from fearing that we'd be canceled to saying, "I think we might be around for a while."

MIKE SCHUR: It is wild to think about how many things lined up at exactly the right moment. We teetered on the brink of cancellation so many times, and if one of those things doesn't go well, if *40-Year-Old Virgin* made twelve million fewer dollars, I think we're canceled. It's crazy to think about in retrospect.

But even with everything going right, it was no time to coast. We finally had the attention we'd been craving, but now we had to keep earning it, week after week. We no longer lived in fear of cancellation, but audiences weren't going to keep tuning in if we didn't deliver on the promise of our first and second seasons.

Here goes nothing!

JENNA FISCHER AND JOHN KRASINSKI: NOT A COUPLE.

6

"John and I Are Not a Couple"

THE OFFICE LOVE STORIES

JENNA FISCHER: A lot of people say things to me like, "I think I found my Pam, I think I found my Jim." Using us as . . . I don't know, what do you call that? [*Laughs.*] As like a noun for love. Even today, people don't know how John and I are not a couple in real life. They don't understand it. And I don't know how to explain it, because it's a little bit like telling kids there's no Santa. I don't want to break anyone's heart.

Audiences had such an emotional connection to Jim and Pam—or, as some superfans called them, P.B. & J. (short for Pam Beesly and Jim)—that it still resonates to this day.

Long after *The Office* went off the air, they've created Jim and Pam mash-ups on YouTube with romantic ballad sound tracks like "Crash into Me" (Dave Matthews Band) and "Iris" (Goo Goo Dolls). Two *Office* fans with an uncanny resemblance to Jim and Pam went viral on TikTok in 2020 with their word-for-word re-creations of the TV couple's most memorable moments.

Supermodel Chrissy Teigen is so obsessed that she hosted a Twitter poll in 2019, on the ten-year anniversary of Jim and Pam's wedding, asking fellow fans if the pair were still together. When 70 percent insisted they were, Teigen argued that the fictional couple were either divorced or unhappy. "They never went to Austin," Teigen wrote, referring to the *Office* finale when Jim and Pam decide to make the move to Texas for a fresh start. "You know it and I know it. I talk about moving to Austin every other day and here I am. Not in Austin."

That's a lot of time and mental energy devoted to a couple that only exists on our TV screens.

But people want to believe. They want to think that Jim and Pam weren't just fictional creations but flesh-and-blood people whose love story was genuine and true. One viewer tweeted at both John and Jenna in 2016, writing, "I'm watching *The Office* for the first time and I'm very saddened to hear that you two aren't together in real life."

BRIAN BAUMGARTNER: You should just explain that John's a real pain in the ass in real life. Why would you not just say that?

JENNA FISCHER: [*Laughs.*] No, it's that I am not Pam in real life and he's not Jim in real life. In real life, we're mismatched. He is perfectly matched with Emily [Blunt, his wife since 2010], and I'm perfectly matched with Lee [Kirk, her husband since 2010]. We need our laid-back, easygoing partners.

BRIAN BAUMGARTNER: I also think you were both playing characters on a TV show.

JENNA FISCHER: But I feel like I have to justify why John and I aren't actually in love. The bottom line is, we were playing characters. But when you say that, it destroys some of the magic of Jim and Pam. That's the thing I don't ever want to take from people.

We're not going to destroy the magic of JAM—our other favorite shorthand for Jim and Pam—or at least we'll try not to. We just want to tell the tale of how a little workplace comedy that wasn't trying to reinvent the wheel—only share some stories about everyday people that felt truthful and real—created one (or maybe a few) of the most iconic couples in TV history.

Love on ice: On-again-off-again couple Kelly and Ryan (Mindy Kaling and B. J. Novak) find their footing, 2006.

"A Really Intense Love Story with a Quarter of the Screen Time"
When Jim Met Pam

BRIAN BAUMGARTNER: If you go back and look at those early episodes of *The Office*, the budding romance between Jim and Pam plays out quietly on the sidelines.

MIKE SCHUR: Greg [Daniels] had a lot of theories, and they were all correct. One of the things he pinpointed for us very early on: What makes the British *Office* so good? Part of it is the once-in-a-generation performance from Ricky Gervais and some of it is other incredible actors and a wonderful mockumentary premise. But Greg broke it down even further. He said, "Almost every show in history has had a formula, and the formula is—the center of the show is—a will-they-won't-they Sam and Diane [from *Cheers*] romance. And off in the corner is a wacky boss, and occasionally the wacky boss comes in and does something funny and gets big laughs and then leaves. But the audience's investment emotionally is with the will-they-won't-they couple. The British *Office* inverted it. The wacky boss is the main part of the show, and shoved into the corner is this will-they-won't-they romance.

BRIAN BAUMGARTNER: Does that change how the audience feels about these characters?

MIKE SCHUR: It does two things. Number one, it makes the wacky boss into a viable character worthy of introspection and layering and dimension in a way that the wacky boss traditionally isn't. No one usually cares about what's going on in the wacky boss's emotional life. It also means that when you shove the romance into the corner, it becomes this delicate, gossamer spiderweb of glances and tiny moments. A character getting someone a candy bar from the vending machine becomes an enormous emotional moment. You've fundamentally changed the way audiences relate to romance. "I only got eight seconds of the romance this week. I want more!" So many people got invested in a different way than they're normally invested in TV romances.

The challenge for everyone, from the writers to the actors to the editors, was how to strike the perfect balance, letting this subtle love story of Jim and Pam unfold at the edge of the frame.

JEN CELOTTA: The fact that they weren't front and center made us enjoy it even more. They were the pop of beauty in the gray.

BRIAN BAUMGARTNER: Their story wasn't Ross and Rachel from *Friends*. Jim and Pam was a little moment here, a little moment there.

JOHN KRASINSKI: The stakes were set up so wonderfully, because that's real life. When you're in love with someone, especially someone at work, you look forward to those interactions at the office. When you go home and have a home life with your friends or whatever else you're doing, you will not see that person. So you're sort of, I don't know, tantalized by the idea that when you get those moments with her, you'll savor it.

A little Jim and Pam moment.

GREG DANIELS: You can play a really intense love story with a quarter of the screen time, and you've still got three-quarters for comedy. Think about *Cheers*. They had one lead man and woman and then side characters. The lead had to carry the comedy *and* the romance. That's one of the great aspects of *The Office*, you didn't have to put it all in one person. It's like Zeppo Marx. [*Laughs.*] With the Marx Brothers movies, the main plot would be the Marx Brothers, and they also had a romance, but they gave it to Zeppo. Obviously Krasinski is no Zeppo. He's super funny. But he didn't have to be as crazy as Michael and Dwight. He can be more of an everyman and react to stuff and be in the romance.

BRENT FORRESTER (WRITER, PRODUCER): Greg used to say a thing that I thought was very interesting. "Tonally," he said, "separate out the scenes that are dramatic tone from the scenes that are comic tone. Don't try to do them both at once." That was a big learning curve for me. He called it the McDLT. This is a reference to a thing that McDonald's used to do very briefly. They had this hamburger that was served hot in half of the Styrofoam container and then the other half was the cold lettuce and tomato. The gimmick was you'd put it together and the hot stays hot and the cold stays cold. That's what Greg used to say. "Keep the hot side hot and the cold side cold, the funny side funny and the drama side dramatic. Separate out those scenes."

KEN KWAPIS: The show is a comedy, but within it is a romantic story that's not played for laughs. This is a show with clowns and lovers. In a show like *Friends*, the romantic story lines are all funny. But in *The Office*, we don't love Pam and Jim because of the laughs. We love them because they seemed grounded and real.

Another reason the relationship feels so grounded is the pacing. Many of the biggest Jim-Pam moments happened off the beat, when we didn't expect them.

GREG DANIELS: Surprise is really good for comedy, right? Anything you can do to increase surprise is good. The problem to me with multicamera shows in general is that the rhythms are so ingrained. It felt like Kabuki or some kind of really ritualized thing.

JOHN KRASINSKI: In TV, you know that the big scenes are coming. And Greg wouldn't do it. I remember how bold it was when you thought Jim was going to do something, like propose to Pam, and then it wouldn't happen and you were like, "Oh man."

BRIAN BAUMGARTNER: Or the time you and Pam accidentally kissed at the Dundies.

JOHN KRASINSKI: That's real life. Those are the things you remember. Whereas a regular television show would have a big huge kiss scene, like, "They finally got together!" I remember reading that script and being like, man, that is so smart. To have the audience be like, "Did they just kiss?" And not give them what they thought they wanted. 'Cause that's how I felt. I felt like, "Oh my God, I thought we were going to do some huge kiss scene." And instead she just did it at the Dundies. I guess this is where I'm very much like Jim, because I would've stewed on that for months and been like, "Was it a real kiss?"

BRIAN BAUMGARTNER: Did that count?

JOHN KRASINSKI: Was she just drunk? That's real life. Rather than if it was a big kiss scene where I took her out back and made some huge overture. You'd be like, "Oh good, I'm being entertained by this moment. But I don't feel anything. I'm not connected."

For someone watching this unfold on TV, it was obvious that Jim had it bad for Pam from the pilot. But in the second season, the tension in this will-they-won't-they relationship really started to build. That was partly due to the addition of a new writer in season two, someone who loves nothing more than a complex psychological story line, Jen Celotta.

Jen Celotta

Job Title: Writer, co-executive producer

Hometown: Gaithersburg, Maryland

Training: Boston University, Class of 1993, communications major

Previous Employment: Writer for *Home Improvement* (1996–1999); writer and producer for *Andy Richter Controls the Universe* (2002–2003) and *Malcolm in the Middle* (2004–2005), among other series

Post-*Office* Credits: Consulting producer on *Space Force* (2020) and *The Newsroom* (2014); director for martial arts comedy-drama series *Cobra Kai* (2018–2021)

Special Skills: "That's what she said" jokes, writing Jim-Pam story lines, or maybe Michael Scott story lines, or maybe all of the above

Career Aspirations: To play a Schrute, which she did in the *Office* finale, playing Dwight's relative Jen Celotta Schrute

JEN CELOTTA: Hi!

BRIAN BAUMGARTNER: Yay!

JEN CELOTTA: Yay, ya, yay! I'm so excited!

That is Jen in a nutshell. Mike Schur sums her up this way.

MIKE SCHUR: Jen Celotta was the beating heart of the show. Her superpower was her incredible connection to Pam and to the sweetness of that character.

But Greg disagrees.

GREG DANIELS: When I think about Jen, I think about Michael Scott stories. I think about the funeral for the bird and stuff like that. She was super into the psychology of Michael. Jen is fascinating. She's the child of a physicist and very brainy. All of her work after *The Office* is like . . . she has a screenplay where every scene is from a different year of a guy's life, and she's doing an animated show with trees as the protagonists.

JEN CELOTTA: I've heard some people talk about how I particularly loved writing Pam and Jim. I did love finding the shades and the colors and the dynamics between the two of them. One of my favorite things I got to do with them was the jinx episode where they didn't speak.

One of the shared office games between Jim and Pam is jinx. After two people unintentionally say the same word or phrase simultaneously, the first one to say "Jinx, buy me a Coke" forces the other to remain entirely silent until a Coke is purchased for the jinxer. In "Drug Testing," episode twenty of season two, Jim and Pam both utter the same Stanleyism ("I do not think that is funny") and Jim is jinxed. Following the "unflinchingly rigid" rules, Jim makes his way to the vending machine but discovers it's sold out of Coke, and so he must spend the day not saying a word to anyone.

> **JEN CELOTTA:** There's a moment with Jim and Pam where she says, "Oh, what, are you going to tell me something?" And he wanted to say that he liked her, but he has to be silent. And she says . . .

```
        PAM: You look like you have something
        really important to say and you just
        can't for some reason.
```

> **JEN CELOTTA:** He looks like his stomach drops and he turns white and looks down, and then you see her know what that means and she reacts. They could be silent film stars.

While these magical Jim and Pam moments felt organic and effortless on-screen, working on them on a day-to-day basis was not. Nothing brought production to a screeching halt like a big Jim-Pam scene.

> **JENNA FISCHER:** It's true.

BRIAN BAUMGARTNER: I would be like, "Please get me out of here before they film this, or it's going to be seven hours."

MATT SOHN: There was a lot of emotion and discussion that went into the Jim and Pam scenes.

BRIAN BAUMGARTNER: I had a very specific Tom Waits impression that I would do, which would be something like [*with a Tom Waits gravelly baritone*], "There's a discussion at the monitor," and the writers would get so aggravated.

MATT SOHN: It was true, though.

BRIAN BAUMGARTNER: You would see it happen. You would see people start assembling.

MATT SOHN: The writers would get called; they would all come down to huddle. Everybody would go to craft services to get coffee. The set would clear out. We'd sit around, we'd wait, we'd talk, we'd chat, we would dissect the scene and we would rebuild it.

BRIAN BAUMGARTNER: Why do you think those scenes were so important?

MATT SOHN: It was a slow burn early on, and they didn't want to go too far too fast. Jenna had strong feelings on what it should be, as did John and Greg.

JENNA FISCHER: We cared very deeply. Everybody cared very, very much. John and I would fight hard for what we believed and we were usually on the same page. We had a singular mind when it came to Jim and Pam.

MATT SOHN: It was finding that exact tone that kept everybody happy, that kept their relationship on point to give it that slow build. It wasn't one of these ridiculous, romantic, silly things that you see in a lot of shows.

GREG DANIELS: I didn't want to do a romance like in so many shows, where they come together and break apart and come together and break apart. It didn't seem real. I felt when Jim and Pam finally get together, they're going to be together. I don't see anything breaking them up because they're so in tune with each other. So then the question was: How do we spin this out for a certain number of years? What are the obstacles?

JENNA FISCHER: There was often one Jim-Pam moment per episode. And it was either where they're going to connect in some super special swoony way or they're going to misstep in some way where one of them gets their feelings hurt. And there was this very fine line that we had to walk all the time. So for example, shooting a scene over and over and over again, where this time they can touch hands, but then we have to do one where they don't touch hands. 'Cause it might be too much if their hands touch, that might be going too far. Do we end it with a hug, or should he kiss her cheek before he leaves? How

HUMAN RESOURCES FILE

Lee Eisenberg

Job Title: Writer, director, co-executive producer

Hometown: Needham, Massachusetts

Training: Connecticut College, Class of 1999, English major

Previous Employment: Writer for the 2001 short film *Flush*

Post-*Office* Credits: Creator, executive producer, and writer for the HBO series *Hello Ladies* (2013–2014); executive producer of CBS series *Bad Teacher* (2014); cowrote the (as yet unproduced) screenplay *Ghostbusters III*

Career Plan B: Culinary school

Writing Partner: Fellow *Office* scribe Gene Stupnitsky, whom he met at the copy machine while a production assistant on the 2000 Harold Ramis-directed comedy *Bedazzled*

First *Office* Assignment: "The Fight" (2005), season two, episode six, cowritten with Stupnitsky

Recommendations: "They write dumb characters really intelligently," said *Office* director Harold Ramis.

Promotions: Ramis hired Eisenberg and Stupnitsky to write the 2009 film *Year One* and the script for *Ghostbusters III*.

much were they allowed to literally touch one another, look into each other's eyes, swoon at each other? I mean, we would spend hours debating and shooting alternates of these Jim-Pam scenes.

LEE EISENBERG: When you look back and you watch it, it feels like some of the choices are so confident and so inevitable.

This is Lee Eisenberg, who joined our writers' room at the beginning of season two.

LEE EISENBERG: But that inevitability makes it feel like it takes months and months and months of going down all these different avenues. When you finally make the choice and it goes through multiple rewrites, and then you have these actors do it and everything comes together, it feels like, oh, that was the exact right choice. But we debated Jim and Pam in "Casino Night" for weeks and weeks and weeks. What does he say and what doesn't he say, and what does she say, you know? There were multiple drafts of it and different versions of it.

Ah yes, "Casino Night," the season two finale, which first aired on May 11, 2006. It gave us the quintessential Jim and Pam moment, the one we'd all been anticipating with every under-the-radar flirtation and furtive glance.

"What I Was Shooting Looked Real"
The "Casino Night" Kiss

GREG DANIELS: "Casino Night" is when Jim says he likes Pam for the first time to her face in the parking lot. The writing staff kind of went nuts. Everybody wanted to write it, first of all. This was, to me, one of the most charming and likable aspects about the writing staff. They cared so much about the show. A lot of times, you get in a situation where they're just trying to get out and go home. And these guys were young. It was Mike [Schur] and Mindy [Kaling] and Paul [Lieberstein] and B.J. [Novak] and, at that point, Jen [Celotta] and Lee [Eisenberg] and Gene [Stupnitsky]. Everybody wanted to be the person to write it.

But Greg went with a first-time writer on the show, Steve Carell.

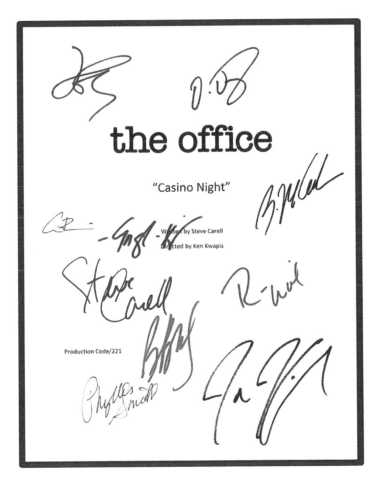

A copy of the "Casino Night" script.

GREG DANIELS: And Steve wrote it really well.

The pivotal scene happens near the episode's end, when Jim and Pam run in to each other outside a company party. It's a simple moment, just two people in a parking lot, spanning no more than two minutes of screen time. But behind the scenes, it became a tug-of-war between director Ken Kwapis and the writers.

GREG DANIELS: Ken wanted to shoot it in a very straightforward fashion. And his reasoning, I think, was very sound. Which was, yes, yes, everybody loves the conceit and the mockumentary part. But now it's about the characters, and the most entertaining and interesting thing is to see their faces. But the writing staff desperately wanted to lean in to the mockumentary. They thought it was our secret weapon.

JEN CELOTTA: I like it when you have to fill in the blanks. In the parking lot scene with Jim and Pam in "Casino Night," I didn't want to miss *everything*, I just wanted to be late to the party or find the shadow of them and hear them talking.

GREG DANIELS: Whose contributions do you want to really push at this moment? The concept and the writing? Or maybe this cast? Should you trust these two great actors and let them do their thing?

DAVID ROGERS (EDITOR): Originally the concept was we would just see the aftermath of it. There was a huge discussion with Greg and Ken and the actors, and it was like, yeah, it's cool to do something as a documentary and just capture the moment after. But there's something unsatisfying for an audience member to not see a piece of this. I think we made the right choice in letting [Jim and Pam] have a conversation.

`JIM: I was just . . . I'm in love with you.`

PAM: What?

JIM: I'm really sorry if that's weird
for you to hear, but I needed you to
hear it.

GREG DANIELS: There are a lot of different versions. But one version which we actually shot was that the cameras are covering Casino Night and, like on a reality show, somebody is monitoring the sound 'cause everybody's mic'd. They realize Jim is about to confess something to Pam and they tell one of the cameramen, "Get it, get it, we don't know where it is!" And the camera guy runs out of the warehouse and down the alley and around the corner of the building just in time to see Jim be told no and walk away. We did shoot that and it was interesting. But ultimately, we went with the faces.

JOHN KRASINSKI: I remember not knowing where Matt [Sohn] was and Ken wouldn't tell me. He was like, "Don't worry about it. Just do the scene."

PAM: What are you doing? What do you
expect me to say to that?

JIM: I just needed you to know. Once.

PAM: Well, I um . . . I . . . I can't.

DAVID ROGERS: You think that's it.

BRIAN BAUMGARTNER: We're done.

DAVID ROGERS: We're done. But then at the end, I mean, talk about an ending.

MATT SOHN: The kiss? Oh my God.

David Rogers

Occupation: Editor, director, and producer

Training: Ithaca College, Class of 1992, B.A. in cinema and photography

Previous Employment: Editor for *Seinfeld* (1998), *NewsRadio* (1999), and *Andy Richter Controls the Universe* (2002)

Post-Office Credits: Director, editor and co-executive producer on *The Mindy Project* (2014–2017); editor and consulting producer on *Upload* (2020) and *Space Force* (2020)

Movie That Inspired Him to Become a Director: *Superman: The Movie* (1978), which he saw when he was eight

Possible Disciplinary Action: Took the *Battlestar Galactica* model that Dwight built and displayed in his office after being promoted to manager, which he had personally selected. Rainn Wilson signed it for him with "David, Galactica loves you. Rainn Wilson, Dwight."

The next thing we see on-screen is Pam, back in the office, quietly talking to her mom on the phone. And then Jim walks in and kisses her.

JOHN KRASINSKI: Nobody was on set, nobody was around the craft service table. I didn't know that was happening. So I walked on, you know, ready to joke with folks, and nobody wanted to make eye contact with me. I was like, "What happened?" I was so nervous.

KEN KWAPIS: There was a lot of conversation about the kiss. I think that John and Jenna had a lot of, uh, what's the right word? They were anxious about the scene.

JOHN KRASINSKI: I was like, "What's happening? Is no one going to call action?" Randall [Einhorn] and Matt [Sohn] were two of my favorite people on earth and I couldn't see them. I was like, "What are we doing?" It was really weird. I was so freaked out. I was on set for a while before Jenna showed up, 'cause Jenna was taking her moment. I didn't know that I could take thirty minutes in my trailer to prepare mentally. And then I got even much more scared. You start to think like, "Oh God, I didn't do my homework."

When they were ready to shoot, everyone disappeared. It was just John and Jenna in the room. Randall Einhorn, the director of photography, was tucked away, just peeking through the blinds.

RANDALL EINHORN: I was so far away from them. And they're really heavy cameras. The cameras weighed like thirty-eight pounds. Ken Kwapis was directing, and I was in the kitchen and all the lights were out. It was a really long lens shot. It was probably a 300-millimeter long lens shot.

KEN KWAPIS: If you shoot a kiss, any kind of kiss, traditionally you want to be able to see two faces. But we decided, and I don't remember if it was Greg's suggestion or if the actors came up with it, that we don't see Jenna's reaction to the kiss. We're at her back. We see John, right? They kiss and then they break. I think they look at each other for a beat. And that's the end of the scene. One of the things I've often thought about with that shot is, as an audience, you get the pleasure of being Pam. You're being looked at by Jim. You don't see her reactions. So you get to, as an audience, kind of write it yourself.

RANDALL EINHORN: I was actually getting choked up. I knew very well that it was John Krasinski and Jenna Fischer and that there was craft service just out the door. And I would see John and Jenna there in a minute. But I would still get emotionally involved. I would get invested because, to me, what I was shooting looked real. I was with those characters and it all felt real.

DAVID ROGERS: It's that moment where they look at each other after and it's like, "What now?"

It was a moment for fans to think about what could be in store for Jim, for Pam, for their future.

JEN CELOTTA: You're so rooting for them. You feel like they're kind of stuck in a place where they both could be—just like everybody—could be doing more.

"They Would Repel a Lot of People, but Not Each Other"
Love Secrets of Dwangela and Phyllis and Bob

Jim and Pam were far from the only promising (or potentially catastrophic) relationship that blossomed at Dunder Mifflin. On most TV shows, secondary characters generally exist to support the main characters' story line or add a little color to the fictional world. But on *The Office*, every character had complex dimensions waiting to be discovered, and desires almost certain to complicate their lives.

BRIAN BAUMGARTNER: When did Dwight and Angela's relationship start?

RAINN WILSON: Boy, Angela would know this a lot better than me.

BRIAN BAUMGARTNER: When were you aware that this relationship was going to be something that lasted?

RAINN WILSON: I think it was the episode where there was a party at Jim's house.

"E-mail Surveillance," the ninth episode of the second season, first aired on November 22, 2005.

RAINN WILSON: Dwight finds Jim's hide-a-key rock, the fake rock where you hide a key in. I brought it in and was like . . .

> **DWIGHT:** Jim! You really think this is a good idea, huh? A hide-a-key rock?
>
> **MARK:** Hey, you must be Dwight!
>
> **DWIGHT:** You don't work with us.
>
> **JIM:** That's because Mark's my roommate.

RAINN WILSON: That's when Pam looks out the window and sees my feet and Angela's feet sticking out of the tree house or whatever it was in the backyard.

JEN CELOTTA: It was in a doghouse or tree fort. I wish I could remember whose idea it was. It had been something that writers were talking about for a while.

RAINN WILSON: They told me an episode before that they were going to get Dwight and Angela together. I'm like, "Oh, that's hysterical." I just thought it would be a little seasoning, a little

Dwight and Angela: A secret love affair.

flavoring. I had no idea that Dwangela would become a phenomenon that would last another seven or eight seasons.

LEE EISENBERG: Every show and every movie has "Oh, here's the weird guy," right? And the weird guy only does weird things. And the weird guy wouldn't get girls 'cause the weird guy doesn't like girls. And the weird guy wouldn't like music because music is discordant to them.

BRIAN BAUMGARTNER: But Dwight loves women.

LEE EISENBERG: And some women really liked Dwight. He's super confident. Dwight has a swagger in his own way that's weird and cool.

ANGELA KINSEY: Our characters look around for the camera. There are times when we see that we've been caught and then we react to being caught. That was always a really fun thing to play off of. It was always something we had to consider when Dwight and I had scenes together. Are we camera aware? Do we know that the camera's picking this up? And sometimes we never saw the camera. They truly were hidden and doing a spy shot. And then there were times where one of us would find it, usually me, and I'd walk off in a huff.

BRIAN BAUMGARTNER: How did that relationship change Angela?

ANGELA KINSEY: I think it just opened her up. In the beginning, you could see her as one note. Like, "Oh, she's just the office bitch." It's sort of true, but the office bitch can be a bitch in love. There's the sneaky bitch, the superstitious bitch, the madly-in-love bitch. There are layers to her grumpiness. She's someone who's very fear based, and I think falling in love with Dwight and having to step out of her comfort zone and trust someone and let someone in, it made her more three-dimensional.

JEN CELOTTA: I couldn't see Dwight with anyone and I couldn't see Angela with anyone. Maybe it was one of the things they had in common. They would repel a lot of people, but not each other. There was some fascination in terms of how un–Jim and Pam they were and how it could be played for even more comedy.

ANGELA KINSEY: But in their own way, their story isn't much different than Jim and Pam. It's two people that love each other and are both a little too scared to let the other person know how much they love each other, so they find ways to throw up all these roadblocks, until they finally just step out into that scary place and say, "All right, you got me." I have a card that we hole-punched whenever we had sex. What was it called? An intercourse punch card.

> **ANGELA:** Dwight and I have a
> contractual agreement to procreate five
> times, plain and simple. And should
> he develop feelings for me, well, that
> would be permissible under item 7C,
> clause 2, so I would not object.

ANGELA KINSEY: We had our own weird ways of stalling what was ultimately what we both wanted.

Healthy relationships weren't easy to find at the Dunder Mifflin Scranton branch, from Pam and Roy's never-ending engagement to Ryan and Kelly's on-again, off-again affair to Kevin's "complicated" relationship with Stacy (who leaves him after he claims the Eagles could win the NFC East). The one couple that was free of emotional complications from the very beginning was Phyllis Lapin and Bob Vance of Vance Refrigeration.

PHYLLIS SMITH: When they wrote Bob into my life, I remember the auditions we had for Bob Vance. Because I was matronly looking, they wanted somebody that had a little bit of pizzazz to them, to be on the handsome side. It worked out great because all of a sudden you had this rich guy who went for the unassuming person on the lot.

From his first appearance on the season two episode "Christmas Party"—where he repeatedly introduced himself as "Bob Vance, Vance Refrigeration"—Bob and Phyllis's relationship was mutually respectful and, well, normal.

> **PHYLLIS SMITH:** Yeah, we were kind of normal. We just hit it off. I always said, "I helped him change a tire in the parking lot." Here's this big handsome guy who couldn't get his tire changed, and I walked along—'cause we shared the same lot at Dunder Mifflin—and helped him change his tire. And that was the beginning of our romance. [*Laughs.*] In my mind, if the story continued, Phyllis and Bob Vance of Vance Refrigeration are still together.

"You're So Stupid, but I Like That"
Michael Scott's Search for Love and Family

Love was running rampant at Dunder Mifflin, but there was one person who just couldn't seem to find his soul mate: Michael Scott.

> **GREG DANIELS:** In the beginning, we were playing his love life for comedy. It was like a comedy of errors, and he would always jump in too far and scare people off.

And then came Jan Levinson-Gould, Dunder Mifflin's vice president of sales. From her first appearance in the pilot, Greg and others noted a sexual chemistry between Michael and Jan, played by longtime TV vet Melora Hardin.

MELORA HARDIN ("JAN LEVINSON"): I remember, after the pilot aired, being at lunch with Steve and Greg, and we talked about the interesting spark between Michael and Jan. We were all like, "Yeah, if we get an opportunity, if we get picked up, we should really have them hook up sometime at a convention or something." We were all laughing about this idea.

But their attraction remained unrequited until season two, in the episode "The Client," written by Paul Lieberstein. It began, like all great love stories, with a drunken make-out sesh at Chili's.

PAUL LIEBERSTEIN: Jan and Michael was a great love story, one that had to end in disaster. It was about Jan lowering her standards because life wasn't working out, but told through Michael's point of view.

Melora Hardin

Occupation: Actor

Hometown: Born in Texas, raised in Los Angeles

Training: Sarah Lawrence College, Class of 1989

Previous Employment: Guest appearances on shows ranging from *The Love Boat* (1978) and *Little House on the Prairie* (1981) to *Matlock* (1994) and *Judging Amy* (2002); cast as "Baby" in the TV adaptation of *Dirty Dancing* (1988–1989)

Post-Office Credits: Roles in *Transparent* (2014–2019), *The Blacklist* (2017), and *A Million Little Things* (2019)

Terminations: Cast as the female lead in *Back to the Future* (1985) but fired for being taller than Michael J. Fox

Special Skills: Singing, as seen in both Disney movies (1991's *The Rocketeer*) and on Broadway (*Chicago* and *Les Misérables*)

MIKE SCHUR: The fun of this isn't, "Maybe Michael has found his life partner." The fun of it is, "Oh no, this is going to be terrible." [*Laughs.*]

MELORA HARDIN: I remember it was somewhat of a struggle for Greg. He talked about it with me and the costume designer and makeup and hair people. He used to say a lot, "Make sure she's not too pretty. Take the makeup down a little." He grappled with that. Greg always wanted to know what I thought. "Why would Jan be attracted to someone like that?"

BRIAN BAUMGARTNER: Did you have any theories?

MELORA HARDIN: I feel like Jan was, well, she was brought up in a man's world. She became more masculine in her behavior than she actually was inside. Some part of her was really sort of sad about the loss of her femininity. Michael's puppylike adoration of her made her feel more feminine and more womanly, like she could be softer with him. She could let down a little bit of that masculine guard that was learned behavior for her.

BRIAN BAUMGARTNER: Was there real love between Michael and Jan?

MELORA HARDIN: It was completely dysfunctional, but there was, yeah, there was. She didn't even know that she was in love with him, but I think she was. She just was really focused on climbing that corporate ladder and forgot about her need for companionship. Michael was all wrong for her in every way, and there was

Michael and Jan: A not-so-secret love affair.

something undeniably attractive about that for her. She needed that adoration. He was just so proud of having sex with her and having a relationship with her, and she was like, "You're so stupid, but I like that." She kind of liked being his trophy wife even though she found him ridiculous.

> **JAN:** I am taking a calculated risk. What's the upside? I overcome my nausea, fall deeply in love, babies, normalcy, no more self-loathing. Downside? I date Michael Scott publicly and collapse in on myself like a dying star.

JEN CELOTTA: We had so many fights in the writers' room [about Michael and Jan], and the fights seemed to be about reality versus comedy. It felt to me like if we're doing a documentary, if we're leaning into that, we would want Michael to keep growing. Jim and Pam evolve to where they are, right? So we want Michael Scott to keep evolving. But if we're just thinking with our comedy glasses on, Jan and Michael are hilarious. So there's this tension of: Should we keep him stuck in this relationship because we can mine it for ridiculous humor, or should we evolve him? As a viewer, I start disconnecting a little if I feel that somebody is stuck in a thing that they wouldn't be in real life.

The Michael-Jan relationship clearly wouldn't last. But not just because they were an imperfect pairing. Michael yearned for something more than just a soul mate. He wanted a big, unconditionally loving family, a search that always led him back to the office.

MIKE SCHUR: It was important that he was single, had never been married, and didn't have any kids. His entire emotional self-worth was tied up in the office, in his job and in those people. Even though there was very little evidence that they thought of him as a family member, he thought of them as his best friends and family members. That's the essence of the show and the British version too, at some level.

GREG DANIELS: I drew something for the writers and it was basically a horrible sinking abyss. And I'd draw Michael running on the edge of it, trying to run out of it but falling in. To me, this is what was going on in his brain. He was desperately trying to avoid thinking of the fact that he was lonely and he was in his forties and, you know, the life he wanted wasn't happening for him. That was key to his personality from the get-go. Why is he being so intrusive with all of the other people in the office? Why can't he just leave them alone and be professional? Well, a positive spin on it is he's lonely and these people are his family, but they all have other lives outside the office.

STEVE CARELL: I think Michael's a decent dude with a lot of heart, but based on his childhood and the things he lacked growing up, things he was deprived of, he was so hungry for acceptance.

We got a hint of his childhood in the season two episode "Take Your Daughter to Work Day," when Michael shows the office a video of himself as a kid, being interviewed on the *Fundle Bundle* TV show.

> **EDWARD R. MEOW (A CAT PUPPET):** So tell me, what do you want to be when you grow up?
>
> **YOUNG MICHAEL:** I want to be married and have a hundred kids so I can have a hundred friends and no one can say no to being my friend.

EDWARD R. MEOW: [*Jaw drops, awkward pause.*] Uh, ah . . . oh, okay! Well uh, nice talking with you, Michael.

STEVE CARELL: I don't think he had the strongest templates in the world to go by, but I think he also learned and evolved and became a better person along the way.

GREG DANIELS: I identified a lot with Michael. Like for instance in the "Halloween" episode, this notion that you would have to fire someone but you'd want to stay friends with them. I was the boss of the writers, so it was funny 'cause there'd be times when they'd be rolling their eyes at me, mocking me, and I was like, "Yeah, you can use it for the show." Steve used to say, "If you're in a situation where you don't see a Michael Scott, *you're* the Michael Scott."

Michael was definitely a work in progress, and early on he'd be oblivious to his deep need to be loved. Nowhere was that clearer than in "Grief Counseling," the fourth episode of the third season, which first aired in October 2006. Michael learns that his Dunder Mifflin predecessor, Ed Truck, was decapitated in a car accident. But nobody else at the office is as horrified, and they continue going about their business as usual, which sends Michael into an emotional tailspin.

GREG DANIELS: That episode was very tricky, because Michael did not know what the story was. He was in complete denial that he was really upset that the guy who had his job had died and nobody cared in the office. He fixated on the bird.

When Toby tries to explain to Michael that death is a part of life, using as an example the bird that flew into the building's first-floor window that morning, Michael insists on giving the dead animal a proper funeral.

MIKE SCHUR: That was [writer] Jen [Celotta] from beginning to end. We kept tinkering and tinkering and tinkering. And eventually she was like, "I think I understand this and I want to write it." We were like, "Great."

GREG DANIELS: I remember Jen on the whiteboard. There was a trailer in the parking lot where we had the table readings, and it was sometimes the room where writers would go to work something out. Jen went into that trailer [to write "Grief Counseling"], and we came in and it looked like she was tracking a serial killer. She had all these lines and diagrams on the whiteboard, and it was about every moment: "What does Michael think is happening subconsciously? What is *really* happening?" It was a very complex story.

JEN CELOTTA: It was steering Michael through the stages of grief. What I always thought about with that episode in particular was: this is a story on a network television show that is an internal story where the character that it's happening to is not even aware of it. My brain was exploding.

MIKE SCHUR: The part of it that she really locked into was Pam understanding what Michael was going through and giving the eulogy and trying to make Michael feel better by talking about this dead bird.

> **PAM:** Lastly, we can't help but notice
> that he was by himself when he died,
> but of course, we all know that doesn't
> mean he was alone. Because I'm sure
> that there were lots of other birds out
> there who cared for him very much. He
> will not be forgotten.

MIKE SCHUR: It's a really complicated emotional moment, but Jen understood it at some fundamental level.

JEN CELOTTA: I love Pam and Michael's connection. I love their relationship. What excites me is the psychology and the insides of a person. How the insides of two people relate to each other is my favorite thing.

GREG DANIELS: What I loved was when Pam had a kindness for non-Jim characters. You know what I mean? I loved when she cared about Dwight when he got a concussion or when Dwight was trying to comfort her when she's crying on that bench. Or "Business School," which I think was maybe one of our best episodes, where Michael buys Pam's painting.

"Business School," episode seventeen of the third season (which aired February 15, 2007), follows Michael as he speaks to Ryan's business school class (not realizing that Ryan has predicted Dunder Mifflin will become "obsolete within five to ten years") and Pam as she tries (and fails) to get her coworkers to attend her first art show.

JEN CELOTTA: That moment at the art show is probably one of my favorite moments. It's genius.

MIKE SCHUR: The ending of that episode, Michael has been just absolutely beaten up [at Ryan's business school class] and no one has come to Pam's art show. But Michael shows up and sees her drawing of the office and he's blown away by it. It's so meaningful 'cause no one else showed up. Jim didn't show up, nobody showed up. And Pam hugs him. And then there's that great joke that I think they added on the set, where she's like, "What's in your pocket?" And he goes, "Chunky," and he pulls out an actual Chunky bar.

MIKE SCHUR: The moment where Michael shows up at Pam's art show, I think it's maybe the best moment we ever did. We were always looking for the off-ramp for Michael. Like, how does he get out of whatever miserable circumstance he's put himself in? And it was like, oh, he goes to Pam's art show. And then the idea that she drew the office and he takes it back and hangs it up, it was the emotional solve.

> **MICHAEL:** [*As he hangs Pam's portrait of the office in the office.*] It is . . . a message. It is an inspiration, it is . . . a source of beauty. And without paper, it could not have happened. Unless you had a camera.

MIKE SCHUR: It should be the thing that he sees every day before he goes to work.

BRIAN BAUMGARTNER: Greg, Jen, and Mike Schur, they all told me that their favorite or the best episode of *The Office* was "Business School."

BRENT FORRESTER: Wow. I'm humbled.

Brent Forrester, already a TV veteran when he joined us in season three, wrote this episode.

BRENT FORRESTER: Watching the scene now, I really feel like it's the relationship between a young aspiring artist and a father. That's really what you see in Pam and Michael. She's celebrated this thing that's been denigrated for him and so it redeems him, and he's buying her failed piece of art, which redeems her to some degree. She feels like she's failed and her art has been called "motel art" by somebody whose tastes she might respect. And here's a guy who she doesn't respect who's saying, "Honey, you're great." That's so beautiful and tragic.

"Beautiful" and "tragic." Two words that perfectly summed up the relationships—both romantic and otherwise—on *The Office*. And we were just getting warmed up. We were still a few seasons away from Holly, the woman who would become the love of Michael's life, and the weddings of both P.B. & J. and Dwangela, the two most unlikely relationships at Dunder Mifflin.

The best was yet to come. But as with everything on *The Office*, it would happen slowly, on its own terms.

HUMAN RESOURCES FILE

Brent Forrester

Job Title: Writer, co-executive producer

Hometown: Malibu, California

Training: Columbia University, Class of 1989

Previous Employment: Writer for *The Ben Stiller Show* (1992–1995), *The Simpsons* (1995–1996), *Mr. Show with Bob and David* (1997), *Undeclared* (2002)

Post-Office Credits: Executive producer and writer for *Space Force* (2020) and the Judd Apatow-created Netflix series *Love* (2016–2018)

Extracurricular Research: Attended Lollapalooza as research for the 1996 *Simpsons* episode "Homerpalooza" and was singled out by fellow concertgoers as a narc

Notable Accomplishment: Directed *The Office* episode "Casual Friday," executing the famous "Kevin's Chili" cold open in one take (Brian is forever grateful)

WHEN TRAGEDY STRIKES, FAMILY IS THERE:
A STILL FROM "GRIEF COUNSELING."

7

"Inheritors of the History of Comedy"

THE COMEDY TROPES THAT INSPIRED AND SHAPED *THE OFFICE*: SEASON THREE

BRIAN BAUMGARTNER: Angela and I went to the Emmys together that first year we were nominated, and we were given a limousine that didn't have air-conditioning.

ANGELA KINSEY: You were sweating your ass off.

BRIAN BAUMGARTNER: Why were we going together? To save money?

ANGELA KINSEY: We were fucking idiots to save money. Sorry. You can edit that out.

BRIAN BAUMGARTNER: No, I don't think so.

It's August 2006, just a few weeks before season three was set to premiere, and *The Office* is nominated for three Emmys: Steve Carell for lead actor, Michael Schur for writing the episode "Christmas Party," and all of us for Outstanding Comedy Series. It's the biggest validation we've gotten as an ensemble since starting this crazy journey. And unlike the Globes, we even got to sit inside the auditorium this time. But in true *Office* fashion, we just couldn't manage to do things the easy way.

BRIAN BAUMGARTNER: The limo kept breaking down. There are all of these issues and it was a hundred degrees out.

ANGELA KINSEY: We got to your house and then the limo wouldn't start. So we get to the Emmys late.

BRIAN BAUMGARTNER: It's our first Emmys and—

BOTH: We miss the red carpet.

BRIAN BAUMGARTNER: It's just started and we're an Emmy-nominated television show and we are locked out of the building.

ANGELA KINSEY: And we're like, "We're on *The Office*." And the guy's like, "Whose office do you work for?" I'm like, "No, *The Office*."

The cast members who made it inside the Shrine Auditorium in L.A. are having an equally surreal experience.

JENNA FISCHER: We were the new kids on the block. The critics loved us, but we were not a frontrunner to win. So it was a complete surprise when we won. Many people there had no idea who we were. I remember running into the cast of *Scrubs,* and they were like the big-deal guys and we were the newbies. They were super nice to us. Cut to eight years later. I remember being at an awards show and running into the next batch, the new freshman class of TV darlings. And I remember thinking, "Oh, I'm *Scrubs* now."

Meanwhile, outside the theater.

BRIAN BAUMGARTNER: We're not allowed to go in. So we're standing there, sweating.

ANGELA KINSEY: We were disintegrating.

BRIAN BAUMGARTNER: Conan O'Brien was hosting and we miss the opening monologue.

ANGELA KINSEY: And we're *in* the opening monologue! Conan came to our set and shot a whole thing.

In the prerecorded bit, Conan, dressed in a tux, emerges from the ceiling air ducts in the Scranton office and drops onto Dwight's desk. He has a brief

Conan O'Brien (*left*) on the set of *The Office.*

flirtation with Pam, confessing during a talking head interview that "if I didn't have an award show to host, I could easily see having two or three seasons of will-they-won't-they sexual tension that ultimately goes nowhere."

BRIAN BAUMGARTNER: And we miss it. We're not there. It started out a disaster, but we ended up winning.

The Office beat out *Arrested Development, Curb Your Enthusiasm, Scrubs,* and *Two and a Half Men* to win Outstanding Comedy Series.

BRIAN BAUMGARTNER: We all swarmed the stage, which took a while because they put us waaay in the back of the theater. Greg Daniels accepts the award, and we head offstage in total disbelief.

BEN SILVERMAN: It was the greatest, it truly was. We were so joyous. We were so young. We were so happy. I remember holding that trophy on that stage. And I don't think I let go of it for the entire night. It was like, "Mom, we made it."

JENNA FISCHER: I remember backstage lifting up Kevin Reilly and holding him up like you would at a sporting event. 'Cause Kevin was the person who kept us on the air when we didn't have great ratings. He was the one who fought for us.

ANGELA KINSEY: All you guys lifted him in the air and that's the photo that made the *L.A. Times*.

KEVIN REILLY: Yeah, I have that picture in my office.

BRIAN BAUMGARTNER: The look on your face is just priceless.

KEVIN REILLY: I did ultimately get fired. So [*The Office* winning an Emmy] didn't save my job. But those moments are rare, where you're doing good work with good people and everyone is doing it for the right reasons.

BRIAN BAUMGARTNER: And yet you still got fired.

Despite a track record of 235 Emmy nominations and fifty wins for the network, Reilly was released from his contract with NBC in May 2007.

KEVIN REILLY: Life is full of ironies.

It felt like we were finally a hit. But were we really? Even with the accolades, could we finally just relax and enjoy the ride?

MELORA HARDIN: I didn't even believe we were a hit after we'd won the Emmy. I didn't believe it until we won the SAG Award [in January 2007], and I had to walk around with that fifty-pound statue all night. The next morning I woke up and my biceps was so sore that I couldn't lift my arm. It was like I needed physical proof. I had done so many things in my career that were like semi-successes. I just didn't believe it.

SEASON THREE
Episode Guide

TITLE	DIRECTED BY	WRITTEN BY	ORIGINAL AIR DATE
"Gay Witch Hunt"	Ken Kwapis	Greg Daniels	September 21, 2006
"The Convention"	Ken Whittingham	Lee Eisenberg & Gene Stupnitsky	September 28, 2006
"The Coup"	Greg Daniels	Paul Lieberstein	October 5, 2006
"Grief Counseling"	Roger Nygard	Jennifer Celotta	October 12, 2006
"Initiation"	Randall Einhorn	B. J. Novak	October 19, 2006
"Diwali"	Miguel Arteta	Mindy Kaling	November 2, 2006
"Branch Closing"	Tucker Gates	Michael Schur	November 9, 2006
"The Merger"	Ken Whittingham	Brent Forrester	November 16, 2006
"The Convict"	Jeffrey Blitz	Ricky Gervais & Stephen Merchant	November 30, 2006
"A Benihana Christmas"	Harold Ramis	Jennifer Celotta	December 14, 2006
"Back from Vacation"	Julian Farino	Justin Spitzer	January 4, 2007
"Traveling Salesmen"	Greg Daniels	Michael Schur and Lee Eisenberg & Gene Stupnitsky	January 11, 2007
"The Return"	Greg Daniels	Lee Eisenberg & Gene Stupnitsky and Michael Schur	January 18, 2007
"Ben Franklin"	Randall Einhorn	Mindy Kaling	February 1, 2007

"Phyllis' Wedding"	Ken Whittingham	Caroline Williams	February 8, 2007
"Business School"	Joss Whedon	Brent Forrester	February 15, 2007
"Cocktails"	J. J. Abrams	Paul Lieberstein	February 22, 2007
"The Negotiation"	Jeffrey Blitz	Michael Schur	April 5, 2007
"Safety Training"	Harold Ramis	B. J. Novak	April 12, 2007
"Product Recall"	Randall Einhorn	Brent Forrester & Justin Spitzer	April 26, 2007
"Women's Appreciation"	Tucker Gates	Gene Stupnitsky & Lee Eisenberg	May 3, 2007
"Beach Games"	Harold Ramis	Jennifer Celotta & Greg Daniels	May 10, 2007
"The Job"	Ken Kwapis	Paul Lieberstein & Michael Schur	May 17, 2007

BEN SILVERMAN: *The Office* became a darling of the network, but it was still not at the level of other hits in the history of broadcast comedy. Its ratings were good, but it wasn't the number one show on TV ever. But we never spiraled out of control cost-wise. It was easy to produce and a well-priced show. We were never going to blow up a building.

BRIAN BAUMGARTNER: I don't know if you remember this, but in 2007 the entire cast and crew did a panel at PaleyFest [an annual television festival hosted by the Paley Center in Los Angeles], and we were all sitting in the semicircle and being idiots, just telling jokes and making the audience laugh. And then the moderator addresses a question to Ben, and Ben goes into this effortless five- to seven-minute speech about the history of comedy and tracing *The Office*'s roots from *All in the Family* and making all of these just incredibly artful and insightful comments, like a dissertation on comedy. Then he stops talking and it's quiet, and then Greg turns to the moderator and says, "That's why he's my boss." That moment has resonated with me forever.

BEN SILVERMAN: The connection that both Greg and I had was about the architecture of television and our shared love of television.

GREG DANIELS: When I grew up in New York, on PBS, you'd get *Monty Python* and *Fawlty Towers* and you'd go, "Oh my God, British TV is so great. It's so smart." And they would only get our best stuff. The UK would only get *Friends* and *Seinfeld*. They grew up with the exact same feeling of, "Oh my God, we can never compete. American TV is only the best, the best of the best." When I was expressing at some point to Ricky and Stephen how much I was a fan of British TV, they were like, "Most of it stinks." They'd seen all of the failures.

Greg and Ben, just like Ricky and Stephen, were students of TV comedy: the good, the bad, and the ugly. Both the British and American versions of *The Office* may have seemed like true originals, but they were filled with comedy archetypes and conventions that had been around for decades and, in some cases, for centuries.

"The Social Contract Is Broken in Tiny Little Ways"
Cringe Comedy and the Hilarious Tragedy of "Scott's Tots"

JENNA FISCHER: In some ways *The Office* was ahead of its time, but we couldn't have existed without shows like *The Larry Sanders Show,*

Freaks and Geeks, Arrested Development. These were all shows that helped develop a trust in the single-camera comedy. And all of the Christopher Guest mockumentary movies. There were things conspiring in our favor before we came along.

BRIAN BAUMGARTNER: I always felt like our deepest roots were with *Cheers.* The only difference was our show was about people who *had* to show up every day, whereas on *Cheers,* they chose to show up at this particular place. But we both had the familiarity and constant interaction.

GREG DANIELS: I agree with you. I also used to compare us to *Hogan's Heroes* in the beginning. 'Cause the staff were like prisoners, all trying to outwit the boss. I don't think that's the main influence at all, but it's fun to think about it.

All of those shows and movies had one thing in common, which was also one critical element of *The Office:* cringe comedy. A guy who knows a lot about that is Ed Helms.

ED HELMS ("ANDY BERNARD"): Testing, testing, testing. This is why I like headphones. 'Cause I can get really intimate.

Ed joined the show in our third season as Andy Bernard, the Nard Dog, a graduate of Cornell (ever heard of it?) and a man known to break into unsolicited a cappella.

ED HELMS: For some reason, our generation embraced the comedy of failure and awkwardness and poor communication. My parents never got *The Office.* They were mortified by it, all of the awkwardness and the tension that we think is so funny. For our parents, especially southern parents—repression is a very powerful force in southern families—awkwardness is so intolerable that they weren't able to see the humor in it.

Ed Helms

Occupation: Actor, director

Hometown: Atlanta, Georgia

Training: Oberlin College, Class of 1996, B.A. in film theory and technology; studied improv with the Upright Citizens Brigade

Previous Employment: 207 episodes as a *Daily Show* correspondent (2002–2009); small roles in *Evan Almighty* (2007) and *Night at the Museum: Battle of the Smithsonian* (2009)

Post-*Office* Credits: Starring movie roles include *Together Together* (2021), *A Futile and Stupid Gesture* (2018), *Vacation* (2015), and the titular hero in *Captain Underpants: The First Epic Movie* (2017)

Side Projects: Bluegrass group the Lonesome Trio with pals Jacob Tilove and Ian Riggs

Medical Records: Had open-heart surgery at fourteen to fix a heart murmur

Scholastic Honors: Delivered the 2014 convocation speech at Cornell University, Andy Bernard's alma mater

Special Skills: Harmonica, banjo, disaster preparedness

ED HELMS: On the *Daily Show*, especially with the correspondent field pieces, it was all about finding extremely tense moments. We would revel in the awkwardness because that tension is funny.

In one of Ed's most infamous *Daily Show* segments, from 2004, he gets drunk at a firing range and argues with the owner of a biker bar in Arizona about whether patrons should be allowed to drink while armed. "Logic tells you that alcohol and firearms don't mix," the heavily tattooed bar owner tells him. "Yeah," Ed responds, "if you're a pussy."

ED HELMS: We would try to make the bad guy squirm, whoever the villain of a field piece might be. I don't know why that's funny.

PAUL FEIG (DIRECTOR): To me, the most awful, embarrassing moments in your life are so hellish when you're going through them, but to watch somebody else go through the same thing is so liberating.

Paul Feig directed some of *The Office*'s biggest episodes ("Office Olympics," "Halloween," "Dinner Party") and later became an executive producer on the show. He's one of the most influential producers and directors in comedy today. But before all that, he was involved in bringing a new wave of American cringe to TV with *Freaks and Geeks*.

Paul Feig and Ken Kwapis on the set of *The Office*.

HUMAN RESOURCES FILE

Paul Feig

Occupation: Writer, director, producer

Hometown: Mount Clemens, Michigan

Training: USC School of Cinema-Television, Class of 1984

Previous Employment: Universal Studios Hollywood tour guide; appeared as "Mr. Pool" the science teacher in twenty-nine episodes of *Sabrina the Teenage Witch* (1996–1997); producer/creator/director of *Freaks and Geeks* (1999–2000)

Post-Office Credits: Executive producer on *Zoey's Extraordinary Playlist* (2020–present), *Love Life* (2020–present), and *Other Space* (2015); directed *Bridesmaids* (2011), *A Simple Favor* (2018), *Ghostbusters* (2016)

Financial History: Used his winnings from a 1985 appearance on *The $10,000 Pyramid* game show to fund a year of doing stand-up

Failed Projects: Unsuccessfully pitched an action comedy movie about Wonder Woman, who "keeps hitting the glass ceiling" of the superhero world, to Universal

Emergency Contact: Melissa McCarthy, longtime collaborator on films like *Bridesmaids* (2011), *The Heat* (2013), *Spy* (2015), and *Ghostbusters* (2016)

PAUL FEIG: On *Freaks and Geeks*, I re-created this car accident I got into when I was sixteen years old. Lindsay [played by Linda Cardellini] is driving and she gets distracted and this car hits her. I remember when we were shooting it, I couldn't stop laughing. It was just this release of all the angst I'd kept ever since I was a teenager, by making somebody else have the same terrible experience. So there's maybe a cruelty to it, but to me at least, I find it very cathartic.

I thought, "Who wouldn't love to watch the most embarrassing, cringey moments of their teen years re-created for them?" And the answer was *nobody* wanted that, at least back then.

Freaks and Geeks, which averaged less than seven million viewers (compared with eighteen million for its time slot competitor *Who Wants to Be a Millionaire*), was canceled in 2000 after just twelve of the first season's eighteen episodes had aired. Garth Ancier, the NBC exec who canceled the show, called it "an awful decision that has haunted me forever."

PAUL FEIG: Every time I'm going through something horrible, I'm like, "You're going to have the greatest story to tell later." All this terrible stuff happened to me in high school, with bullies and embarrassing moments. But in my twenties, when I would hang with friends, I would bring down the house every time with my stories, because they were so much worse than everybody else's stories. And that was the moment when you go, "There's something in this."

EMILY VANDERWERFF (TV CRITIC FOR VOX): Really this tradition comes from the Brits. *Fawlty Towers* is a show that kind of plays in that vein. And people didn't really want to see that on American television in the eighties.

American TV at the time was more hopeful. Even *M*A*S*H*, a show about military surgeons during the Korean War, was full of unironic optimism.

We started to get hints of cringe in the U.S. during the '90s with shows like *Seinfeld*.

> **ELAINE** [TO THE BLACK WAITRESS]: Long day?
>
> **WAITRESS:** Yeah, I just worked a triple shift.
>
> **ELAINE:** I hear ya, sister.
>
> **WAITRESS:** Sister?
>
> **ELAINE:** Yeah. It's okay, my boyfriend's Black.
>
> **(From the 1998 *Seinfeld* episode "The Wizard")**

EMILY VANDERWERFF: *Seinfeld* is a big breakthrough for a show that had cringe elements and you were supposed to fundamentally find those four people . . . I won't say likable, but relatable. And then the British *Office* is the big breakthrough for what we think of as modern cringe comedy.

STEPHEN MERCHANT: It was not our intention to make people squirm. It was just that, for us, it was so much funnier when someone who was trying to be funny, for instance, said a joke and then you just sat in silence. I don't know why, Ricky and I just found that so funny. It was only when we started hearing from people, "Oh, that made me feel really uncomfortable," or "I had to watch it through my fingers," only then did it occur to us, oh, maybe this is not always as enjoyable for other people as it is for us.

They weren't even aware of how realistic all of these cringey moments felt.

STEPHEN MERCHANT: I think maybe it was like, if you work on a horror movie and the blood is fake and the knife is not real, you can just keep adding more violence and more bloodshed. And you go, "Ha, this is great." And then when you watch it with an audience, they're like, "Oh, this is horrible." I think for us, it was a bit like that. It was so funny to us to just keep turning the screw and making this world uncomfortable. I don't think it occurred to us that people would find it cringe-worthy until they started telling us. And then of course we just doubled down and were like, "Oh, well now we're going to *really* lay it on."

The center of cringe on the British *Office* was the boss, David Brent. Ricky Gervais says that the cringey aspects of Brent came from the wide gap between who Brent wanted to be and who he actually was.

RICKY GERVAIS: David Brent wanted to be a philosopher and a teacher, he wanted to be cool. He wanted to be sexy. He wanted to be funny. He wanted to be all those things that he wasn't quite, and that is comedy at its most basic, particularly in a sitcom. A sitcom is about an average guy or gal trying to do something that they're not equipped to do. That's what we're laughing at, the blind spot. So I just made David Brent all about the blind spot.

Which brings us to David Brent's descendant, Michael Scott, who had to be different from Brent in some key ways. Michael couldn't completely alienate himself from his employees, for instance. That would end the show.

PAUL LIEBERSTEIN: I think one of the biggest changes was Steve's performance. To the extent that Ricky's character could just straight-out insult someone and not care, that would never happen with Michael. He could insult someone thinking he was complimenting them. He could be unaware, but he could never be mean.

EMILY VANDERWERFF: Because we simultaneously identify with him and with all the people working under him. We're getting both sides of this relationship, which is where cringe comedy lives. Michael is frequently awful. His employees have to work under him and we watch how that relationship shifts and changes, how they negotiate the spaces between them, and the ways that social contract is broken in tiny little ways.

Like when Michael replaces his girlfriend's ex-husband with himself in a family photo.

> **MICHAEL:** That is my Christmas card. It's a picture of you and me and your kids on a ski trip, having a blast. Ski-son's greetings.
>
> **CAROL:** No, see, we never went on a ski trip.
>
> **MICHAEL:** I know, I know.
>
> **CAROL:** I went on a ski trip, two years ago, with my kids and my ex-husband.

Or when Michael insists on hoisting a new, larger employee onto a conference table as part of a welcoming ceremony.

> **MICHAEL:** Bend at the knees. Okay. Here we go! Here we go! I'm under this. I'm under this hock here. I don't know what I'm grabbing here!

Or when Michael, under oath during a deposition for Jan's lawsuit against the company, describes his girlfriend's . . . assets.

> **JAN'S LAWYER:** Did Ms. Levinson ever say why she thought she was being fired?
>
> **MICHAEL:** She thought it had to do with the twins. That's what I call them.
>
> **JAN'S LAWYER:** Can you be more specific? Who are the twins?
>
> **MICHAEL:** Um, to be delicate, they hang off milady's chest. They make milk.

Sometimes the cringe factor wasn't something we could so easily separate from as a viewer. Greg wasn't just about singling out Michael for ridicule, but finding the ways in which we all, embarrassingly, behave like Michael.

MELORA HARDIN: They would take things that we would say and turn them into jokes. The whole breastfeeding-at-the-office scene happened because I was breastfeeding my daughter at a brunch with Greg and his wife and Steve and his wife at Greg's house. I think it made Steve uncomfortable, and I was just like, "Dude, my child needs to drink." I felt very feminist about that. We can carry guns in this country, but you can't breastfeed a baby? That's what our boobs are for, you know? I think I even said that at the brunch. And Greg was like, "Oh my God, this is amazing. We're doing this."

A breastfeeding scene was shot for the season five episode "Baby Shower," in which Jan breastfeeds her daughter in the office, while

Michael Scott with his photoshopped Christmas card.

Kevin (and eventually Creed) watches a little too creepily, but it was eventually cut.

And then there's the season six classic, an episode that's become a classic for being unwatchable, even among die-hard fans: "Scott's Tots." It took cringe to the extreme, with Michael unable to keep a promise he made years ago to some third graders.

> **MICHAEL:** I didn't want to see them fall victim to the system. So I made them a promise. I told them if they graduated from high school, I would pay for their college education. I have made some empty promises in my life, but hands down that was the most generous.

There's even a subreddit called "CannotWatchScottsTots," with (as of this writing) almost seventeen thousand subscribers, where *Office* fans bond over their inability to sit through the cringiest of all cringey episodes. "I'm only around 9 minutes in the episode," one person wrote, "and can I just say how excruciating this is to watch?" Another noted that despite their "super-strong stomach" and love of horror films, they couldn't sit through the entire thing.

BRIAN BAUMGARTNER: There are so many people who come up to me and they're like, "I'm the biggest fan of *The Office*, but I can't watch 'Scott's Tots.'" "Dinner Party" is straddling the line, but "Scott's Tots" is the one where people are like, "No."

GREG DANIELS: I think Ricky and Stephen put it in the bones of the show, right? Michael does the wrong thing. The show knows what the right thing is, but he doesn't and he's always doing the wrong thing. Michael intended to be successful and to be a hero and a philanthropist and to make a big, positive impact in these kids' lives. That was his intention. It was a good intention. If you get that right, you can get all your jokes but still protect the character. It really hurt Michael that he wasn't able to be the guy he thought he was going to be when he made those promises. So you got all your "he's a jerk" jokes, but you were also like, "Aww."

"Scott's Tots" was written by Lee Eisenberg and Gene Stupnitsky, who also wrote "Dinner Party," the other *Office* episode considered among the most cringey in the series' entire run. That can't be a coincidence.

LEE EISENBERG: Gene and I really liked the cringe comedy of the British *Office*. That's a comedy engine that we really dug, trying to make it as grounded as possible, but also sitting in a moment for a really long time after a character says the wrong thing. And then you can't get out of it. Both of those episodes are very claustrophobic, because you're in a condo ["Dinner Party"] or you're in the classroom ["Scott's Tots"].

BRIAN BAUMGARTNER: "Scott's Tots" is considered the most difficult to watch by a lot of fans. Are you proud of that?

LEE EISENBERG: Incredibly, yeah. Nothing makes me happier. I mean, other things make me happier, but I'm very pleased.

BRIAN BAUMGARTNER: No one wants to watch it, and you're *pleased* about that?

LEE EISENBERG: Well, I think that the comic premise is so strong and it's like, what can you do to keep turning the screw and make it feel worse and worse? Like when they start dancing. Michael was just sitting there and he also loves performance and he loves dance, but he also knows that he can't get out of this. It was incredible.

Incredible is one way to put it, super awkward is another. Cringe was an essential part of Michael Scott's character. And as with many leading men over the history of comedy, so was his handling or mishandling of sensitive social issues.

"It Makes Us Think About Television Differently"
Michael Scott as the Next Archie Bunker

Another comedy archetype that influenced *The Office* is the lovable yet un-PC leading man. There have been many throughout the history of TV comedy: Homer Simpson, Fred Sanford, Al Bundy. And then there's the granddaddy of them all, the character that redefined just how unlikable a TV lead could be and still make audiences love him: Archie Bunker, the patriarch of *All in the Family* (1971–1979) and its spin-off, *Archie Bunker's Place* (1979–1983), and perhaps the least woke leading man to ever grace prime-time TV.

PAUL FEIG: It's a real close race between Carroll O'Connor and Steve Carell for me. There's other people who were great, like Danny DeVito on *Taxi*. But that was a supporting character. Characters like Archie Bunker are always convinced they're right. And when they say something terrible, it's like, "What? What did I say that's so terrible?" It's that weird innocence of thinking you can get away with it.

GREG DANIELS: Archie is a man with some good human qualities but some bad, bigoted opinions. But Michael Scott wasn't a bigot, he was a nine-year-old that repeated jokes he heard without thinking.

EMILY VANDERWERFF: The thing about Michael Scott is that he has un-PC moments, he has moments when he's racist and sexist and

Michael Scott dancing at Kelly's Diwali party.

whatever, but it makes those things look pathetic. Like he's trying too hard to be funny and doesn't understand the line between like a good joke and actual overt offensiveness.

> **JAN:** We get that money for hiring an ex-convict.
>
> **MICHAEL:** I didn't hire an ex-convict. Unless they mean Toby. Convicted rapist. [*Jan sighs.*] . . . I'm just kidding.

EMILY VANDERWERFF: Michael Scott came out of a culture where a lot of jokes were that kind of joke. We still had a lot of comedians who were deliberately thumbing their nose at societal conventions, who were saying, "This is bad, and we should say that." Michael Scott is trying to be that kind of comedian and utterly failing at it. And that's the joke about him. You'll sometimes see people talk about homophobic jokes on *Friends*. You don't really get that with *The Office*. When Michael Scott says something homophobic, the joke is on him in a way that has allowed the show to sustain itself in this era of people being more aware of the harm that kind of humor can do.

RICKY GERVAIS: It's important that people know the difference between the subject of a joke and the actual target. The target was actually people pretending to be all those good things, but not quite getting it right. We were taking a stab at this false notion of pretending to be about equality and fairness, but getting it wrong.

STEPHEN MERCHANT: The big problem for Michael Scott and the David Brent character to some degree is they just didn't know when to stop. They didn't know what to say but they always have to be talking. Sometimes silence is golden, but not for them. They just have to speak. And they think they are great joke tellers. They think they have great personalities, they want to show off for the cameras that are filming them. And so they never shut up. They don't realize how they're coming across to the world.

BRIAN BAUMGARTNER: Michael Scott made us look back and see all those earlier comedy heroes in a different light, which was a broader trend in the early 2000s.

EMILY VANDERWERFF: *The Office* came out in the era of antihero television. Antihero television often asked us to consider actions we considered heroic in other characters in a new light. We've seen a million action heroes kill people and just be like, yeah, whatever. But if Tony Soprano's killing somebody, now we have to think about the morality of that. It deepens our understanding of the kinds of characters, not just on *The Sopranos* but on other shows. It makes us think about television differently. There's a similar quality in Michael Scott. He's obviously not killing people, but he's definitely making us think about the ways that the emotional and psychological behavior of other TV comedy heroes in real life would be kind of pathetic and sad.

It's a difficult tightrope to walk. How do you make a character both represent all that is ugly and un-PC in our culture, but at the same time make him somebody sympathetic, somebody we want to root for and can't help but cringe when he says the wrong thing yet again? Well, it helps when he's played by somebody with the comedic brilliance of Steve Carell.

ED HELMS: Steve's character on *The Daily Show* was at its best when he was a version of Michael Scott. Not self-aware and usually less informed than everyone around him. On *The Daily Show*, he really pioneered the segments in which the correspondent is the butt of the jokes, as opposed to making fun of somebody else, which is easy and mean-spirited. Usually it's shooting fish in a bucket and it's not interesting.

> **STEVE CARELL:** Senator, how do you reconcile that you were one of the most vocal critics of pork-barrel politics and yet while you were chairman of the Commerce Committee, that committee set a record for unauthorized appropriations?
>
> **JOHN MCCAIN:** [*Says nothing, looks confused.*]
>
> **STEVE CARELL:** [*Bursts out laughing.*] I'm just kidding! I don't even know what that means.

(From *The Daily Show* interview with presidential candidate John McCain, December 1999)

ED HELMS: Steve shifted that and found a way of being an idiot news reporter and still getting great satire into his pieces. That was hugely instructive for me.

JEN CELOTTA: We could get away with more because Steve was so gifted. We could push things because he could have that undercurrent of humanity. I mean, certainly there were lines, but we could push that so far and still have it read true.

We knew we were working with one of the all-time greats, but the Academy of Television Arts & Sciences apparently did not.

PAUL FEIG: Steve Carell never won an Emmy. It makes me mental. Alec Baldwin [who won the lead actor in a comedy Emmy in 2008 and 2009, for *30 Rock*], I love him, he's the funniest guy in the world. But that was a showy part. People would say to me, "Steve just shows up and he's crazy." Are you fucking kidding me? First of all, he's not crazy at all. He's one of the most even-tempered guys I've ever met in my life. But for comedy to be good, it's gotta look easy. If it looks sweaty and like people are trying too hard, it's terrible. But when it's so great that it looks real, people go, "Well, you're not doing anything."

BEN SILVERMAN: It's a disgrace. The guy was and is a comedic tour de force, but also a pathos-ridden empath who just delivered on emotion and sadness and real feelings through his portrayal that was as good as there's ever been on television, and television didn't think so.

BRIAN BAUMGARTNER: Ricky, what do you think about the fact that Steve never won an Emmy?

RICKY GERVAIS: Didn't he?

BRIAN BAUMGARTNER: Never.

RICKY GERVAIS: How many did he get nominated for? He must've gotten nominated every year.

"I'm Only Going to Fail You"

WHEN THE CAST AND CREW COULDN'T STOP FROM LAUGHING

JOHN KRASINSKI: *People always asked me, "What's the hardest you've ever laughed on set?" Without a doubt, it's when Kevin sat on Michael's lap.*

In "Secret Santa," the thirteenth episode of the sixth season, Michael dresses up as Santa for the office Christmas party. He invites Kevin to sit on his lap, an invitation he quickly regrets.

BRIAN BAUMGARTNER: *There was this noise that Steve made every single time we shot that scene. As I sat down, he went, "Gwarwaw," and it just got me every time.*

JOHN KRASINSKI: *I would laugh so hard that I had to walk off set.*

BRIAN BAUMGARTNER: *Diving into the entryway of the office.*

JOHN KRASINSKI: *Diving! And I'm a cry-laugher. I have that high-pitched girl laugh.*

BRIAN BAUMGARTNER: *[Laughs.] That's right, that's right!*

JOHN KRASINSKI: *I was just the most unprofessional. Steve said something about attaching balloons to you or something.*

They whipped [the camera] to me for a reaction, and I was like, "Dude, don't do it. I'm only going to fail you." That was one of the only times that I just literally gave up on doing my job.

KEVIN: I didn't even get to tell you what I wanted.

MICHAEL: Okay, you know what you get? You get a thousand helium balloons attached to you so Santa doesn't have to go through this again.

Matt Sohn

Occupation: Camera operator, director of photography, and director

Training: Washington & Jefferson College in Washington, Pennsylvania, Class of 1990, psychology major

Previous Employment: Cinematographer and/or camera operator on *Cops* (1989–2009), *The Amazing Race* (2001), *The Bachelor* (2002), *Survivor* (2001–2002), and *The Apprentice* (2004)

Post-Office Credits: Director of *Black-ish* (2014–2016), *The Mick* (2017–2018), *The Kids Are Alright* (2018–2019), and *At Home with Amy Sedaris* (2020)

Special Skills: Lived for two and a half weeks in a nuclear submarine

Medical Records: Contracted dengue fever in Thailand

International Experience: Has been employed in every continent but Antarctica

BRIAN BAUMGARTNER: He probably got six or seven, but he never won.

Steve was nominated for Outstanding Lead Actor in a Comedy Series for *The Office* six times between 2006 and 2011.

RICKY GERVAIS: Wow. In your face, Steve Carell. [*Laughs.*] I hadn't realized he'd never won an Emmy. That is a travesty. But who cares? It doesn't mean anything. It's an amazing performance. He doesn't need Emmys to validate that.

Carell's comedic powers weren't just in making the audience laugh. He had the same ability to make a cast member break character and burst into laughter during filming.

MATT SOHN: The good thing about a talking head scene is the camera was on a tripod, not on my shoulder. The bigger challenge was to not break when the camera was on my shoulder and there were some extra shakes and giggles.

VEDA SEMARNE (SCRIPT SUPERVISOR): We all laughed so much that sometimes it was hard to finish a scene. And I had to put that in my notes. I'd say this scene was great up until they all broke. That was something the editors would mention to me sometimes. You know, "I can't cut this. Somebody's breaking in every take."

RANDALL EINHORN: Once one person goes, then there's somebody else who goes.

BRIAN BAUMGARTNER: We had to take breaks from shooting because of laughing.

RANDALL EINHORN: It was too much giggling.

JEN CELOTTA: I was biting my cheek at times. I would go home with like welts and stuff in my mouth.

BRIAN BAUMGARTNER: I had a trick.

JEN CELOTTA: What was your trick? Why didn't you tell me this then?!

BRIAN BAUMGARTNER: With my index finger and my thumb, I would bury my fingernail into the side of my thumb.

JEN CELOTTA: Oh my God! It worked?

BRIAN BAUMGARTNER: It was just trying to just think about that small amount of pain that was there and not Steve being "Prison Mike" or whatever.

RANDALL EINHORN: Steve was usually the last one holding on to some shred of sanity and not just losing it and giggling. Once he went, it was over.

STEVE CARELL: I'll crack up as much as anyone, but I try not to because I always feel like if I laugh, it's going to ruin whatever they're doing. And if I crack up it's unusable. But there are times that I'm sure you can see tears welling in my eyes. That was one of the hardest things, to not lose it.

Besides Steve, the cast member most likely to send people into hysterics was Rainn.

JOHN KRASINSKI: Rainn had this look on his face that would make me break every time. His face didn't even move, but like some energy came out and I would just lose it.

JEN CELOTTA: There was one moment with Rainn where he's doing a talking head. I cannot remember the topic, but Greg had to leave. He couldn't be in the room. He left the stage. He was outside the building.

We weren't always laughing because something was especially funny. Sometimes it was hard to decipher between what was real and what was acting.

JEN CELOTTA: There was a moment, I don't remember the episode but I think I wrote it. I was on set and Steve was doing a scene with Holly [played by Amy Ryan]. They were having this kind of intimate scene and then they started laughing. And I started laughing because it was so real, I just thought they broke. Steve turned to me and I was like, "Oh my God, I'm sorry." He's like, "We're acting here!"

"Bring Me the Big Tureen"
When Comedy Got Physical at *The Office*

Physical comedy may not be the first thing you think of when it comes to *The Office*—we weren't exactly doing Buster Keaton-style slapstick—but there was a physicality to many of the performances that could be easy to miss.

BRIAN BAUMGARTNER: Rainn Wilson and I were really the only two that came from theater, like Shakespeare and Chekhov.

JOHN KRASINSKI: Don't throw that in my face.

BRIAN BAUMGARTNER: No, what I'm saying is that for him and I, in terms of character construction, the physicality was a conscious decision.

JOHN KRASINSKI: I just tuned you out. It's just highbrow theater garbage. Did you also learn fencing at school? Come on!

BRIAN BAUMGARTNER: I did.

JOHN KRASINSKI: I wasn't trained at all.

RAINN WILSON: I was in the NYU grad program, and I did a lot of clowning and physical theater. I'm not trying to sound pretentious—like, "Oh, Mr. Theater"—but when you get that kind of training, a lot of it is about finding a character in your body. There were certain elements of Dwight that if I needed to get into character, I put my focus in certain parts of my body and I would immediately be Dwight. Like a straight neck and hips forward. I don't know if you notice that Dwight always stands too close to people. If someone's sitting down and he's standing next to them, his hips look really big. He had a little bit of a swagger and the shoulders thrown back. What about you, Brian? Did you have some for Kevin?

BRIAN BAUMGARTNER: For me, it was my jaw. I knew there was a specific place that I could put my jaw that was him.

RAINN WILSON: You had a weird mouth. Your lips would be a little like pursed.

BRIAN BAUMGARTNER: Yeah, exactly. I also had the idea that Kevin was not aware of the size of his body and so he wouldn't think that he could, you know, potentially injure a smaller person. Which to me was always hilarious when I would come up against Angela. I just wouldn't see her there and I'd knock her around. There was something about my torso that doesn't move agilely from side to side.

CREED BRATTON: I thought of my character as a cracked tuning fork. It's fibrillating and it's ready to break. The physical comedy is from [the French mime, actor, and filmmaker] Jacques Tati, the way he physically walks, and the facial expressions are Jack Benny, George Gobel, and Bob Newhart. It's a juxtaposition of all those characters that I loved.

BRIAN BAUMGARTNER: Was there something to the physicality that helped you get into that character?

CREED BRATTON: It was like giving myself a hiccup. It was almost a nervous twitch to be him. I'm much more serious and thoughtful than that character. But when I'm behind the desk, there's chicanery involved. There's escaping from the law. It's thinking, "Are they going to find me out?" That was always my backstory. "Are they gonna find me out?" So every time I would look at anybody, in the back of my mind was "Are they going to see that I'm just faking it here, that I'm cheating them and stealing from them?" After a while it just becomes ingrained in your behavior.

RAINN WILSON: So this is where we could talk shop a little bit, because I love the history of clowns and of clowning. It really started with the comedies of the ancient Greeks. You know, like Aristophanes's *The Frogs* and some of those plays. What's the one where they all have boners? Um . . . the women withhold sex from the men until they stop the war. Anyone?

We looked it up. It's *Lysistrata* (aka *The One Where They All Have Boners*).

RAINN WILSON: Anyway, so it all starts back then and then swiftly moves to commedia dell'arte, which sprang out of Roman theater and had these comic tropes that would travel all over Europe. They always had the dopey clown like Kevin. They had the weird, intense clown like Dwight. Basically all of comedy in the Western world is based on those tropes from commedia dell'arte. They influenced Molière, obviously, but also Shakespeare and vaudeville.

Those tropes eventually made their way to *The Office*. The dialogue may have gotten more attention, but the physical antics happening in the background were just as important.

KATE FLANNERY: It's fun to do physical comedy. And I was thinking about the first Valentine episode, in season two, when Phyllis is getting all these gifts and flowers from Bob Vance, and Pam is really upset and you just see Meredith with her Big Gulp. We find out at the end that she's drinking and she's passed out at her desk with a lime in her hair. What a perfect little C story, just long enough. We get it. I feel like there was so much power in being someone who got to do the physical stuff. Everybody wants to be the star, but there's something to be said for holding that space in the background and not wrecking it.

BRENT FORRESTER: I directed the scene where Kevin spills the chili.

During the cold opening for season five's "Casual Friday," Kevin brings a pot of his "Famous Chili" to the office. It is, he explains in a voice-over, "probably the thing I do best." A line made tragic when he accidentally dumps his chili all over the bullpen carpet.

BRENT FORRESTER: We were going to build a chili tureen with a fake bottom, so it looks like it's filled but Brian won't have to carry seventy-four pounds of liquid chili. But, Brian, you looked at the expensive prop with a slanted bottom so that it seemed to be filled but wasn't, and you were like, "I'm going real. Bring me the big tureen." You carried that incredibly heavy chili container. We only got two takes.

BRIAN BAUMGARTNER: One.

BRENT FORRESTER: One take?

BRIAN BAUMGARTNER: I did that in one take. For whatever reason, it has become the thing for which I am known now.

BRENT FORRESTER: I own a T-shirt with you carrying the chili.

BRIAN BAUMGARTNER: They put down a piece of carpet that went from the hallway around the reception desk and over to Jim and Dwight's area.

BRENT FORRESTER: Because the chili would've screwed up the carpet forever. The moment when you take printer paper and try to mop up the chili is so brilliant. Everybody knows printer paper doesn't absorb at all. It's just this Sisyphean doomed effort to clean up.

RAINN WILSON: One of the things that I said to Greg [Daniels] early on is I really love physical comedy and I think Dwight soars when he's doing physical comedy. I told him, "Please consider writing as much physical comedy for me as possible." I think you could do a compilation episode of *The Office*'s best physical comedy bits. Like the fire drill episode . . .

> **DWIGHT:** People learn in lots of different ways, but experience is the best teacher. [*Lights a cigarette.*] Today, smoking is gonna save lives. [*Throws cigarette into garbage can filled with paper and lighter fluid.*]

RAINN WILSON: Or the "Baby Shower" episode.

> **DWIGHT:** Do you have the Sharpie?
>
> **MICHAEL:** Yes, I do.

DWIGHT: Okay, when the baby emerges, mark it secretly in a kind of a mark that only you could recognize and no baby snatcher could ever copy.

BRIAN BAUMGARTNER: Even you giving Kevin a massage. Do you remember? You climbing up on the wall?

RAINN WILSON: I was on my feet on the filing cabinet behind you as I was doing that. In every episode, I would say we had at least one or two big bits of physical comedy. I don't think that gets quite enough props or attention from people.

"This Perfect Comedy Triangle"

BRIAN BAUMGARTNER: *What do you think made our little group of the accountants in the corner so special?*

ANGELA KINSEY: *I think the dynamic. I always felt like Oscar and I were your parents and you are the idiot son who still lived at home. The three of us were just so in sync from the very beginning.*

BRIAN BAUMGARTNER: *I view the three of us as this perfect comedy triangle. You've got the stern one who's got to be in control. You've got the slower one who kind of likes to get under the skin of the one in control. And then you have the put-upon one, Oscar, who also enjoys bettering the stern one and wants to be in control.*

ANGELA KINSEY: *But he also has to be the referee.*

BRIAN BAUMGARTNER: *Totally. He's the referee in between you and me. But then the alliances keep shifting. There's Kevin and Oscar against Angela, and there's Angela and Oscar against Kevin.*

ANGELA KINSEY: *It's Kevin and Oscar against Angela whenever they want to play, it's Angela and Oscar against Kevin whenever they actually have to get things done.*

BRIAN BAUMGARTNER: *Is it ever Angela and Kevin?*

ANGELA KINSEY: *No, I don't think so.*

BRIAN BAUMGARTNER: *Well, actually, one of my favorite pictures I have is a selfie that we took in a car when we were filming the episode*

at your house with the creepy portrait of Angela.

That would be the season nine episode "Vandalism," in which Angela and her husband, Pennsylvania state senator Robert Lipton, invite a few friends to their home to celebrate their son's birthday.

ANGELA KINSEY: *Oh, that's right. You stand up for me.*

```
KEVIN: Thank you for the food. Oh, and
also, you suck.

SENATOR: I beg your pardon?

KEVIN: You are like a terrible person.
These guys care about you and you're
just using them. Again, the food was very
good.
```

ANGELA KINSEY: *Aw. Yeah, that was really sweet. You know what? It's Kevin and Angela versus Oscar when Angela finds out that Oscar is sleeping with her husband.*

BRIAN BAUMGARTNER: *Yes, but Kevin knew and was happy that he was able to keep the secret.*

ANGELA KINSEY: *Yeah. He was so proud of himself. One of my favorite running bits we did, whenever we had the smallest scene and you would think we were going to get an Oscar or something, that's how serious we took it. There were times I would turn to you guys and be like, "Guys, it's not our show. It's not about us." And one of my favorite things that Oscar would say is, "Well, maybe we'll have a spin-off on Telemundo and it will be Oscar, Anjela, y Kebin." [Laughs.]*

"The Bassoon-Playing Weirdo in the Corner"
The Comedy Duos of Dunder Mifflin

EMILY VANDERWERFF: Comedy teams are as old as comedy. In TV, I think you certainly have to look back at Lucy and Desi. That's the birth of so much TV comedy, *I Love Lucy,* where there are multiple fun relationships to follow: Lucy and Desi, Lucy and Ethel. Fred and Desi, Fred and Ethel. All four of those characters have interesting relationships among them.

RAINN WILSON: Think about *The Honeymooners,* Ralph Kramden and Ed Norton. And the rhythms of the clowns in Warner Bros. cartoons, and the early sitcoms of Dick Van Dyke and Mary Tyler Moore, and these constantly evolving archetypal forms. I really view comedy duos like Michael and Dwight, and Dwight and Jim, as being inheritors of the history of comedy.

EMILY VANDERWERFF: That became sort of the standard for the American sitcom. A British sitcom can be about a single character in a way that an American sitcom cannot. Think about the show *Fleabag.* We're stuck in her point of view and we're seeing the world through her eyes. American TV comedy is built on relationships. And the more interesting relationships there are within a show, the better that show tends to be.

The Office had no shortage of interesting relationships, thanks in large part to Greg Daniels. Here's how he explained it to Rainn Wilson.

RAINN WILSON: We never talked about scenes. Never ever. One of the things Greg said early on is, "It's never about the character,

it's about the duo. How is that character in relation with other characters?" Dwight doesn't have to be funny. Dwight and Jim should be funny. Dwight and Pam should be funny. Dwight and Michael should be funny. Dwight and Kevin should be funny. A lot of mistakes they make in television comedy are funny characters that aren't necessarily funny when they're together.

Dwight and Jim could be funny separately, but the true comedy magic happened when these two polar opposites came together.

PAUL FEIG: It's a classic setup of the person who just wants to drive the other person crazy. But why it worked is that even though Dwight was always upset about it, it never made him hate Jim.

GREG DANIELS: They were equally matched and could stand up to each other. It was like, oh, okay, I see how this is gonna play out endlessly. This is like *Spy vs. Spy.*

Spy vs. Spy, a regular comic in *Mad* magazine since the early '60s, follows two birdlike espionage agents—Black Spy and White Spy—who try to sabotage each other, often with dynamite and other weapons.

JOHN KRASINSKI: What the writers did so well was make those pranks kind of loving and brotherly. I wasn't being mean. I think that Dwight just represented everything I didn't want to be, or so I thought.

PAUL FEIG: There was no malice about it. It was just everybody trying to get through the day and not go crazy, you know?

JOHN KRASINSKI: The beauty of our show is they would allow Rainn's character to have heart. You felt bad for him at times, and then he'd totally not make you feel bad for him because he'd do something crazy.

As the British singer-songwriter Tom Rosenthal sang in "Jim and Dwight," his 2020 love ballad, "You took pleasure in each other's misery / but those pranks were a cover for a synergy."

RAINN WILSON: One of my favorite moments was directed by Paul Lieberstein. I think it was in the episode "Money" [from season four] and it's Dwight and Jim in the stairwell. Dwight is heartbroken over Angela, and Jim gives him some really heartfelt advice, relating it to what happened with him and Pam.

> **JIM:** I lost it, Dwight. I couldn't sleep, I couldn't concentrate on anything. Even weird stuff, like food had no taste. So my solution was to move away. It was awful. It was something that I wouldn't wish on my worst enemy, and that includes you.

RAINN WILSON: Dwight has his head down in his hands and Jim slips away, and then Dwight reaches out as if to put his arm around Jim and hug him. It would've been their first hug ever. It's this awkward kind of moment. I always think if Jim hadn't left and Dwight had put his arm around him, they might have bonded in a way that wouldn't have allowed the show to go on. Because they wouldn't have been the nemesis to each other anymore. They would have connected too deeply. And you can't have that on the show. You want to have them not connecting episode after episode after episode. To me, that little moment defined what *The Office* was. It had absurdity and reality at the same time. It was based in heartbreak, but it was twisted into something odd and awkward.

BRIAN BAUMGARTNER: Probably our most iconic duo was Dwight and Michael. The two of you together were so stupid.

STEVE CARELL: So stupid.

BRIAN BAUMGARTNER: So stupid, but so funny. Michael and Dwight are both clowns. There's no straight man, which is pretty unique, but it's a complicated relationship. Dwight loves Michael and is desperate for his love in return. Michael is desperate for love from *anyone* but Dwight.

GREG DANIELS: I always viewed Michael as a nine-year-old and Dwight as a teenager, in terms of their comic energy.

PAUL FEIG: I mean, there's not really a parallel to them, 'cause it's not Laurel and Hardy and it's not Abbott and Costello. It's this weird thing where they needed each other, but Michael doesn't want Dwight's acceptance.

BRIAN BAUMGARTNER: Part of what made it work was that each of them contributed their own kind of weird, particularly Dwight.

PAUL FEIG: It's a character that could have easily been so over the top, but there's a humanity to him. He's just that guy we all know who's striving and wants it and wants it so much and tries to kind of throw everybody else out of the way. But he's still sensitive.

RAINN WILSON: The thing I hate the most about comedy is when someone knows that they're being funny. I think the key to the comedy on *The Office* is that none of the characters thought of themselves as being funny. I think the documentary element helped with that. I tried to play Dwight as outrageously as possible and as grounded and realistic as possible at the same time. So he could do just preposterous things, but I always tried to motivate them internally.

BRENT FORRESTER: Rainn was not making fun of this guy. He was celebrating him. And it just seemed so obvious to him that that's what one would do. You could see how much he loved Dwight. He brought this energetic adoration for the marginal guy.

RAINN WILSON: Look at any scene with Dwight, no matter how ridiculous, you can always tell what Dwight is feeling and what he's going through on the inside and what he thinks he's hiding. And I think that that allowed people to relate to him. So those moments when Dwight was sad or hurt or disappointed, people really felt for him. Even if he was being haughty or arrogant, there's a big kid in there too.

JEN CELOTTA: In terms of comedy duos, I think Dwight and Michael are up there with the greatest. Their characters are so specific, in Dwight's wanting to be more than he is in Michael's eyes. I mean, I'm thinking of "Drug Testing" [episode twenty of season two], when Michael asked for Dwight's urine.

> **MICHAEL:** I went to an Alicia Keys concert over the weekend, and I think I may have gotten high accidentally by a girl with a lip ring.
>
> **DWIGHT:** Are you serious?
>
> **MICHAEL:** I need clean urine for the lady.
>
> **DWIGHT:** But that's illegal.

JEN CELOTTA: It's the ultimate ask, going against Dwight's ethics and responsibilities as a sheriff. But then this is *Michael* asking him . . .

RAINN WILSON: Steve is like a virtuoso violin player with a Stradivarius. He can be funny and pathetic and sad and moving at the same time. Playing Dwight, I felt more like the bassoonist. Or the cello to his violin, something like that. Part of Dwight's job, and part of my job as an actor, is just to keep him off balance a little bit. I don't need to do what Steve does. I improvise pretty well, but I'm not a virtuoso. I'll do my thing. My thing is to be the bassoon-playing weirdo in the corner.

The real trick to why these relationships felt so real, connected to the comedy past but also uniquely original and fresh, wasn't just what was written on the page.

JENNA FISCHER: It's so hard for me to think about Pam's relationship with Dwight without thinking about my relationship to Rainn, which is very special to me. Rainn is a deeply soulful person. I feel deeply loved by Rainn, and I think Pam felt deeply loved by Dwight as well. They had a real bond. They really cared for one another eventually.

And just like their characters, they could aggravate each other.

JENNA FISCHER: Rainn's also like a curmudgeonly old man. He's cranky sometimes. I remember once we were getting ready to shoot and he said, "Hold on, wait, just hold on, everybody. I have an announcement. On Mondays, you do not need to ask me how my weekend was anymore. All right? Every single person asked me how my weekend was. Just assume it was fine."

We learned from what came before us. And we aimed to contribute something new, whether it was experimenting with comedy duos, creating a new kind of leading man, or adding another page to the playbook of cringe comedy.

We went into season four on a high note. We were a hit with audiences and critics. We had an Emmy on our shelf, not to mention awards from the Screen Actors Guild, Peabody, Writers Guild of America, Producers Guild of America, Television Critics Association, NAACP, and Teen Choice Awards. NBC picked us up for thirty episodes, so we expected a busy and productive 2007.

And then, like the rest of the TV industry, we got blindsided.

8

"I Don't Care, Fire Me!"

INSIDE THE *OFFICE* WRITERS' ROOM . . .
AND THE WRITERS STRIKE THAT NEARLY
ENDED THE SHOW: SEASON FOUR

A CAST FULL OF HEAVY HITTERS: EVERY WRITER'S DREAM.

MIKE SCHUR: Greg's theory was that a writing staff should be like the X-Men. If you have people who have the same comedic powers, you're gonna have one awesome thing about the show. But if everybody has his or her own comedic power, then you get everything.

The superhero metaphor for the *Office* writing staff isn't just an easy way to describe how they all had unique contributions to bring to the show. The writers have a lot of thoughts about their respective comedic superpowers.

MIKE SCHUR: Mindy [Kaling]'s superpower was always the super absurdist stuff, like when Michael burns his foot on the George Foreman Grill.

JEN CELOTTA: I don't know if it's a super strength, but what excites me is the psychology between two people like Pam and Jim. I love finding the shades and the colors and the dynamics between the two of them.

BRENT FORRESTER: Mike Schur is gifted in ninety thousand different directions, but his superpower is his love of funny words. He's like an Eric Idle in that sense. He just couldn't believe how funny words were. I once pointed out to him that we had a character named Jim and another character named Jan, and then we have Stamford and Scranton. And I said, "I've invented a new character named Jam Strandforb." Mike almost had to quit the show because he spent the entire day coming up with other fake names just using those letters.

MIKE SCHUR: Lee [Eisenberg] and Gene [Stupnitsky] were really into the super cringey. "Scott's Tots" was an episode they pitched very early on, and Greg was like, "We're *never* doing this." Paul Lieberstein was really into Michael's worst instincts.

There have been a lot of legendary TV writers' rooms over the years— from *Your Show of Shows* in the early '50s, whose writing staff included future comedy luminaries like Mel Brooks, Carl Reiner, and Neil Simon, to *Late Night with David Letterman* in the early '80s, which launched the careers of writers who'd go on to create *The Simpsons, Seinfeld,* and *Newhart*—and the writers' room at *The Office* was no less extraordinary. How'd they pull it off, crafting a show that was equal parts funny, moving, and smart all at the same time? Was it some sort of Robert Johnson-esque deal with the devil at the crossroads? Or was it just a lot of hard work and not having a life outside the office?

"Scripts Aren't Poems, They're Living Documents"

Stuffing the Sausage, Strange Pairings, and Other Office Writers' Room Tricks

---

The Office's showrunner, Greg Daniels, was the guy who led our writers' room. He was full of methods, games, and theories that he taught to the whole team.

GREG DANIELS: I have a bunch of advice that I'd give to people who wanted to break in and be comedy writers. Like . . . they should find a show they loved and watch it and pause it so you can write down everything, like it's a court transcription.

MIKE SCHUR: When he was young, he would tape episodes of sitcoms that he really liked on a VCR and play them back, line by line, and then write out the script by hand, just to get a feel for how long scenes should be and the rhythms, and how long individual lines of dialogue were and stuff like that. Again, he's just the most meticulous human being alive.

GREG DANIELS: I would develop these different theories. One of the theories I called "Stuff the Sausage." A great show like *Seinfeld* is wasteful of wonderful ideas, you know what I mean? They'll have a great idea and it might just turn into a couple of lines. They don't milk it or make a whole episode out of it. So we tried to do that on *The Office* too.

MIKE SCHUR: Before one of the first days we reported for duty, he sent us an email and said, "Everybody come in tomorrow with ten ideas." And those ideas could just be observations. I remember he said once that he noticed when people who work in offices are eating lunch, they throw their neckties over their shoulder, to keep it out of their soup or whatever. He was like, "That's what I want. I want those tiny observational things."

BRENT FORRESTER: The depth with which he will think about stuff is remarkable. And he's in possession of something brain-wise that mere mortals don't have. His ability to remember what was in the second draft of an episode we'd done six episodes ago was just astonishing. And sometimes he would have these wonderful *Rain Man*–like moments where he used to take the script in the rewrite process and put the pages on the ground in a giant oval, circling the writers' room table, so that he could walk around observing the script in three dimensions. Then one day, he decided that three-by-five cards on the wall corkboard were not enough when plotting out the seasons. So he had the cards removed from the wall and taped to paper cups so he could move the cups around in three dimensions on the table. Like Spock's three-dimensional chessboard on *Star Trek*. It was astonishing to watch.

LEE EISENBERG: The other thing Greg did with us was called "Strange Pairings," which I always thought was so fun.

MIKE SCHUR: Greg would write everyone's name down on cards and then he'd grab two at random and would send us off to write some Stanley-Creed stories or whatever.

LEE EISENBERG: We'd have all the characters up on a board, and he'd be like, "What's a Kevin-Creed story? What's an Oscar-Michael story?" That's how you get weird stuff like Dwight spying on Oscar.

In the season two episode "The Secret," Dwight suspects that Oscar is faking an illness and stakes out his home, eventually catching him returning from an ice-skating date with his boyfriend.

LEE EISENBERG: If all the stories are just the accountants together, that feels like, "Oh, I know where *The Office* is going." But if Kevin and Dwight form a band together—which was something that we talked about at one point—then it's like, okay, Kevin's a musician and Dwight's a musician and now you have a different thing going.

MIKE SCHUR: He'd do that once a week. It was something he did when he was getting annoyed by us. But it also didn't feel like busywork. What happens if Creed and Stanley are in a story? What happens if Meredith and Angela are in a story?

BRENT FORRESTER: Back on *Nurses* [an NBC comedy that aired from 1991 to 1994], I asked one of the senior writers there what makes a story, and the guy called me into his office. His name was Bruce Ferber. He closed the blinds, shut the door, locked it, and he said, "A story is usually about two people." And then he unlocked the door and made me leave. It sounds so commonplace, but it's actually the key, right? My first *Simpsons* episode, I paired Homer versus Patty and Selma. It had never been done before, so I got an episode. On any show, what two characters have never been in a story together? Do that.

MIKE SCHUR: We'd look at episodes like a jigsaw puzzle. There are twenty people in the cast and three stories per episode, and I have twenty-one minutes and thirty seconds. How do I put this all together? Writing for *Saturday Night Live* was great for a number of things, but most don't translate to long-form writing. But *SNL* teaches you to be non-precious with your own writing. You learn that these things are disposable. Greg used to say the scripts aren't poems. They're not architectural blueprints. They're living documents and they change and it's okay for them to change.

GREG DANIELS: You don't live in the blueprint, it's just a means of getting to the house. But a poem is a thing in itself that is valuable in itself.

ANGELA KINSEY: There would be nuggets dropped in and never revisited again. Like, all of a sudden, we find out Creed did action movies in Hong Kong. We start in the middle. We don't explain everything to you. I was just rewatching the "Halloween" episode, and when Michael leaves, he walks right past Hank [the security guard]. No one ever introduced Hank. That's just where he sits, that's who he is. He's the security guy downstairs. But there weren't these big "now we must introduce this person" moments. It was just like life.

STEVE CARELL: I don't know how much footage there is on the cutting room floor, but you could probably edit an entire season of scenes that were hilarious and cut for time. I mean, our scripts were long. Our first cuts had to be, what, forty minutes? Sometimes they just split them in half and we'd have two shows.

MIKE SCHUR: Greg introduced us to this concept called "Double Duty." Bad sitcoms split their lines—some are jokes and some are advancing the story. The best writing does double duty, where you're advancing the story *and* telling a joke. Our cuts used to be forty-one, forty-two minutes long. And you have to tell the story. If you don't tell the story, the audience is like, "What am I watching?" So what ends up happening is, if you've separated the story and the jokes, you cut all the jokes to get the story and then you have nothing but stories. So he was really hard on us. "You have to make the story funny. They have to do double duty. And if they don't, then that's not good enough."

As it turns out, this was an easier rule to agree with than follow. Many of the writers fell in love with jokes that just never served the story.

MIKE SCHUR: We wrote a talking head for Dwight that was, I think, an entire page long. It was insane. It was about how one of his cousins had one leg that was shorter than the other, and when he ran to the bus, he would have to curve in like a long arc because the natural awkward gait of one leg being shorter than the other would cause him to run in a long curve. It was nonsense. And it went on for so long. Paul [Lieberstein] and I were in a crazy giggle fit when we wrote it, and Rainn loved it and memorized the whole thing and nailed it. I wish it could've aired but there was no way to justify it. It had nothing to do with the story at all.

BRIAN BAUMGARTNER: The thing that I got the most pissed about was, to me, one of the greatest jokes that might've been. It's an episode called "Baby Shower," where Jan brings her baby to the office. Kevin asks Jan where she went to get her sperm donor donation and she goes, "Oh, it's a very exclusive place." And Kevin says, "The place behind the IHOP?" The idea being that it potentially could be Kevin's child. I just loved it. I went to the editing bay and they were like, "It's gone, man. They can't." And I was like, "No, no, you cannot!" It's funny, but it's not the story.

STEVE CARELL: That's such a great thing, though. Even if it didn't become a story line, just to dangle it out there as a possibility is so funny.

Another strategy the writers had was to take moments that happened in the writers' room and put them in the show.

LEE EISENBERG: In some ways it was looser [than other writers' rooms]. It would take us a long time to focus. But it's like, you're writing a show about an office and we're working in an office. We just happen to be writing a show about the thing we're doing. We played [the first-person shooter video game] *Call of Duty* a lot, and then we did an episode about *Call of Duty* ["The Coup," episode three from season three].

```
JIM: At the Stamford branch, they
all play this World War II video
game called Call of Duty, and they're
all really into it. I'm told it
started as a team-building exercise.
Unfortunately, I really suck at it.
```

LEE EISENBERG: Everything is fodder. I'd come in and I would talk about my date from the night before and all of a sudden that could be something.

BRIAN BAUMGARTNER: I remember going into the editing bay one time, and I was having a conversation with [editor] David Rogers and somebody kind of whizzed by the door. And they were like, "Ready, Dave?" And I'm like, "What's going on?" And he goes, "It's *Call of Duly* time."

LEE EISENBERG: It was just procrastination. But it all turns into something, you know what I mean? When you're doing a show that's about people trying to make it through the day, everything is up for grabs. I think that's one of the reasons that people dig it. It's like, "Oh, this feels like my job."

JEN CELOTTA: Greg and I were trying to write a script together. I wonder if I should say this. We both usually wrote alone and then we were going to try and write an episode together. My process at the beginning of writing is a lot of procrastinating and then panic and then writing. We sat down to write, and it was one of those writer things where you just make sure the temperature is exactly right. You have all the pencils exactly sharpened. And then we were like, "We should order lunch." Just avoiding getting to it, 'cause it's hard. It's wonderful, but it's hard. He was having some sort of . . . I don't remember if it was a back thing or a shoulder thing, and I was having an ear problem. So we went to WebMD. He got me to put some olive oil from the kitchen in my ear 'cause I was like, "I think that this will help." And we're sitting there and we're on WebMD and we're just not starting. We're not starting. We're just diagnosing what's wrong with my ear and what's wrong with his back, and we're spending a lot of time not writing anything. But we turned it into a Michael and Dwight on WebMD.

> **DWIGHT:** Okay, where does it hurt?
>
> **MICHAEL:** Just . . . all over. I don't want to do anything . . . I'm dying . . .
>
> **DWIGHT:** No, that's not how it works. You have to point to a specific part of the body.

JEN CELOTTA: That's what was happening in our lives.

All of these methods, games, and theories helped build the dynamic in the writers' room. But because our writers had different superpowers, they were bound to clash.

BRENT FORRESTER: Writers' rooms are a very competitive environment. We are trying to impress each other that we're smart and talented. I definitely remember the first day I walked into the *Office* writers' room. I knew it was going to be brutal. So I brought in a prop. I brought in an army survival manual. There's an acronym that the army has: S.U.R.V.I.V.A.L. And each of those letters has a thing you're supposed to do. S is survey the situation, understand the risks. One of the *V*s is vanquishing fear and panic. It was my way of surviving. I figured if it got tight in there, I'd have a whole bit I could do. I never busted it out, but I remember on the first day, Mike Schur and I, we were arguing over some plot point. Should the story go this way or that way? I just went into an English accent. That was my move.

BRIAN BAUMGARTNER: Did it help?

BRENT FORRESTER: Absolutely it helped. I mean, it defused everything. And then on some level it kind of says, "We're playing a game of performative cleverness and this is just a move in that dimension."

MIKE SCHUR: There's only a couple of times in my life where something didn't really play well and I still fought for it. One of them, I wrote a talking head for Dwight in the "Dunder Mifflin Infinity" episode [of season four] where he gets into the backstory of his maternal ancestors and how they were maybe Nazis.

> **DWIGHT:** I'm gonna live for a very long time. My grandma Schrute lived to be 101. My grandpa Manheim, he's 103. He's still puttering down in Argentina. I tried to go visit him once, but my travel visa was protested by the Shoah Foundation.

MIKE SCHUR: It got like a moderate laugh 'cause a lot of people probably didn't know what the Shoah Foundation was.

The Shoah Foundation—Shoah is a Hebrew word for the Holocaust—is a nonprofit organization dedicated to preserving survivor testimony of the Holocaust and other modern genocides.

MIKE SCHUR: The idea that the Shoah Foundation would get involved in a travel visa for a random guy, that's how bad his maternal grandfather was. I remember fighting really hard for that in the edit. Greg wanted to cut it and I was like, "Please, please, please, please, please!"

BRIAN BAUMGARTNER: Was the Shoah Foundation in there?

MIKE SCHUR: Yeah, that aired. I was basically like, "I will never ask you for anything for the rest of my life if you leave this in."

JEN CELOTTA: I didn't hear this from [Greg], but somebody said that he wanted to hire people that could replace him. He wasn't scared of somebody who would constantly challenge him. Like, he wanted to have people who would fight him on stuff in the room. He wanted to have people who are passionate. They all gave a shit and they all fought.

PAUL FEIG: I remember just standing and watching [the writers] from the other side of the room. And everything they came up with was brilliant. Occasionally I tried to pitch a joke and they looked at me like, "Okay." I'm suddenly the dad in the room, pitching some shitty old hacky joke.

SEASON FOUR
Episode Guide

TITLE	DIRECTED BY	WRITTEN BY	ORIGINAL AIR DATE
"Fun Run"	Greg Daniels	Greg Daniels	September 27, 2007
"Dunder Mifflin Infinity"	Craig Zisk	Michael Schur	October 4, 2007
"Launch Party"	Ken Whittingham	Jennifer Celotta	October 11, 2007
"Money"	Paul Lieberstein	Paul Lieberstein	October 18, 2007
"Local Ad"	Jason Reitman	B. J. Novak	October 25, 2007
"Branch Wars"	Joss Whedon	Mindy Kaling	November 1, 2007
"Survivor Man"	Paul Feig	Steve Carell	November 8, 2007
"The Deposition"	Julian Farino	Lester Lewis	November 15, 2007
"Dinner Party"	Paul Feig	Gene Stupnitsky & Lee Eisenberg	April 10, 2008
"Chair Model"	Jeffrey Blitz	B. J. Novak	April 17, 2008
"Night Out"	Ken Whittingham	Mindy Kaling	April 24, 2008
"Did I Stutter?"	Randall Einhorn	Brent Forrester & Justin Spitzer	May 1, 2008
"Job Fair"	Tucker Gates	Lee Eisenberg & Gene Stupnitsky	May 8, 2008
"Goodbye, Toby"	Paul Feig	Jennifer Celotta & Paul Lieberstein	May 15, 2008

"I Had This Boss Once . . ."
The Collaboration Between the Actors and Writers

When it came to scripting, a big part of Greg's philosophy was to blur the lines between actors and writers.

GREG DANIELS: [On other TV shows], the actors and the writers didn't really hang out. And they'd always resent each other. The writers would try and write actor-proof jokes because they didn't trust that the actors could get laughs on behavior. It was very dysfunctional. The first thing I really wanted to do was create comedy television in a different pattern so that you could get more laughs off performance and not jokes.

JOHN KRASINSKI: I remember when the writers did come, I was always struck by how little they would talk. You know what I mean? I was always kinda surprised that they weren't saying things like, "No, we've got to do that line again." They were more just smiling and almost seemed like fans of the show. And now that makes sense that they were actually probably thinking, in their head, "Let's see what happens to the thing we wrote based on what these people are doing."

GREG DANIELS: The biggest laugh of all time was Jack Benny, where he's getting mugged.

> **MUGGER:** Don't make a move, this is a stickup. Now, come on—your money or your life.
>
> **BENNY:** [*Silence.*]

MUGGER: Look, bud! I said, your money or your life!

BENNY: I'm thinking it over!

[CROWD ROARS WITH LAUGHTER.]

(From *The Jack Benny Program*, March 28, 1948)

GREG DANIELS: To me that's great. 'Cause it's not a joke, right? You're bringing to bear everything you know about the character. I thought those were such cooler things than jokes.

ED HELMS: The creation of Andy's profile was one of the most thrilling creative endeavors of my life, because the writers would give Andy some weird thing and I would take it and run with it on set and improvise and do some crazy thing. If it was the a cappella thing, I would just start singing on set at wrong times. And then the writers would see that and be like, "Oh, that's fun." And then they'd write in more singing. That's just one example. There were so many little details that started to slot in, like a *Tetris* game about who Andy was. And it was this feedback loop, and Mike Schur in particular had a real shine for Andy and we just had so much fun. I would go to the writers' room and just joke around with Mike about who Andy is and what made us laugh about

Ed Helms in character as singing sensation, Andy Bernard—aka the Nard Dog.

him. The collaboration between the writers and the cast was next level.

ANGELA KINSEY: Jenna and I pitched an idea to Greg one day on set about these ridiculous "women in the workplace" workshops we'd have to do when we were both in corporate America. He was like, "Hold up, hold up. B.J., come here and write this down." B.J. took it and ran with it, and it became the episode "Boys and Girls" from the second season.

> `PAM:` Today's a "women in the workplace" thing. Jan's coming in from corporate to talk to all the women about . . . um . . . I don't really know what. But Michael's not allowed in. She said that about five times.

JENNA FISCHER: I remember the first time Greg called me at home, it was early on in season one and I thought, "Oh my God, I'm being fired." The only reason a showrunner calls you at home is to fire you. They don't call for any other reason. And Greg called and he was like, "Jenna, I was just wondering . . . why do you think Pam is still with Roy?" And I was like, "Oh, Greg, I've got a document. I've got a whole—"

BRIAN BAUMGARTNER: "Would you like to read the book I've written?"

JENNA FISCHER: I told him, "Greg, in my mind, the reason they never got married was because they had saved up some money for the wedding, and then Roy bought some WaveRunners with his brother. He spent their wedding money on a pair of WaveRunners." And Greg was like, "Oh my God, oh my God, that's amazing." And then he wrote it into the show. Greg truly believed that no one knew our characters more than we did. He would ask us questions all the time. He also knew that I worked in offices and that I had worked as a receptionist, and he used to ask me questions. "What's the craziest thing one of your bosses ever made you do?" There's an episode where Michael is refusing to sign all of his documents until the end of the day [the season two episode "The Fight"]. He keeps putting it off and putting it off and putting it off. And I told Greg, "I had this boss once, every month at the end of the month, he had to turn in this boilerplate report and he would put it off and put it off. And one time he put it off so long I had to drive to LAX because that was the last FedEx pickup and I was so pissed."

> **PAM:** Michael tends to procrastinate
> a bit whenever he has to do work.
> Time cards, he has to sign these every
> Friday. Purchase orders have to be
> approved at the end of every month.
> And expense reports, all he has to
> do is initial these at the end of
> every quarter. But once a year it
> all falls on the same Friday.
> That's today. I call it the perfect
> storm.

JENNA FISCHER: Greg loved those stories. He was always very curious.

STEVE CARELL: To be able to trace the evolution of a character and have something in mind and be able to talk to the writers and Greg Daniels and say, "What if next season my character went in this direction?" And then it happened. To be able to chart your own course as a character rather than just have it laid on you, that was really special. I think everyone trusted each other to such a degree that they were willing to not be too precious about anything.

It wasn't the only time that a script was changed while it was being shot. Just as Greg had told the writers, scripts were living documents that could change and evolve at any moment. This happened in a pivotal scene from "Gay Witch Hunt," the first episode of the third season, in which Michael inadvertently outs Oscar to the entire office and then tries to reconcile by hugging him and then . . .

BRIAN BAUMGARTNER: He kissed you. And that wasn't scripted, right?

OSCAR NUÑEZ: That was not scripted. No, Steve just did it. He just did it.

BRIAN BAUMGARTNER: Why? Why did he do it?

OSCAR NUÑEZ: Because the scene was flat. Nothing was happening.

BRIAN BAUMGARTNER: What do you mean?

OSCAR NUÑEZ: Well, I thought at the time it was just messing around. He kept hugging me. And that's nothing, not for an *Office* scene. Something's got to happen.

> **MICHAEL:** [*Embracing Oscar.*] You know what, I'm going to raise the stakes.
>
> **OSCAR:** You don't . . .
>
> **MICHAEL:** I want you to watch this. And I want you to burn this into your brains.

> **OSCAR:** I don't think we need to do
> this . . .
>
> **MICHAEL:** Because this is an image that
> I want you people to remember for a
> long time to come.

OSCAR NUÑEZ: Michael always has good intentions, but he's an idiot with a God complex. He's the only one who can fix problems. He knows better than anyone, so he's going to fix it. That beautiful kissing scene, it was like the ultimate acceptance. It was like, "Look at what I'm doing, everyone."

JEN CELOTTA: Michael kissing Oscar was one of the best moments of the whole show. It was funnier than what was scripted. Steve had great respect for the text, but he also had this ridiculous ability to understand everything in such a depth that if he was going to change things up, it was always going to honor the intention.

STEVE CARELL: For me, the hardest part of it was servicing the script. I'd get dialogue every day and think, "I can't screw this up." I think we all felt a responsibility to get it right. We all had a barometer as for what rang true and what didn't. And I think the things that ring true are the things that are reflected in society, but to do it in a way that wasn't too heavy-handed and felt organic to what we were doing as characters.

In that same episode, Angela Kinsey had a line that didn't feel right to her.

ANGELA KINSEY: There was a pretty harsh dig from me at Oscar's expense about his sexual orientation. I went to Greg and I was like, "Angela is a lot of things, but she does care for Oscar. He's her only ally in that corner of accounting and she knows it. She wouldn't say that. She might not agree with his lifestyle choice. She might not understand it. Because she has some fear, she might be a little put off by it, but she does care for him. That can exist all at the same time in someone." He really heard me and we changed the line. Instead she said:

> **ANGELA:** Sure, sometimes I watch *Will & Grace* . . . and I want to throw up. It's terribly loud.

The topic of "Gay Witch Hunt" was obviously risky: 2006 was a time of "Don't Ask, Don't Tell," and same-sex marriage in the United States was nearly a decade away. But the episode ended up being both very funny and a sharp social commentary on homophobia in the workplace.

EMILY VANDERWERFF: The reason that episode works is because it's reinforcing the belief that it's totally fine to have gay friends in your life. The gay guy in your office is just like you, because he is also put-upon by Michael Scott. It's very progressive in its values and very progressive in the way it talks about what it is to be a gay man in America.

BRIAN BAUMGARTNER: At the time, Oscar was the only LGBT person of color to be a regular on any sitcom. Were you aware of that?

OSCAR NUÑEZ: No! That's a big deal. That's fantastic. I'm like Jackie Robinson.

BRIAN BAUMGARTNER: You won awards for that, right?

OSCAR NUÑEZ: I was nominated for a GLAAD award. I took my two gay friends with me, Michael and Joel. They were rolling their eyes. They're like, "You asshole, you're not even gay." [*Laughs.*] Joel was in ACT UP [AIDS Coalition to Unleash Power], fighting the fight for real.

He was like, "Good Lord, what is happening?" And I'm like, "Don't be jealous, I'm just better than you guys." [*Laughs.*]

BRIAN BAUMGARTNER: Do you ever meet fans who are surprised that you're not gay?

OSCAR NUÑEZ: All the time. I get a lot of people coming up to me going, "I came out because of you." It's trippy. Years ago, right around the third season, [my future wife] Ursula and I are walking around New York and these two adorable Puerto Rican guys were like, "Oh my God, you're Oscar from *The Office*!" And they look at Ursula and go, "Who's this?" I'm like, "This is my girlfriend," and they were so disappointed. I'm like, "Come on, you guys. You ever hear of acting?" [*Laughs.*]

"Gay Witch Hunt" was just one example. The writers loved to poke at social issues most TV comedies avoided, like workplace health care and sexual harassment. That kind of writing won us some pretty big awards. When we won a Peabody, this is how the committee described the show: "*The Office* explores the monotony and inanity of the daily grind while highlighting the simple pleasures that make the working world bearable. All the while, sharp observations about American society slip through in the guise of comedy."

GREG DANIELS: The Peabody is like legit.

BRIAN BAUMGARTNER: That's a thing.

GREG DANIELS: I remember going to that and we didn't really know too much about it. We got in the room, and the other people that were nominated were like news organizations that were digging into really important stories and war-torn places.

The other Peabody recipients in 2006 included shows and movies about the Galapagos Islands, pan-Asian immigration to the United States, urban schools, Iraq War military hospitals, and AIDS in Black America.

GREG DANIELS: You looked around that room and you were like, "Oh my goodness."

It was humbling, sure, but it was also reinforcement that the writing really was as good as we hoped it was. As Greg often said, he wanted *The Office* to be real, to reflect what was happening in the real world. It's an instinct he'd had since his days as a writer on *The Simpsons*.

GREG DANIELS: The way that one *Simpsons* writer won respect from another *Simpsons* writer was when you did something super real, and somehow in contrast to the cartoony-ness of it. When I got to *King of the Hill,* we used to do a lot of research. I'd take the writers to Texas every season and we'd fan out with our reporter's notebooks and try to dig up unique stories. Because I always felt the shows that I really liked, the stories seemed like something that had happened to one of the writers. It wasn't just, "What did *Cheers* do?" You had to go out and do your own work and dig up your own stories.

This is what our writers and actors were so good at. We tackled real, relatable topics and made them funny. We were a team. So when it came time to defend the show, we stood together.

"He Called Their Bluff"
The Writers Strike of 2007

BRIAN BAUMGARTNER: You may have forgotten this, but you and I share an Emmy.

MIKE SCHUR: We do?

BRIAN BAUMGARTNER: We do. Yes.

MIKE SCHUR: For the webisodes?

BRIAN BAUMGARTNER: For the webisodes, yes.

In the summer of 2006, we developed a web series called *The Office: The Accountants*—written by Schur and Paul Lieberstein, and directed by Randall Einhorn—which follows Angela, Oscar, and Kevin as they try to solve the mystery of a missing $3,000 from the company books. The series won a Daytime Emmy for Outstanding Broadband Program—Comedy in 2007.

BRIAN BAUMGARTNER: Did you ever get yours?

MIKE SCHUR: I don't think I have an actual trophy for it.

BRIAN BAUMGARTNER: I do, because we were invited to the ceremony and we accepted it and it came home with me.

MIKE SCHUR: How does it look?

BRIAN BAUMGARTNER: It's great actually. It's really special.

MIKE SCHUR: Those webisodes were really fun. We did like ten episodes over three days.

BEN SILVERMAN: The webisodes were launched because we didn't have a ton of episodes for that summer, having only produced a season and a half or so. And we decided to do these webisodes, which would be original and deepen the audience's relationship to other cast members and would open the door to more connectivity. And it was amazing. It was the first of its kind and we started something no one had ever done before.

BRIAN BAUMGARTNER: We were showing the network that we could be valuable over multiple platforms. I remember NBC.com that summer grew exponentially.

BEN SILVERMAN: People tuned in to our webisodes on [NBC's] online platform and [NBC was] getting revenue from the iTunes platform, which they hadn't had as a revenue stream during the initial cycles of shows before. The audience was growing and the advertisers were loving it.

MIKE SCHUR: We shot those webisodes with union labor and no one got paid.

Not the actors, the writers, even the camera people. NBC considered it "promotional material," even though the videos were monetized with YouTube ads and included on the DVD release of season two.

MIKE SCHUR: It wasn't because of those webisodes that the writers went on strike. Those webisodes were an example of the way things were going. We've got to do something about this. Networks at the time were saying, "We don't have enough information. Let's just wait three years from now." And we were like, "No, you're basically trying to grandfather in the internet as a thing that you don't pay for."

On November 5, 2007, the Writers Guild of America went on strike. It was fighting the networks and studios over compensation for new media, like web originals and streaming.

MIKE SCHUR: It was a huge deal and it was very scary. It happened pretty quickly.

BRENT FORRESTER: I had a memorable showdown with Jim Brooks [cocreator of *The Mary Tyler Moore Show, Taxi,* and *The Simpsons*] where he said, "Hey, man, I hear you're on strike." He got enraged, his beard was shaking. He said, "Don't go down that road! Don't float that balloon!" I've never heard that phrase in my life.

BRIAN BAUMGARTNER: "Don't float that balloon"?

BRENT FORRESTER: "Don't float that balloon." It might be like a World War II reference. If you ever meet him, please tell him I'm sorry and ask him what that means.

Greg Daniels, however, was more than willing to float that balloon.

MIKE SCHUR: Greg was like, "We're going to picket our own show."

BRENT FORRESTER: We would go out in the cold and picket together. And there was this feeling of solidarity and shared purpose. And we felt like what we were doing was right. I will eternally praise our catering guys, who made the writers a bunch of breakfast burritos on the first day of the strike. It brought a lot of people together.

But a major concern around the strike was that the crews would suffer. If the production shut down, the non-writing staff—hair and makeup, catering, props, set design—none of them could earn a living.

The Office cast picketing in solidarity alongside the writers.

LEE EISENBERG: We're friends with the crew, and the crews are walking past us into the studio, and some of them are kind of looking at us like, "Fuck you." The writers are among the highest-paid people, and all of a sudden someone's going to not work for three months because we're complaining about our DVD residuals or our health care and it doesn't matter to them. They just want to work and we shut down production.

JEN CELOTTA: It was a little scary. It was confusing. I remember very specifically driving to the studio at 4:30 in the morning, and [the Bob Seger song] "Night Moves" was playing on the radio. Super weird. I'm on the 134 [Ventura Freeway], nothing's around me. I remember getting there and seeing Paul Lieberstein all bundled up, with like a scarf and gloves. It's so cold, I can see the breath coming out of his mouth. I'm like, "Oh shit, this is our new future."

DEBBIE PIERCE: Everybody was like up in the air about whether we're going to have jobs or not.

Debbie Pierce was one of our key hairstylists, along with Kim Ferry, who became the head of the hair department.

KIM FERRY: I remember the first day, we didn't want to cross because all the writers were there. Literally, the whole cast was there. I was like, "I don't want to cross. I'm union. We're *all* union." B.J. was there and he was like, "It's okay." I'm like, "It's not okay." I remember getting choked up, like, "I don't want to do this to you. You guys are my family. I don't want to pass." And he said, "No, look, [the network] is telling you to cross. We don't want you to get in trouble." So we sat on the stage and just waited.

DEBBIE PIERCE: 'Cause there was nothing else we could do.

KIM FERRY: I think about six, seven hours later, they said, "You can go home." As a mom of two young kids and the person supporting my household, it was terrifying. I will never forget.

On the other side of the strike were the networks and the studios. Problem was, the head of our network was Ben Silverman, executive producer of *The Office*, the guy who started our whole show.

BEN SILVERMAN: I was thirty-six years old when I was asked to be the cochairman of NBC [in 2007]. I thought it was my dream job and I really did see where the business was going. The future was coming hard and fast, and technology was going to enable an absolute transformation of how people consume content. And I was eager to lead that transformation. I was rudely awakened to the reality that no one wanted to change the status quo because it had been working so well for so many of the people who were part of it, and there was real fear in the decisions I was making.

BRIAN BAUMGARTNER: If you knew what was happening in terms of technology, then you had to know that what the writers were fighting for was inevitable, right?

BEN SILVERMAN: The problem was the networks feeling they were going to fall off a cliff. They hadn't yet decided to be Disney+ or Peacock or HBO Max or whatever. They thought, "Oh my gosh, our ratings are going down rapidly and we are going to lose our shirts." What was clear to me was it was bad for both sides to shut it down at that moment. It eventually did hurt both sides, but it hurt the writers more at that time. I don't think it was clear yet what there was to fight for.

BRIAN BAUMGARTNER: It was also really confusing for the actors, because we had our union, but we were not protected by the strike. We were still supposed to show up to work.

MIKE SCHUR: And we [the writers] knew that. I remember Ed [Helms] came out and hung with us. And then he was like, "I'm really sorry, but I need to go back inside," and we were like, "No, no, no, we get it. Your union is not on strike here. No one's mad at you." No one had any animosity towards any of the actors. You were in breach of contract if you didn't show up.

ED HELMS: I remember going that first day of the strike and being like, "Oh, wow, this is real." There's Lee and Gene and Mike and Greg, everybody's just out on the sidewalk with picket signs. I think everyone felt a lot of tension in a way that's baked into any union conflict, like, "Am I a part of this fight?" Obviously I support the writers, but it's scary a little bit. It just felt so right and natural to jump out of the car and sidle up to everybody and be like, "Let's do this!" In hindsight, I really appreciate how courageous that was for so many people.

JEN CELOTTA: There was something that happened at the strike that still bothers me to this day. [At a different picket line,] I remember that there were people with drums and loud musical instruments to disrupt a production that was going on inside. That was just not cool to me. I was very upset. I understood what we were fighting for, but other people were making their money to shoot things that had already been written. That part of it was very complicated to me because I wanted everybody to be able to continue to do their job.

Over at our studio, we could have shot another episode even as the strike was going on.

MIKE SCHUR: We had a finished script. That script was ready to go and could have been shot. The actors and the directors weren't on strike and the crew wasn't on strike.

Lee Eisenberg and Gene Stupnitsky had written a soon-to-be classic for the fourth season called "Dinner Party." Michael and Jan invite several couples, including Pam and Jim, to their condo for a dinner party, and the evening devolves into a hilariously uncomfortable affair, like Edward Albee's *Who's Afraid of Virginia Woolf?* but with more laughs. It culminates with Michael's tiny plasma television getting destroyed with a Dundie and the cops showing up.

Michael Scott hosting his infamous "Dinner Party."

LEE EISENBERG: It's probably to this day the thing that we're most proud of writing. We did the table read of it, and in the beginning it's good, not great. Then you get to the condo and you start feeling something. It became electric in a way. I'm thinking about it now and it makes me emotional.

MIKE SCHUR: It was the best read-through I think we ever had. It was like a rock concert.

LEE EISENBERG: Gene sweat through his shirt. And it was just like, it was the greatest moment of our career. Greg pulled us into his office 'cause we were getting notes from the network and we got on the phone with some executives. They said, "Hey, so we read the script, very funny." And Greg said, "Thank you." And they said, "It's really dark." And Greg goes, "Yeah." And they go, "Just the thing is, it's *really* dark." And Greg goes, "Yeah." And then he says, "Is there anything else?" And they go, "Nope." He goes, "Okay, great. Thanks, guys. Bye." And hung up. I was like, "Wow, that was fucking cool."

JOHN KRASINSKI: Amazing. That's like some Jedi mind trick.

The episode was ready to be filmed. And then came the writers strike. Production certainly could have gone on during the strike, and it possibly would have, if not for one man.

MIKE SCHUR: Steve Carell said no. The way we make this show is collaborative. There are writers on the set and producers on the set and we change things and we work out new little moments and pitch new jokes. He didn't want to make the show without the writers. And he didn't show up.

Steve refused to cross the picket line.

MIKE SCHUR: They shot a couple scenes from the episode that Michael Scott wasn't in. And then there was nothing else to do and the show shut down. That was such a heroic thing. He just stayed home and he got calls from a lot of lawyers and a lot of studio executives, all the way up the ladder. He got calls from the head of the network, from people at GE corporate, from really, really powerful people, saying, "You have to do this." And he was like, "No, I don't. Watch me."

It wasn't the first time Steve had stood up to the network.

STEVE CARELL: I remember when one executive came in and said, "Hey, for budgetary reasons, we would like to do some product integration." I raised my hand and said, "I'm very much against this, because it changes the show." If we are serving a corporate master, there's no way the show will be the same. It's going to alter how we write the show, how we perform the show. I was dead set against it. They went ahead and did a couple of things anyway. And each time they were disasters. They were terrible.

Well, they weren't all disasters. When Dwight quits his job at Staples to return to Dunder Mifflin in the season three episode "The Return," Staples, which had a product placement deal with NBC, released this tongue-in-cheek memo: "Despite his promising start in business machines (selling 2 printers in one morning), it was soon clear he wasn't a good fit with the Staples culture."

STEVE CARELL: I feel we were all very protective of the show. I was just in a position more often than not to be the voice of the show. Like to say something and not just let things transpire without any sort of representation.

MIKE SCHUR: Greg called him and was like, "I know that you've had a lot of pressure coming at you. Are you okay?" And he was like, "Yeah, I'm home. I'm playing with my kids." He was totally unfazed by it. He had the attitude of like, "This is a collaborative effort. This is a thing that we do together. Without writers on the set, we don't make the same show and I'm not going to make that show." "Fire me" was basically what he was saying. He called their bluff.

Without Steve Carell, production on *The Office* shut down, which left the actors standing in solidarity with the writers.

> **MIKE SCHUR:** The story of what he did spread like wildfire. He did not have to do that. There were very few people in his position—the star of a very popular, successful, gigantic, monolithic hit show—who would do that. He didn't have to. No one would've been mad at him. The actors weren't on strike.
>
> **JEN CELOTTA:** I mean, what a dude. Steve's just a class act outside of being so ridiculously talented. It really was a family and he was going to support his people. Greg and Steve were like the dads.

One hundred days later, on February 12, 2008, the Writers Guild and the studios reached an agreement. Writers would finally get a share of digital revenues, and we could finally go back to work. Not everybody came out unscathed. Some studios and networks severed writers' contracts and many shows in development never got made. Was it worth it?

> **MIKE SCHUR:** There's still people in the Writers Guild who think the strike didn't accomplish anything. But literally one-third of all TV that's produced now is for streamers. To think that none of that would be covered by our contracts is lunacy. It was a crucial and vital action that saved the union and all of entertainment.

But the lasting impression, at least among the cast and crew of *The Office*, isn't about what was won or lost at the negotiating table. It's about what we learned about just how strong our connection really was, and how we could count on our fearless leaders even when the future seemed uncertain and scary.

LAVERNE CARACUZZI-MILAZZO (MAKEUP ARTIST): It was like, "We have to do this because we have to make a point, but we also want you to know that you're appreciated." Like when every crew member got a check out of Greg Daniels's personal checking account.

BRIAN BAUMGARTNER: Wait, what was that?

LAVERNE CARACUZZI-MILAZZO: Am I allowed to talk about that?

BRIAN BAUMGARTNER: Sure.

LAVERNE CARACUZZI-MILAZZO: Greg Daniels went into his personal checking account and wrote the crew [*starts to tear up*] each an individual check because we were going to be out of work.

KIM FERRY: A thousand dollars for every family. I was floored, because that made such a difference to my household.

DEBBIE PIERCE: I went to the mail that day, and people were sending Christmas cards and stuff. I looked at the cards and I saw this card from Greg Daniels. I'm going, "Oh, isn't that nice? He thought of us." I opened it up and I saw this check and I didn't really look at it really clearly at first. I thought it was $100. And then I started counting the zeros and I could not believe it.

LAVERNE CARACUZZI-MILAZZO: You knew that it was his personal checking account because when you received the check, it had the address up in the corner. Why wouldn't you want to keep working for these people, regardless of how long the strike is? You're taking care of us now. My tears are more tears of joy, because I felt so appreciated at that point.

DEBBIE PIERCE: I told that story to quite a few of my friends who worked on other shows and they were like, "Are you kidding me?" That was unheard of.

KIM FERRY: You know why? Because we were family.

DEBBIE PIERCE: That's absolutely true.

Speaking of family, not everybody on *The Office* spent those hundred days on the picket line or hanging out at home. Angela Kinsey got pregnant during the strike. She would be giving birth to her daughter, Isabel Ruby Lieberstein, in May 2008. Amazing news for our dear friend, but for a show where she played a character who was absolutely not pregnant, well . . .

ANGELA KINSEY: I was completely showing. I remember thinking, "Okay, how do we hide this?" Because it wouldn't have made sense for my character to all of a sudden be pregnant. I had one of the most hilarious conversations with Paul Feig, who was directing an episode where Phyllis walks in on Dwight and Angela making out in the office and they're caught.

In the season four finale, "Goodbye, Toby," Phyllis catches Angela and Dwight having sex on one of the office desks after Toby's farewell party.

ANGELA KINSEY: I was seven and a half months pregnant and they were trying to have Rainn hide my belly with his body as we're making out. We're supposed to be in stages of mid-undress. At first the writers were like, "Well, what if Angela got on all fours," or "What if we put her here?" It was like, "Where do you put the giant pregnant belly? What do we do so it doesn't look *really* inappropriate instead of just mildly inappropriate?"

Another day, another *Office* writing challenge.

Well, the strike was behind us, but we were far from done with the surprises and emotional tailspins. What awaited us would make the first four seasons seem like a walk in the park.

9

"The Moment That My Life Changed"

A WEDDING, NEW HIRES (AND LOSSES), AND OTHER SHAKE-UPS: SEASONS FIVE AND SIX

CELEBRATING THE SHOW'S ONE HUNDREDTH EPISODE.

By the late aughts, *The Office* was hitting its stride. Seasons five and six are often ranked by critics and fans alike as among our best. We weathered unexpected storms, witnessed pivotal moments for our characters, made new hires at Dunder Mifflin, and faced some major shake-ups behind the scenes.

How did we navigate those winds of change? In the words of Michael Scott, when asked by Dunder Mifflin CFO David Wallace to explain his secret to success (in the fifth season episode "The Duel"), "Sometimes I'll start a sentence, and I don't even know where it's going. I just hope I find it along the way."

That might as well have been our motto before every season: We don't know where it's going, we're just hoping to find it along the way.

Which isn't to say we faced the challenges with a confident shrug. The more attention we got, the bigger the stakes. And now more than ever, we knew how much there was to lose. Or as one soon-to-be *Office* showrunner put it . . .

JEN CELOTTA: We did not want to screw anything up.

"It Feels Like Mozart Wants to Design a Piano with Me"
Office Spin-offs and New Hires

When you have a TV show as popular as *The Office*—a staple of NBC's newly branded (as of 2006) "Comedy Night Done Right" Thursday lineup—it's only natural that the network would come knocking for a spin-off. Ben Silverman, who replaced Kevin Reilly as cochair of NBC Entertainment in the summer of 2007, was eager to double down on the show that had made his reputation at NBC. Just as *Cheers* had its *Frasier*, *All in the Family* had its *Jeffersons*, and *The Daily Show* had its *Colbert Report*, *The Office* would have its . . . well, Greg wasn't sure yet. But he knew whom he wanted to help him create it.

MIKE SCHUR: [Greg asked me] during the writers strike. We were picketing at Paramount, and Greg was like, "Hey, I want to talk to you." And he basically said, "The network wants me to do a new show and I want to do it with you." I remember thinking, "What does this feel like? Oh, it feels like Mozart wants to design a piano with me."

That's the closest analogy I could come up with. "This is the moment that my life changes."

GREG DANIELS: Mike could produce, he could write, and he wasn't one of the main characters [on *The Office*]. I felt very responsible to the cast and to Steve [Carell]. If Steve was going to stick with it and not bug out and go do movies, I didn't want to be the guy who was doing something to the detriment of the show.

MIKE SCHUR: I was very nervous, because *The Office* is the best job I ever had in my life by a factor of a thousand. There's a thing in this business of like, if you've got a bird in the hand, just leave it in your hand. What are you doing? But again, you don't turn down the chance to develop a show with Greg Daniels. So it was very scary, but it was also the right move. And if it blows up, I'll bet he'll hire me back [on *The Office*].

GREG DANIELS: There was a lot of pressure to do an *Office* spin-off. And I was worried, because it felt like spin-offs are never as good.

Mike Schur (*right*) as Mose Schrute.

Why are you doing it? 'Cause you're trying to take advantage of the [original show's] popularity.

MIKE SCHUR: It's classic Greg. If the best idea is to do a spin-off from *The Office*, great. But if the best idea is something else, then we should do something else. Greg is a man of enormous creative integrity and personal integrity. He could have cashed in so easily. He could've taken the [Scranton branch] accountants and spun them into their own show. He could have taken Kelly [Kapoor, played by Mindy Kaling] and spun her into a show. He could've taken Jan [Levinson] and spun her into a show. He could've been the Dick Wolf of comedy.

Dick Wolf is the creator and executive producer of the lucrative (and seemingly endless) *Law & Order* franchise.

MIKE SCHUR: But he was like, "I don't want to harm the integrity of *The Office* proper."

The next vital steps of the creative process took place in a diner.

GREG DANIELS: I used to go to NORMS all the time up in Van Nuys. There's a terrific NORMS on Sherman Way that would be my hangout.

NORMS is a chain of twenty diners in the SoCal area started in the '50s by used-car salesman Norm Roybark. It's the place where Tom Waits claims he enjoyed "strange-looking patty melts" in the *Nighthawks at the Diner* song "Eggs and Sausage."

GREG DANIELS: I started going to NORMS trying to think of a different show.

MIKE SCHUR: We met for breakfast like three times a week. And I pitched him, I don't know, 275 ideas for TV shows. And he pitched me, it wasn't a one-way street. We just kept pitching and pitching and pitching. Some of them were like, "Maybe we could do something with the warehouse," or "Maybe a different branch." The reason the show was [originally] called *The Office: An American Workplace* is because Greg was thinking a thousand chess moves ahead. If this works, you could do *The School: An American Workplace* and do a show about teachers. Or *The Team: An American Workplace* about a minor league baseball team, whatever. He was thinking globally at that level, even before he made the pilot.

GREG DANIELS: I had an idea that I thought was good. The workplace is a good genre of TV comedy, but an even bigger genre is the family show. What about a mockumentary about a family? There's that *American Family* one from the seventies that was on PBS.

An American Family, a 1973 PBS television documentary that's often called the first American reality series, followed Bill and Pat Loud and their five children from Santa Barbara, California. Audiences watched as the couple went through a divorce and their son Lance came out to them.

GREG DANIELS: We had worked it out. Ed Helms was gonna maybe be the lead with [British actress] Catherine Tate as his wife. It was going to be a mockumentary looking at some suburban cul-de-sac.

BEN SILVERMAN: We were talking about having Amy Poehler and her husband at the time, Will Arnett, do a family-like spin-off. We had debated and discussed what the mothership [i.e., *The Office*] could support and how to set something that wouldn't be competitive with it but would be consistent with it.

MIKE SCHUR: Because he's Greg, he didn't commit to anything. He's like, "Okay, good, we've got that, let's keep pitching and try to come up with something else." Day after day after day after day after . . .

Mike was starting to feel anxious. At least until he talked to someone who knows Greg's quirks better than anyone: his wife, Susanne.

MIKE SCHUR: She told me about a time early in their marriage, when they were driving from Chicago to New York. It's ten o'clock at night and they're driving through Schuylkill [County], Pennsylvania. They pull off the highway and find a diner. The waitress comes over and Greg says, "What do you guys serve here? What's everyone's favorite dish?" And she goes, "Oh, people really like the meat loaf." And he goes, "How do you prepare it?" She goes into the meat loaf, and he's like, "What else do people like?" And Susanne says, "Can we just eat?" And he goes, "I want to know what kind of food they have." So he asks a hundred more questions and she goes, "Honey, I'm starving." And he goes, "Susanne, this might be the only time we're ever here. We have to get the best dining experience in Schuylkill, Pennsylvania." And they don't sit down. They drove to another restaurant and he asked more questions. "What do you serve here? What do people like?" She tells me this story and my mouth is agape. She goes, "That's the man I chose to marry. And that's the man you've chosen to develop a TV show with."

It was beginning to seem like they'd never come up with a premise for the spin-off.

BEN SILVERMAN: And then Mike Schur came up with an idea set in the world of small-town politics.

That idea, in part inspired by Barack Obama and the '08 presidential election, would become *Parks and Recreation*. "Documenting" the lives, loves, and adventures of the parks and rec department in the fictional town of Pawnee, Indiana, the series, which starred Amy Poehler, ran from 2009 to 2015.

MIKE SCHUR: The show isn't just about local government, it's about a whole town. Like we can invent Dunder Mifflin, but an entire town, an entire ecosystem with media outlets and restaurants and city hall and local celebrities and a history. It set our brains on fire. It's like a comedy *West Wing*. If the stakes of the *West Wing* are Russia and China going to war in Kazakhstan, the stakes of this show are the boys' soccer team and the girls' soccer team are both trying to use the same soccer field.

It wasn't technically an *Office* spin-off, since the two shows shared no similar characters.

BEN SILVERMAN: I had made a deal with Amy Poehler, who I was pursuing to be part of *The Office* cast originally.

Amy was briefly considered for the role of Jan Levinson. It didn't worry Greg that Amy and Steve Carell, both alumni of the Second City comedy theater in Chicago, could be very convincing (and sympathetic) at playing well-meaning morons. Amy's character on *Parks and Rec* wouldn't just be the female Michael Scott.

GREG DANIELS: I don't think Amy can hide her intelligence. One of Steve's real gifts is you can stare at his face and he's doing something really stupid and you can't tell that he's aware that it's stupid. He completely hides his intelligence. Amy probably could if she wanted to, but chooses not to. She just doesn't hide it. Maybe it's also being a woman. It means something different to hide your intelligence.

Parks and Rec was taking shape. But Greg knew he couldn't run two shows by himself. Luckily, he'd been planning for this moment for years and had his eye on two writers in particular.

JEN CELOTTA: We were . . . I'm terrible at military things . . . lieutenants? Is that like a person like underneath the captain? Greg's the captain and we're underneath him and take on some responsibilities.

Jen Celotta and Paul Lieberstein were perfect for the job of co-showrunners, or cocaptains.

PAUL LIEBERSTEIN: Greg and I went on a walk on Saticoy [Street in Van Nuys], and he asked if I wanted to do it with Jen.

BRIAN BAUMGARTNER: You took a *walk* with him?

PAUL LIEBERSTEIN: That was not unusual. Did you not walk? We had a real running club [for the *Office* cast and crew] for a month.

BRIAN BAUMGARTNER: When Greg asked you to take over, did it scare you?

PAUL LIEBERSTEIN: Definitely.

JEN CELOTTA: We felt an enormous amount of responsibility. But it wasn't like Greg was getting on a boat and leaving. He would help us navigate this and we'd be able to ask questions. The main responsibilities would be to Paul and me, so we certainly felt like there was a lot on our shoulders. But Greg would still be involved.

That involvement began early, with weekly meetings between Greg, Mike, and the two newly appointed *Office* showrunners.

JEN CELOTTA: Greg passed out a memo about the meetings that was like, "Say things in the quickest amount of time that you can say them," or something like that. It was very polite and basically like, "Try to stay on track." I was thinking about it—Mike likes to talk but he's very succinct in everything he says, and Paul doesn't talk that much.

SEASON FIVE
Episode Guide

TITLE	DIRECTED BY	WRITTEN BY	ORIGINAL AIR DATE
"Weight Loss"	Paul Feig	Lee Eisenberg & Gene Stupnitsky	September 25, 2008
"Business Ethics"	Jeffrey Blitz	Ryan Koh	October 9, 2008
"Baby Shower"	Greg Daniels	Aaron Shure	October 16, 2008
"Crime Aid"	Jennifer Celotta	Charlie Grandy	October 23, 2008
"Employee Transfer"	David Rogers	Anthony Q. Farrell	October 30, 2008
"Customer Survey"	Stephen Merchant	Lester Lewis	November 6, 2008
"Business Trip"	Randall Einhorn	Brent Forrester	November 13, 2008
"Frame Toby"	Jason Reitman	Mindy Kaling	November 20, 2008
"The Surplus"	Paul Feig	Gene Stupnitsky & Lee Eisenberg	December 4, 2008
"Moroccan Christmas"	Paul Feig	Justin Spitzer	December 11, 2008
"The Duel"	Dean Holland	Jennifer Celotta	January 15, 2009
"Prince Family Paper"	Asaad Kelada	B. J. Novak	January 22, 2009
"Stress Relief"	Jeffrey Blitz	Paul Lieberstein	February 1, 2009
"Lecture Circuit: Part 1"	Ken Kwapis	Mindy Kaling	February 5, 2009
"Lecture Circuit: Part 2"	Ken Kwapis	Mindy Kaling	February 12, 2009
"Blood Drive"	Randall Einhorn	Brent Forrester	March 5, 2009
"Golden Ticket"	Randall Einhorn	Mindy Kaling	March 12, 2009
"New Boss"	Paul Feig	Lee Eisenberg & Gene Stupnitsky	March 19, 2009

"Two Weeks"	Paul Lieberstein	Aaron Shure	March 26, 2009
"Dream Team"	Paul Feig	B. J. Novak	April 9, 2009
"Michael Scott Paper Company"	Gene Stupnitsky	Justin Spitzer	April 9, 2009
"Heavy Competition"	Ken Whittingham	Ryan Koh	April 16, 2009
"Broke"	Steve Carell	Charlie Grandy	April 23, 2009
"Casual Friday"	Brent Forrester	Anthony Q. Farrell	April 30, 2009
"Cafe Disco"	Randall Einhorn	Warren Lieberstein & Halsted Sullivan	May 7, 2009
"Company Picnic"	Ken Kwapis	Jennifer Celotta & Paul Lieberstein	May 14, 2009

I was like, this is for *me*. Greg wrote the memo for me. It was saying, "Jen, stop talking all the time."

PAUL LIEBERSTEIN: Jen and I wrote "Goodbye, Toby" together [the season four finale], and I remember Greg saying something to me that shocked me 'cause I hadn't thought about it this way. He was like, "Really kill it with this one. 'Cause a lot of people will be looking. This will set the tone for next year." I was like, holy shit. Well, *that* makes it harder.

LEE EISENBERG: Paul and Jen had been our coworkers for three years and we loved them and we thought they were incredible. So it felt like a natural progression rather than like the show is now a different show.

Paul and Jen had no intention of overhauling *The Office* or changing it radically from Greg's vision.

PAUL LIEBERSTEIN: It wasn't like, "Finally, we get to do it *our* way." We loved Greg's writing. Even though he gave me authority, I wanted him to like the show, you know? If he came to a table read and didn't like something, I would change it. I don't think I ever said, "Well, I like it so we're doing it." We would always find the overlap.

It was a good thing they did, because season five threw us some big curveballs. Remember back in our first season, when NBC ordered a measly six episodes? Well, now it wanted twenty-eight.

JEN CELOTTA: We ended up doing nineteen in a row. It was just like, "Oh shit. Oh shit. Oh shit." Greg is very good about signing on to things and then just figuring it out. With me, I pre-panic and pre-worry, and then once things get rough, I'm okay. When we were first asked to do nineteen episodes in a row, I remember panicking a little and they [Greg and Paul] were like, "It's going to be okay, it's just more episodes. It's more exciting. It's more for everybody to do. It's more money, it's more everything." I remember telling Paul and Greg, "I feel like I'm in a horror movie with you guys, but I'm the only one that sees the monster." And then I remember there was a particularly hard patch and Paul was like, "I see the monster, I see the monster!"

Thankfully, they had help. Paul Feig came on board as a co-executive producer. And with editors Dean Holland joining *Parks and Rec* and Dave Rogers starting to direct as well, we brought in a new editor, Claire Scanlon. Today, Claire is a major TV director—*Unbreakable Kimmy Schmidt, The Good Place, Brooklyn Nine-Nine*, and the Netflix romantic comedy *Set It Up*—but back in early 2009 when she joined our show, she had done only reality shows and documentaries.

CLAIRE SCANLON (EDITOR AND DIRECTOR): This was the very first scripted television show I ever edited, period. I literally went from not scripted to the number one company.

She got the gig after passing along an editing friend's name to Paul Lieberstein, whom she'd known in social circles since their twenties. Claire's friend was hoping to join the *Office* spin-off.

CLAIRE SCANLON: I told Paul, "Hey, my friend wants to put his name in the hat for the new show." And he's like, "Well, what about you? You're an editor too." It didn't even cross my mind that I'd even have a chance. I'd met Greg and Susanne at Paul's birthday party one year. To me, they were like the grown-ups. They had a kid already, and I was in my twenties and they were just so mature. When I went in to my interview with Greg, I remember thinking, "He's a dad."

There's a seven-year age difference between Claire and Greg.

CLAIRE SCANLON: I told him, "I don't have any narrative editing background. This isn't my forte. I come from documentaries. In fact, I've worked with a lot of your camera operators on *The Apprentice*." Greg's like, "That's a

Claire Scanlon

Occupation: Editor and director

Hometown: Chicago, Illinois

Training: University of Chicago, Class of 1992, English major; University of Southern California film school

Previous Employment: Editing documentaries for PBS and the Discovery Channel, like *Lenny Bruce: Swear to Tell the Truth* (1998), *Bodybuilders* (2000), and *Las Vegas Weddings* (2001)

Post-Office Credits: Director for series like *Unbreakable Kimmy Schmidt* (2016–2018), *Fresh Off the Boat* (2015–2018), *Black-ish* (2014–2019), *Brooklyn Nine-Nine* (2015–2020), and *GLOW* (2017–2019); directed several Netflix features including *Set It Up* (2018) and *Unbreakable Kimmy Schmidt: Kimmy vs the Reverend* (2020)

Special Skills: Directing and editing while pregnant; finished filming *Set It Up* a month before giving birth, and completed editing episode of *Last Man on Earth* in the hospital while getting induced

Sales and Marketing Experience: Directed Jack Daniel's commercial lobbying for Lynchburg, Tennessee, to get its own NBA franchise

plus." I can see now in retrospect why that was an attractive quality. He wanted people willing to thwart the script structure, who don't think the script is the Bible.

DAVID ROGERS: She hit it out of the park right away. She just got it.

CLAIRE SCANLON: It was a trial by fire. Dave Rogers was amazing, and he'd always watch my cuts and give great advice like, "Don't cut away. Stay on the joke till the end." Things it would take a more seasoned editor to know. But because of my background, I was very comfortable with the shooting style. Whereas I think other editors would come on and be like, "Whoa, what the heck?"

Claire stepped in, Paul and Jen stepped up, and Greg and Mike stepped back. Our show was changing, but we always managed to find our footing. A good thing, because as we'd soon find out, there were choppy waters ahead.

"How Does It Make You Feel?"
The Office and the Great Recession

GREG DANIELS: I want to be realistic. I want to be relatable. I want to be observational. I want to do research and look at the real world. What's happening in the real world? How do you connect that so that it feels relevant to people? If you're going to follow those principles, you're going to end up commenting on what's around you.

What was around us in the summer of 2008, as we prepared for our fifth season, was a mix of hopefulness and anxiety. NASA landed a spacecraft on Mars. Folks from around the world flocked to the Beijing Olympics.

Barack Obama was running for president. It was an optimistic time. But also, we were in the midst of a terrible recession.

The Office had been reflecting this economic anxiety for a while, such as in the season three classic "Business School," where Michael has to defend Dunder Mifflin to business school students.

> **MICHAEL:** David will always beat Goliath.
>
> **BUSINESS STUDENT:** But there's five Goliaths. There's Staples, OfficeMax . . .
>
> **MICHAEL:** You know what else is facing five Goliaths? America. Al-Qaeda, global warming, sex predators . . . mercury poisoning. So do we just give up?

There was "Money" in the fourth season, where Michael takes a second job as a telemarketer to make ends meet . . .

> **MICHAEL:** Yes, money has been a little bit tight lately. But, at the end of my life, when I'm sitting on my yacht, am I going to be thinking about how much money I have?

. . . and "Customer Survey," episode six of the fifth season, where Jim buys his parents' house in the middle of the housing crisis.

> **JIM:** If history tells us anything, it's that you can't go wrong buying a house you can't afford.

BRENT FORRESTER: I think it was in the DNA of the show even before the recession. Scranton was deliberately chosen as this struggling working-class town, with paper being an obsolete industry. For sure we were aware of the recession, but Scranton was already an economically precarious place. I don't recall us ramping that up during the recession, but I do remember people talking about it.

BRIAN BAUMGARTNER: The story line of Sabre came at a time Comcast was coming in and taking over.

The fictional Florida-based printer sales company Sabre bought out the Scranton branch in season six, just as Comcast was buying stakes in MGM and Disney and becoming the nation's largest internet service provider.

SEASON SIX
Episode Guide

TITLE	DIRECTED BY	WRITTEN BY	ORIGINAL AIR DATE
"Gossip"	Paul Lieberstein	Paul Lieberstein	September 17, 2009
"The Meeting"	Randall Einhorn	Aaron Shure	September 24, 2009
"The Promotion"	Jennifer Celotta	Jennifer Celotta	October 1, 2009
"Niagara"	Paul Feig	Greg Daniels & Mindy Kaling	October 8, 2009
"Mafia"	David Rogers	Brent Forrester	October 15, 2009
"The Lover"	Lee Eisenberg	Lee Eisenberg & Gene Stupnitsky	October 22, 2009

"Koi Pond"	Reggie Hudlin	Warren Lieberstein & Halsted Sullivan	October 29, 2009
"Double Date"	Seth Gordon	Charlie Grandy	November 5, 2009
"Murder"	Greg Daniels	Daniel Chun	November 12, 2009
"Shareholder Meeting"	Charles McDougall	Justin Spitzer	November 19, 2009
"Scott's Tots"	B. J. Novak	Gene Stupnitsky & Lee Eisenberg	December 3, 2009
"Secret Santa"	Randall Einhorn	Mindy Kaling	December 10, 2009
"The Banker"	Jeffrey Blitz	Jason Kessler	January 21, 2010
"Sabre"	John Krasinski	Jennifer Celotta	February 4, 2010
"The Manager and the Salesman"	Marc Webb	Mindy Kaling	February 11, 2010
"The Delivery"	Seth Gordon	Daniel Chun	March 4, 2010
	Harold Ramis	Charlie Grandy	
"St. Patrick's Day"	Randall Einhorn	Jonathan Hughes	March 11, 2010
"New Leads"	Brent Forrester	Brent Forrester	March 18, 2010
"Happy Hour"	Matt Sohn	B. J. Novak	March 25, 2010
"Secretary's Day"	Steve Carell	Mindy Kaling	April 22, 2010
"Body Language"	Mindy Kaling	Justin Spitzer	April 29, 2010
"The Cover-up"	Rainn Wilson	Gene Stupnitsky & Lee Eisenberg	May 6, 2010
"The Chump"	Randall Einhorn	Aaron Shure	May 13, 2010
"Whistleblower"	Paul Lieberstein	Warren Lieberstein & Halsted Sullivan	May 20, 2010

BRIAN BAUMGARTNER: Was that intentional or a happy accident?

BRENT FORRESTER: B. J. Novak was very aware of these trends in technology. WUPHF [Ryan Howard's fictional website, introduced in season six] is such a perfect takedown of the internet start-up. And Greg is always way ahead of trends. I don't know where he finds the time to read *The Economist* or whatever he's doing. We did an episode, I think it was called "China" [from season seven]. That was Greg realizing, "Oh shit, China's gonna take over the world economy. What if Michael reads an article about this in a dentist's office?"

> **MICHAEL:** My whole life, I believed that America was number one. That the saying. Not "America is number two." England is number two. China should be like eight.

BRENT FORRESTER: I'll tell you a writers' room joke. There are things that become a reference that never leaves the room. When webisodes became a thing and people were talking about them, the writers' room joke was there should be a form of entertainment called "silosodes," where they just project *The Office* on the front of a grain silo. [*Laughs.*] So we were always talking about the silosodes money.

There were even times when the line between life in *The Office* and life in the real world became a little blurred. Take Andy Buckley, for instance. He played Dunder Mifflin's chief financial officer, David Wallace. And he didn't just look like a finance guy. He was an actual financial adviser at Merrill Lynch.

Andy Buckley as Dunder Mifflin's CFO, David Wallace.

ANDY BUCKLEY ("DAVID WALLACE"): Michael Schur loved that I was in the financial world. And I stayed at Merrill Lynch the whole time I was on the show. We filmed the last episode in March of 2013, and I officially left Merrill Lynch in December of 2012. I worked at Merrill Lynch the whole time.

ANDY BUCKLEY: One time we're at home and I'm looking all scruffy, playing with our son Xander, who at the time was two. The doorbell rings and I answer it and it's Courtney Love. She was having a meeting with some big director about a movie role and she wanted to be prepared. I told her, "Nancy's coming down. You can wait in the kitchen." And I go back to playing with our little guy. Nancy comes down and they walk back to the studio, and the first thing Courtney says to my wife is, "Why is the guy from *The Office* in your house?"

Andy wasn't just "the guy from *The Office*." He was working at Merrill Lynch when everything went south in the fall of 2008.

Andy Buckley

Occupation: Actor, financial consultant

Hometown: Born in Salem and raised in Marblehead, Massachusetts

Training: Stanford University, Class of 1987, B.A. in political science

Previous Employment: Small roles in *Silk Stalkings* (1993), *Melrose Place* (1997), and *The West Wing* (2000); appearances in several music videos for Reba McEntire (1997); wealth management adviser for Merrill Lynch (2001–2012)

Post-*Office* Credits: Movie roles in *Bombshell* (2019), *Lady Bird* (2017), and *Jurassic World* (2015)

Special Skills: Played golf for Stanford; did improv comedy with Melissa McCarthy and Dax Shepard at the Groundlings Theatre in L.A.

Marital Status: His wife, Nancy Banks, is an acting coach who's worked with celebs like Channing Tatum, Jennifer Aniston, Jared Leto, and Margot Robbie, among many others

ANDY BUCKLEY: The weekend that Lehman Brothers went out of business [on September 15, 2008], it was nuts because this was when I was on *The Office* all the time. It was my busiest year on the show. Luckily I did have partners. There was one day the stock market was down over seven hundred points in just three hours.

It happened on September 29, 2008, just days after our season five premiere. The Dow Jones Industrial Average suffered the largest point drop in its 112-year history.

ANDY BUCKLEY: That was the day that I was sitting there and it was . . . I think it was the Michael Scott negotiation, when we're buying out the Michael Scott Paper Company.

It was "Broke," an episode from the fifth season—the first, coincidentally, directed by Steve Carell—in which Michael's offshoot paper company, on the brink of financial ruin, gets a buyout offer from his former employer.

ANDY BUCKLEY: Every time they were like, "Okay, let's take five," I'd duck out to make a call for work. "Dr. Wilson, it's Andy Buckley. We're going to be fine, it's a temporary thing." And meanwhile, I've got a huge scene. I wanted to tell them, "You cannot believe what I'm getting to do today!" But of course I couldn't say that.

It was a stressful time, but *The Office* was a place where people could go for comfort. CNN in late 2009 claimed that the recession-era themes in *The Office* offered "a sense of solidarity for the viewing public and a new type of coping mechanism for dealing with recession-related stress." And on February 1, 2009, we got to provide that on the biggest stage in TV, the hour after the Super Bowl.

This was the most coveted time slot in network television. Lassie owned it first in the late '60s, getting the prime TV real estate on three different years, and soon the postgame programming became as popular (a record-setting 52.9 million viewers tuned in for the post–Super Bowl *Friends* in 1996) and talked about (an ass-kicking Jennifer Garner in lingerie wowed audiences who stayed for *Alias* in 2003) as the game itself.

Super Bowl XLIII included a pregame interview with President Obama and a halftime show with Bruce Springsteen. After the game, NBC aired a two-part *Office* episode called "Stress Relief." It's the one where Dwight surprises his coworkers with a fire drill so frighteningly real, it gives Stanley a heart attack.

EMILY VANDERWERFF: It has one of the great jokes that is now a time capsule, but at the time was so timely, which is Michael yelling at Stanley, "Stanley, Obama is president!" I think it was the first Obama joke on television.

PAUL LIEBERSTEIN: "Stress Relief" is the episode most people tell me is their favorite.

BRIAN BAUMGARTNER: Well, it was special, coming on right after the Super Bowl.

PAUL LIEBERSTEIN: Yeah, but I think that's irrelevant now. It was a really big deal at the time. We were so focused on this opportunity to get more eyeballs on the show.

TERI WEINBERG (NOW EXECUTIVE VICE PRESIDENT OF NBC ENTERTAINMENT): We needed to do something completely outrageous to make sure that people watching the Super Bowl who'd never seen *The Office* before would say, "Oh my God, I love this! I'm staying!" I was getting a little pressure from [NBC president] Jeff [Zucker] to make sure we had some celebrities in there. But we never had celebrities on our show. It was always about making sure that it felt like we were dropping into a world of human beings.

Our casting director, Allison Jones, wasn't thrilled with the idea of including celebrities. In fact, she'd been resistant to stunt casting since day one.

ALLISON JONES: I would not shut up about how it's a documentary, and suddenly Matt Damon is gonna show up in Scranton? It drove me crazy. As the network started getting more involved with sweeps week and stuff, they started saying, "You have to use Ben Affleck," or blah blah, blah blah. I never agreed with that at all. To me, it broke the DNA of the show. So we never did it much at all.

BRIAN BAUMGARTNER: Until the Super Bowl episode.

ALLISON JONES: That pissed me off. I would never normally talk back to a studio executive, but I believe I did it on a conference call. I was like, "Are you effing kidding me?" I was vociferous about not wanting that.

TERI WEINBERG: But in Greg's brilliant fashion, he found a way to bring in celebrities without it feeling like celebrities were a part of *The Office*.

Jim, Pam, and Andy watch a pirated movie called *Mrs. Albert Hannaday*, in which Jack Black's character has a torrid affair with his fiancée's (Jessica Alba) grandmother, played by Cloris Leachman.

TERI WEINBERG: For me personally, I didn't care if there were stars in the episode. That was a boss [Jeff Zucker] trying to mandate. And I understood it as a programming thing. But we found a way to make the boss happy without fucking with the integrity of the show. I had to learn how to balance both of those things, give my bosses what they felt like they needed, but most importantly, protect the show.

The show delivered as promised. According to Nielsen, 22.9 million viewers tuned in to watch, our biggest audience ever. The reviews were glowing—the *A.V. Club* summed up the episode in three words: "Holy motherfucking shit"—and Jeffrey Blitz won an Emmy for directing the episode. But Teri is proudest that they did it without abandoning the creative principles that Greg instilled in them from the beginning.

TERI WEINBERG: He used to tell me, "What's most important to me is that you tell me how you feel. How does the episode make you feel? How did the characters in this episode make you feel?" So I would look at the script and think about how it made me feel. I didn't look at it and say, "Well, the structure isn't so much blah blah blah." It was all about: Are we accomplishing this really quiet moment between Jim and Pam? Is there something going on with the accountants in the corner that we're peeking in on? It was really about how it made me feel.

"A Pigeon-Toed Person Dancing with a Bow-Legged Person"
The Many Loves of Erin Hannon

Season five of *The Office* saw a lot of staff changes at Dunder Mifflin. Both Ryan Howard and Toby Flenderson returned to the Scranton branch, and Michael quit to form his own business, the Michael Scott Paper Company, somehow convincing Pam and Ryan to follow him. We also saw new faces join the team, like Charles Miner, the new vice president of the northeast region (played by Idris Elba), and Toby's replacement in HR (and Michael's soul mate) Holly Flax (played by Amy Ryan).

We also met our new receptionist, who would stay with us for the rest of the series. Erin Hannon, played by Ellie Kemper, couldn't have been more different from her Dunder Mifflin coworkers, most of whom were just counting the minutes till they could leave.

ELLIE KEMPER: Erin loved being there. You can imagine her getting ready for work in the morning, just wanting to excel at her job. Stanley was maybe a little bit over it. Oscar was over it. But Erin *lived* for it. Within thirty seconds of meeting her [Erin joined the Scranton branch in the "Michael Scott Paper Company" episode from season five], she agreed to change her name. Her full name is Kelly Erin

The newest addition to *The Office*.
Ellie Kemper as Erin Hannon.

Hannon, but there's already a Kelly in the office. So she's like, "I'll go by Erin." She just wanted to be there.

BRIAN BAUMGARTNER: She just wanted to impress Michael. Like she never felt beaten down by him or rolled her eyes at him.

ELLIE KEMPER: Oh my gosh, no. On the contrary. She adored him. He was an inspiration to her. Remember when Erin meets Holly [in the season seven episode "The Search"] and it's almost like she's territorial? Like, this is the lady who's stealing Michael's heart.

ERIN: Holly is ruining Michael's life. He thinks she's *so* special, and she's *so* not. Her personality is like a three. Her sense of humor is a two. Her ears are like a seven and a four. Add it all up and what do you get? Sixteen.

ELLIE KEMPER: She's just so skeptical of this woman because she feels like no one is good enough for Michael.

HUMAN RESOURCES FILE

Ellie Kemper

Occupation: Actor, writer

Hometown: Born in Kansas City, Missouri, raised in St. Louis

Training: Performed with Jon Hamm in a high school production of *Stage Door*; Princeton University, Class of 2002, B.A. in English

Previous Employment: Performed in sketches on *Late Night with Conan O'Brien* (2007) and *Important Things with Demetri Martin* (2009–2010); contributed to *The Onion* (with headlines like "Dog in Purse Stares Longingly at Dog in Yard"); had a hit one-woman show, *Feeling Sad/Mad with Ellie Kemper* (2008), at the UCB Theater

Post-Office Credits: Star of Netflix series *Unbreakable Kimmy Schmidt* (2015–2020); author of autobiographical humor book *My Squirrel Days* (2018)

Special Citations: Named one of *Variety* magazine's "10 Comics to Watch" in 2009

Sales Experience: Appeared in commercials for Dunkin' Donuts and Kmart

BRENT FORRESTER: Ellie was one of those guest characters that every writer instantly wanted to write for. Everybody started pitching stories for her. It was like a shot of adrenaline to us. Some performers are so gifted and special that they create their own longevity.

PAUL FEIG: She's got a real different energy from everybody on the show. So it was like, "Is this going to work?" But that was really the brilliance of Greg and Paul [Lieberstein], seeing that and going, "Yeah, let's play with this." [Directing] her first talking head, I just had never done a talking head with anybody with that kind of attitude on *The Office* before. It was refreshing but also disorienting.

BRIAN BAUMGARTNER: Her character is someone who's actually optimistic and enthusiastic.

PAUL FEIG: That's why we put her against the window. We gave her the Jim window because she was so happy. The Jim window was something that Randall came up with, I think, which was putting Jim's talking heads against the wall with a window, because he has a future and isn't trapped, and the others are mostly against a wall with no exterior window.

CLAIRE SCANLON: When Ellie came on, we were like the new girls. I didn't know how you guys introduced new characters, which was really by hook or by crook. They waited for the actor to show them who they were and it either worked or didn't. I remember cutting "Secretary's Day" [the twenty-second episode of the sixth season], and Erin had a scene where Michael took her out to lunch and he told her that [her boyfriend] Andy had been engaged to Angela, and then Erin has a meltdown.

> *[ERIN COVERS HER FACE WITH HER HAIR.]*
>
> **MICHAEL:** What are you doing?

> **ERIN:** In the foster home, my hair was my room. [*Starts yelling under her hair.*]

CLAIRE SCANLON: I remember thinking, "She's going to make it." I hadn't seen much of her work before that, but cutting that scene, I was like, "She's got the chops, she can play with Steve, she's going to make it." It was a great scene and she was definitely driving it, and he was the reactor to everything she was doing.

ELLIE KEMPER: Oh, you're gonna make me cry. That's the sweetest compliment. "Secretary's Day" was my favorite episode.

BRIAN BAUMGARTNER: You were going toe-to-toe with Steve, maybe one of the best improvisers on the planet.

> **MICHAEL:** Andy, you know, come on. Andy, his butt looks big in those khakis.
>
> **ERIN:** Oh, I like his butt.
>
> **MICHAEL:** You said butt.
>
> **ERIN:** You tricked me!
>
> **BOTH:** Ahh!

ELLIE KEMPER: It was one of the best days of my life. The whole time I felt a little bit giddy.

The writers liked Erin and the new story lines started following, including a complicated office romance with Andy Bernard, played by Ed Helms. He first started pursuing Erin in season five, even getting into a "Take Me Home, Country Roads" sing-off with Dwight for her affections. It wasn't until season six that Andy finally mustered the courage to ask her out.

ED HELMS: I don't think there was an arc spelled out early on, but Erin's energy was just so funny and it felt right for Andy in a way, both of them being very left-footed socially. It made them perfect for each other. It's like a pigeon-toed person dancing with a bow-legged person.

BRIAN BAUMGARTNER: Ellie, do you think Erin and Andy were a good match?

ELLIE KEMPER: I never thought so. Is that terrible to say?

BRIAN BAUMGARTNER: No.

ELLIE KEMPER: I felt like Andy was a bit too childish. I don't think he was ready to take care of Erin the way she needed to be. And Erin was ready to take care of him, so it felt uneven in that respect. I love that we got to be in so many scenes together, but that relationship never felt fair to me.

She soon drifted to Gabe Lewis, director of emerging regions coordination for Sabre (played by Zach Woods), but he wasn't a much better match.

ELLIE KEMPER: I don't know who Erin should be with. Someone who's odd but also able to take care of her. I didn't feel like she ever quite got her right match in that show. So that's why we need one Christmas special to see who she picked. I want that to happen. I don't know if anyone else does, but I do. Just one episode.

BRIAN BAUMGARTNER: Do you know that I pitched Kevin and Erin getting together?

ELLIE KEMPER: I think that would be a pretty reasonable relationship.

BRIAN BAUMGARTNER: I went up to the writers' room. And I said, "If Kevin could mature *just* a little." There was something about their energy that I thought was right. It's almost like the static being and the hummingbird, but somehow their energies matched in a weird way.

ELLIE KEMPER: Brian, that actually makes perfect sense to me. I love that pitch.

Kevin and Erin actually came close to becoming the next great *Office* romance. In the season six episode "The Delivery," Michael attempts to play matchmaker, setting up new couples in the office. He matches Kevin with Erin, and sparks don't exactly fly on their first "date."

> **ERIN:** Did you grow up around here?
>
> **KEVIN:** No.
>
> **ERIN:** So, you must have grown up around somewhere else?
>
> **KEVIN:** Yes.

Let's have a moment of silence for "Krevin."

"We Basically Blew the Entire Budget with One Shot"
The Proposal

Over the next few seasons, we would see some of the biggest changes yet for our other favorite couple, Jim and Pam.

PAUL FEIG: It wasn't a Sam and Diane situation. It wasn't a Ross and Rachel situation where that was the centerpiece of the show. It was this nice thing that was happening as a sideline. So you didn't get worn out on that story line. You just kept investing in it, wanting it to happen more.

The moment we'd all been waiting for finally came in the premiere of season five, an episode called "Weight Loss."

PAUL FEIG: One of the greatest honors for me was also getting to direct the proposal.

It happened, as you likely remember, at an interstate rest stop in the pouring rain, somewhere between Scranton and New York City.

PAUL FEIG: It was the most expensive shot we ever did in the show's history. That was the very first episode of that season, and we basically blew the entire budget with one shot, which cost like half a million dollars.

Why so much for what became a fifty-two-second scene? The original plan was to fly the cast and crew out east to shoot at an actual rest stop on the Merritt Parkway, but they wouldn't be able to create fake rain for the scene. So our production team built an entire rest stop on a parking lot behind a Best Buy in Los Angeles. Greg guesstimates the cost at around $250,000.

DAVID ROGERS: We built this on a huge parking lot and we had eighteen-wheelers doing figure eights, to make it look like they're passing.

But once they got that shot in the can, that's when things *really* got complicated.

DAVID ROGERS: We did a version where you couldn't hear them, you would just see it. And then we had a version where you would hear it.

GREG DANIELS: I couldn't decide whether you should hear it or just see it. You could tell what it was from seeing it. We recorded the audio and then we were like, well, maybe it should just be the sound of rain. What's the most effective?

BRENT FORRESTER: One of the great debates of American history.

JEN CELOTTA: It was the craziest discussion, and there were people on both sides. It was about fifty-fifty on whether we should have sound when we saw Jim propose to Pam, or just see the visual of him in the rain getting on one knee.

BRENT FORRESTER: They went back and forth and tested and A/B-ed it and firmly concluded it should be one way and then revised it. I think it's possible that objectivity finally gets lost in that process. It's hard to remain objective about anything, but in a subjective medium like the arts and comedy, who knows? You just make a decision at the end.

GREG DANIELS: It went back to that "Casino Night" thing. How much do you lean into the docu device? Is it going to make it cooler or less cool?

JEN CELOTTA: The side that wanted to hear Jim's words were like, "We've been waiting forever to hear him propose to Pam. Why would you take that moment away from people and not hear his actual words?" You want to give them what they'd been waiting for, which might be slightly more of a comedy show kind of thing. With a mockumentary thing, it was, "God, it's so beautiful and subtle to be across the street and have to reach for it." Because Jim would turn his mic off in this moment. It's a *big* moment. Or [the camera guys] missed the exit and they're trying to get it and they can't get it exactly. But you see what's happening and you know what's happening. And once you see him down on one knee, what is he going to say other than what *everybody* says [during a proposal]? We know what he's saying. Actually filling in the blank is more beautiful.

PAUL FEIG: I was a pro-sound guy. It was so emotional to me and their performance was so good, and we were already dealing with so much with the highway and all of these cars zooming past. I remember fighting really, really hard for that. I think Greg was always on the fence about whether we should have done it [with sound].

JEN CELOTTA: There was one moment where Greg was getting into his car, after the discussion had gone on for a month and we had to settle on it. I was coming from a trailer and he was getting into his car, and I said, "Greg." He turned and he was trapped between his car door and his car. I was like, "Did you decide on sound or no sound?" And he was like, "No, no, I haven't." It was literally like a horror film. I was stalking him to find out if the decision had been made.

GREG DANIELS: I went back and forth on that. I had so many versions. I tested it with different people, brought in everybody to look at it.

JEN CELOTTA: I remember being in the office and I saw a list of people who wanted sound and a list of people who wanted no sound. His wife and two kids were on one side of the list, and his other two kids were on the other. His family was split down the middle. So he was interviewing everybody and saying, "What should we do? What should we do?"

PAUL FEIG: We were literally like, "Hey, guy who fixes the cars for the show, come on in. What do you think?"

DAVID ROGERS: Ultimately, Greg went with the version where you can't hear them. And then he changed his mind that morning that we were airing. He's like, "No, I've slept on it and I want to put the one where they can hear them."

BRIAN BAUMGARTNER: The *morning* we're airing?

DAVID ROGERS: Yeah. I think both of them were great versions, but it's probably better to hear. I mean, we waited so long for this moment, it was probably better to hear it and not just see it, because you didn't want any kind of confusion of what happened.

GREG DANIELS: And we sorta did a half and half I think at the end. Right. They can kind of hear it, but the audio's got a lot of rain in it.

[JIM GETS DOWN ON ONE KNEE.]

PAM: What are you doing?

JIM: I just . . . can't wait.

PAM: Oh my God.

BRIAN BAUMGARTNER: Do you think they made the right decision?

BRENT FORRESTER: I think it could've gone either way. That's why directing is not a fraudulent art form. All of those questions, whether you see the actor or don't see him, all these different ways you can do it. And then to have the conviction at the end to go, "Yeah, there's clever ways to do this, but what matters most is this performance."

DAVID ROGERS: I think we made the right choice. But I'll tell you this, they didn't destroy the one with no sound. And when it was time to make the DVDs, they almost screwed up. It almost got burned on the DVDs. They were doing QC [quality control] and some heads rolled because, you know, this [alternative take] needs to be labeled so it doesn't get mixed into syndication cuts or Netflix or whatever.

"You Can't Have a Horse Die at the Moment of Maximum Romance"
Jim and Pam's Wedding

BRIAN BAUMGARTNER: Were you worried that when Pam and Jim finally got married, it would screw things up?

JENNA FISCHER: I wasn't, because we had been together now for a couple seasons. So I think the question was: Can they get together and be a stable couple, and will we still care? I remember having a conversation with Greg, and he was like, "What's going to lose people is if we just keep manufacturing these weird ways to keep them apart. That's exhausting and it's not realistic. And so what we're going to need to do is bring them together and then give them obstacles to overcome as a couple." So rather than obstacles that keep them from being a couple, give them obstacles to break through as a couple. Like Pam wanting to go to art school or Jim wanting to start his own business or having their first kid or whatever. Things where they'd have to weather the storm together, which is more interesting and realistic. What's not gonna be satisfying is if they get together at the end of season nine after multiple affairs. Everyone's going to be like, "Yay . . . I guess. Congrats? I hope you enjoy your marriage with all your horrible baggage." Not a happy ending.

In season six, it was time for Jim and Pam to finally tie the knot, and the entire office went to Niagara Falls for the wedding. Much like Jim and Pam's relationship, the shoot for this episode had many obstacles. It was a real "everything that makes it harder makes it better" situation.

PAUL FEIG: We were going to shoot on this boat, the Lady of the Mist or whatever.

BRIAN BAUMGARTNER: *Maid of the Mist.*

The *Maid of the Mist* has been taking tourists on a boat tour of Niagara Falls (well, the river below the falls) since 1846, and it's carried passengers like Marilyn Monroe, Stephen Hawking, Princess Diana, and Mick Jagger.

Jim and Pam plan a church wedding, but when they realize that it is becoming more about the guests than each other, they sneak off to get married in secret on the *Maid of the Mist*. So the first obstacle? Shooting on location on an actual boat on the river below Niagara Falls.

PAUL FEIG: It brought so many logistical things that it was hard to invest in the emotion of it at first. I was so worried, like, are we going to get soaked? Is the camera going to screw up?

The camera didn't screw up. But they did get soaked, which was not ideal for our hair department head, Kim Ferry.

KIM FERRY: Both [Jenna and John] got soaked the first take, it was awful. There was no electric on the boat and it was for the wedding scene. We were told by the producers, "Look, we did three runs [on the boat] to test everything, and it's going to be fine because no water ever came up on the boat." And then we get out there and we're near the falls, and all of a sudden it's like *whooooosh*. It just soaks both of them.

DEBBIE PIERCE: What did you do?

KIM FERRY: I started laughing. And then we just went with it. That's why [Jenna's] hair changed, because it was so drenched on the boat, we couldn't go back again. We had to keep filming. They're like, "Can you fix it?" I'm like, "Are you kidding me right now? With *what*?"

And if everything wasn't complicated enough, John Krasinski had the flu.

JOHN KRASINSKI: I remember showing up and I can't walk, I'm so sick. One of the most romantic moments in the show, I'm not actually kissing Jenna. I'm kissing her cheek because I didn't want to get her sick. I was like *dire* sick.

BRIAN BAUMGARTNER: I think for that moment, you should have just gotten her sick.

JOHN KRASINSKI: That's an awful thing. But that's why I did a big Humphrey Bogart–like twist kiss away from the camera.

BRIAN BAUMGARTNER: When you walked on the boat, the two people behind you were my parents in real life. Do you remember that?

JOHN KRASINSKI: Oh my God, now I remember, yes. Paul [Feig] was in his suit in the blue tarp and, as nicely as he does, he was like, "These are Brian's parents."

Jim and Pam return to the church to have a second ceremony in front of all their friends and family. What viewers don't know is that another scene was supposed to happen in that moment.

JOHN KRASINSKI: The horse was going to go off the cliff.

That's right. Greg's idea was that Roy would interrupt the ceremony with a grand gesture, riding in on a horse. Somehow Dwight gets a hold of the horse and rides it away from the church.

PAUL FEIG: Originally, Greg had this insane idea that Dwight was going to ride a horse over Niagara Falls.

GREG DANIELS: Dwight is at the hotel, and he's looking at all these photos of animals going over the falls, and Roy shows up on a horse to try and win Pam back. He abandons the horse, and Dwight puts it together and he gets on the horse and he starts going over the falls, riding a horse, and then he realizes it's a terrible idea. He jumps out at the last minute. And while Pam and Jim are getting married, a horse goes over in the background. Everyone's just screaming at me. They were like, "You can't have a horse die at the moment of maximum romance!"

PAUL FEIG: We were just like, "I don't know if we want to kill a horse at Jim and Pam's wedding." He fought for it and fought for it.

GREG DANIELS: I was really committed to this story line of Dwight riding a horse over the falls, to the extent that I scouted the pool of water that the horse was going to fall into.

JOHN KRASINSKI: Up until shooting, that was in there. I think it was Rainn, he was like, "Even I think this is nuts."

BRIAN BAUMGARTNER: The moment of you standing there on the boat is so beautiful. Do you want a horse diving over a cliff? And it seemed like, yes, Greg *did* want a horse diving over the cliff.

GREG DANIELS: We routinely made changes of that size after a table reading, just not with such big stakes. Basically, the script that Mindy and I wrote, and we read at the table, had a horse going over the falls in the background after all the romantic stuff with Pam and Jim having their own private ceremony on the *Maid of the Mist* after their wedding. But it was beset by problems. It was part of a Dwight story and I meant for it to balance the unabashed romance of the A plot, but after the table reading, the cast sat me down and told me I was wrong and I listened to them. It was like an intervention of normal people in the life of a comedy addict.

Greg changed his mind, which meant Paul Lieberstein and the writers had to come up with a totally new concept for the wedding ceremony.

PAUL FEIG: It was a very last-minute thing. We had like a day or two. And that wedding video was all over the internet.

"That wedding video" captured the nuptials of Jill Peterson and Kevin Heinz, who picked Chris Brown's "Forever" for their walk down the aisle—with a choreographed twist. The bridal party danced and strutted, and the groom even somersaulted. The video was uploaded to YouTube in July 2009 and, as of this writing, has been viewed more than one hundred million times.

PAUL FEIG: It was kind of the perfect setup. And then when we were shooting in that church all day, I mean, it was so much to shoot that we were running out of time. Literally, I had like a half hour left. I was like, "I don't even have time to get this dance number!" So we're going to have maybe two takes at it. And the first time they did it, it was gold. It's just like, that's it. Drop the mic.

Now they had footage of us dancing down the aisle at the "official" wedding and separate footage of Jim and Pam's secret wedding on the *Maid of the Mist*. The next challenge came in the editing room, where Paul and Claire had to figure out how to fit both ceremonies together.

PAUL FEIG: We decided to intermix the dance number with the wedding, and we just burst into tears. I mean, I still get so emotional watching that because it's so beautiful. The way that it goes back and forth between the two.

CLAIRE SCANLON: There's the last scene of Niagara where Jim and Pam are on the bow of the boat, and he puts his arm around her and looks right into the camera. It's not even cocky, it's just a sweet smile, like, "I got her." John and Jenna came into my bay to see it. They were like, "We need to see this show. We need to sign off on this." And after they watched it, I turned around and they're both bawling. For the poignant moments, all you want is to make people cry. It was really a sweet moment to be a part of their journey and be a witness to it.

One of the satisfying things about getting to make a TV show for so many seasons is that you have the room to show real change. By the end of season six, the wedding of Jim and Pam, and their discovery that they're pregnant, didn't feel like a check in a box. It felt real. Hundreds of people flocked to the Pam and Jim wedding website (halpertbeesly.com) to write messages in the guest book, congratulating the fictional happy couple. But falling in love with these characters just made it even more difficult when one of them decided to walk away, as we were about to find out.

Jim and Pam with their newborn baby: A life begins as one story comes to an end.

THE OFFICE CAST AT MICHAEL'S LAST DUNDIES.

10

"Losing the Captain of Our Ship"

THE LONG GOODBYE FOR MICHAEL SCOTT (AND STEVE CARELL): SEASON SEVEN

STEVE CARELL: I remember the last take. We were shooting in the bullpen, the main set, and it was basically me saying goodbye to everybody. I started to get this sense of like, "Uh-oh, something's happening." After that last take, the room just filled with people. It was all the writers and crew and cast. It was ridiculously emotional.

It was impossible for us to imagine *The Office* without Steve Carell. It would be like *The Bob Newhart Show* without Bob Newhart. Or *The Simpsons*, but Homer has moved out. We were always an ensemble show, but our ensemble had its fearless leader, and he was number one on the call sheet. (A call sheet, for those of you not in TV production, is a document sent to a show's cast and crew, detailing where they need to be and when for the next day's shoot.)

Steve—or rather, Michael Scott—wasn't just the first face you saw in *The Office*'s opening credits. He wasn't just the boss and lead character. According to some people, he was the heart of the show.

MATT SOHN: Hands down, it was Michael. There were times where that heart was broken, but he was the guy you loved to hate. And there were other moments when he was so fragile that you couldn't help but like the guy.

Saying goodbye to Michael, and farewell to Steve, wasn't easy. There was behind-the-scenes drama, in-front-of-the-scenes drama, and loose ends that needed to be tied up, for both Steve the actor and Michael the fictional creation.

His departure threw our show into a tailspin, transformed our story line, but ultimately reinforced our bonds as characters, as teammates, and as friends.

"They'd Blown Something They Could Have Saved"
Steve Carell's Decision to Leave

RAINN WILSON: We were starting to slip in our ratings even before Steve left. It's not like we were just a ratings bonanza all the way through Steve, and then Steve left and we were in decline. We were in decline for a good year or two with Steve there.

It wasn't just *The Office* taking a ratings hit. Every major network saw its ratings slip by 13 percent during the 2008–2009 season, and the future wasn't looking more promising. But it wasn't that audiences were walking away from TV shows entirely. They just weren't watching them in the typical places.

RAINN WILSON: What we didn't know at the time is that [the ratings on] all shows were declining because people were streaming and they were watching things online.

In August 2009, just as we were heading into our sixth season, online streaming was up 41 percent from the previous year, according to Nielsen. Audiences were also watching shows they'd recorded on TiVos and other digital video recorders.

BRIAN BAUMGARTNER: They were still watching *The Office*, just not in the same ways they used to. But all the network saw was that the ratings were down.

BEN SILVERMAN: The press at that moment really didn't understand where television was going. They were still all rooted in a three-channel, four-channel universe with a couple of cable originals. They didn't have the framework to understand what was going to happen, what Hulu was going to be, what Netflix was going to be.

In December 2009, Comcast announced that it was acquiring a majority stake in NBC Universal. Our onetime savior at NBC, Kevin Reilly, was long gone, having been fired by the network in May 2007.

KEVIN REILLY: NBC invited me to no longer do that job.

BRIAN BAUMGARTNER: Despite your success with *The Office*?

KEVIN REILLY: The thing about *The Office*, the show that was going to be a real problem [for NBC] was one of the only things that endured that was worth hanging on to through that really brutal time for that organization. Everyone kind of felt like, "Great run, great show, let's move on."

Ben Silverman, who'd succeeded him, was also on his way out. He resigned as cochairman of NBC Entertainment in the summer of 2009, in what some news outlets described as "uncertain circumstances."

BEN SILVERMAN: I thought it would be a fantasy to run a network in my youth. I always wanted to run NBC.

BRIAN BAUMGARTNER: NBC specifically.

BEN SILVERMAN: It was the network I had grown up watching. I loved *Cheers, Hill Street Blues*. I didn't realize that I would have to basically just service the corporate part of it, because that was the only way that we could keep it moving without real pressure. And it took me away from the part I love, which was the creative part. I was still able to green-light *Parks and Recreation* and *Community* and all these wonderful shows.

BRIAN BAUMGARTNER: Was it scary to quit?

BEN SILVERMAN: I remember being just so excited to quit and telling Jeff Zucker, "I have a stomachache when I'm in here. I know I don't want to be here." And I said, "I'll help you manage it, but I can't be here anymore." I was in that corporate world and I realized, "Oh, don't do that again. Don't get that far away from the content. Return to what you love."

Jeff Zucker, who was widely blamed for NBC's falling ratings and his mishandling of the Conan O'Brien–Jay Leno *Tonight Show* situation, publicly revealed that he'd been fired on September 23, 2010, which just so happened to be the same day of our season seven premiere, which also happened to be our last season with Steve Carell.

Wait, what?

The news was surprising to many of us. But Steve's decision to leave wasn't entirely out of left field.

RAINN WILSON: I knew that Steve was going to get out of there as soon as he possibly could because he had all of these movies that were wanting to pay him ten, fifteen million a pop.

BEN SILVERMAN: I was shocked that they couldn't work it out. It made me so depressed how they'd blown something that they could have saved.

GREG DANIELS: Everybody else [in the cast] renegotiated and added two years. And I forget when that happened, but that was pretty early. And Steve didn't. So at that point it was pretty clear.

ANGELA KINSEY: I can't remember the exact moment. Maybe they announced it at a table read. I feel like Steve talked to us on set one day and gave us the heads-up before the announcement, 'cause he's just a class act like that. I remember one of the things he said to me was, "I really just feel like I've done everything I can with Michael and Michael's story."

Episode Guide

TITLE	DIRECTED BY	WRITTEN BY	ORIGINAL AIR DATE
"Nepotism"	Jeffrey Blitz	Daniel Chun	September 23, 2010
"Counseling"	Jeffrey Blitz	B. J. Novak	September 30, 2010
"Andy's Play"	John Stuart Scott	Charlie Grandy	October 7, 2010
"Sex Ed"	Paul Lieberstein	Paul Lieberstein	October 14, 2010
"The Sting"	Randall Einhorn	Mindy Kaling	October 21, 2010
"Costume Contest"	Dean Holland	Justin Spitzer	October 28, 2010
"Christening"	Alex Hardcastle	Peter Ocko	November 4, 2010
"Viewing Party"	Ken Whittingham	Jon Vitti	November 11, 2010
"WUPHF.com"	Danny Leiner	Aaron Shure	November 18, 2010
"China"	Charles McDougall	Halsted Sullivan & Warren Lieberstein	December 2, 2010
"Classy Christmas"	Rainn Wilson	Mindy Kaling	December 9, 2010
"Ultimatum"	David Rogers	Carrie Kemper	January 20, 2011
"The Seminar"	B. J. Novak	Steve Hely	January 27, 2011
"The Search"	Michael Spiller	Brent Forrester	February 3, 2011
"PDA"	Greg Daniels	Robert Padnick	February 10, 2011
"Threat Level Midnight"	Tucker Gates	B. J. Novak	February 17, 2011
"Todd Packer"	Randall Einhorn	Amelie Gillette	February 24, 2011
"Garage Sale"	Steve Carell	Jon Vitti	March 24, 2011
"Training Day"	Paul Lieberstein	Daniel Chun	April 14, 2011

"Michael's Last Dundies"	Mindy Kaling	Mindy Kaling	April 21, 2011
"Goodbye, Michael"	Paul Feig	Greg Daniels	April 28, 2011
"The Inner Circle"	Matt Sohn	Charlie Grandy	May 5, 2011
"Dwight K. Schrute, (Acting) Manager"	Troy Miller	Justin Spitzer	May 12, 2011
"Search Committee"	Jeffrey Blitz	Paul Lieberstein	May 19, 2011

PAUL LIEBERSTEIN: Steve would have made a lot of money [with a new contract]. There's only one reason for not doing that. You just don't want to stay. So it was not a huge surprise.

BRIAN BAUMGARTNER: Do you remember how you found out he was leaving?

PAUL LIEBERSTEIN: I remember I was shooting an episode at an airport hangar. We had rented a private plane. I think it was with Kathy Bates and Steve.

It was the season six finale "Whistleblower," directed by Paul and written by his brother, Warren, and Halsted Sullivan, in which Michael meets with Sabre CEO Jo Bennett (Kathy Bates) at the hangar for her private jet.

PAUL LIEBERSTEIN: Steve and Greg went into the plane for a really long time, and we're all just waiting and waiting to shoot. It was very shortly after that I learned. So I think that's when Steve told Greg that he's not coming back.

GREG DANIELS: I don't really have a memory of that. It sounds like a funny story. Did I break something? [*Laughs.*] I remember the vibe of it, though. I couldn't be mad at him. Steve was so graceful and full of integrity. So he may have taken that moment to let me down and prepare me. He also didn't want the show to fold, because everybody loved each other on that show in a very unique way. And he didn't want to be the guy who left the party early and shut it down. We also had some time to think about how Michael leaves. What's the most satisfying arc for his psychology?

"He's Found His True Family"
When Michael Meets Holly

From the very beginning of our show, Michael Scott was the office man-child. He was the one most in need of babysitting, incapable of taking care of himself financially . . .

> **MICHAEL:** I . . . declare . . . bankruptcy!

. . . or professionally . . .

> **MICHAEL:** No, I'm not going to tell them [about the downsizing]. I don't see the point of that. As a doctor, you would not tell a patient if they had cancer.

. . . and definitely not emotionally.

MICHAEL: Two weeks ago, I was in the worst relationship of my life. She treated me poorly, we didn't connect, I was miserable. Now, I am in the best relationship of my life, with the same woman. Love is a mystery.

But while he may have seemed stagnant, he was changing, if only in baby steps.

STEVE CARELL: I wanted Michael to have an arc throughout the series. And I think all the characters did, all the characters evolved and grew. It's not the same group of people at the end as the group that started. And that's what life is like, you know?

STEPHEN MERCHANT: What both Michael Scott and David Brent have in common is, behind all of the things that make them dislikable, they're not bad people. They're just needy people, and that's their great weakness. They want to be your friend, but they also want to be your boss. What Steve Carell and the writers [of the American *Office*] managed to do is bring that out more, bring out that he's a little boy in a world of adults. Once you dive into that and you see that there is a kind of lonely sweetness behind it all, then I think you start to root for the character.

STEVE CARELL: Michael Scott, at his core, wants to be loved.

For most of the series, he didn't have much luck in that department. But then at the end of season four, a new character was introduced who would play a big role in Michael's evolution: Holly Flax, Toby's replacement for HR rep at the Scranton branch.

PAUL LIEBERSTEIN: It was just an idea to put someone next to Michael who likes him and see how that looked.

BRIAN BAUMGARTNER: Did you have an idea of them ending up together?

PAUL LIEBERSTEIN: No, no.

BRIAN BAUMGARTNER: That was born later?

PAUL LIEBERSTEIN: Yeah. And it became one of the strongest relationships in the show.

Finding an actress to play Holly, only slated for six episodes but with the potential to go much longer, created a challenge for casting director Allison Jones.

ALLISON JONES: Who would believably be the female version of Michael Scott, maybe not as obnoxious, and get his jokes and be appealing in the same way?

And then they met Amy Ryan.

ALLISON JONES: Amy was a hard get. She was an expensive actress at the time. It was a tough deal to make.

AMY RYAN: That was the year I was nominated for an Oscar for *Gone Baby Gone* [2008]. I remember saying to my agent, half joking but not really, I was like, "If we have any pull right now, I want to cash it in on *The Office*." And he was like, "Okay." Apparently simultaneously, Paul Lieberstein, who I had known from a sitcom many, many years earlier called *The Naked Truth*—

The ABC series, which ran for three seasons between 1995 and 1998, starred Téa Leoni as a Pulitzer-nominated photographer forced to work for a sleazy tabloid. Amy played Téa's stepdaughter, and Paul wrote several episodes.

AMY RYAN: I'm not sure who called who first, but there was a coincidence of timing.

I felt very, very confident in my decision that this is where I wanted to be next. Because there's not much imagination once you poke through with a role, you know? People are like, "We have this new role for you. She's a drug-addicted mother." You mean like the one I just played [in *Gone Baby Gone*]? Okay. That doesn't sound like so much fun. Making those hard right turns and giving people whiplash is what I was after.

MIKE SCHUR: It was the beginning of season five, and it felt like we're shifting into a different gear with Michael. Like, who knows how long the show will last, but we'd done almost a hundred episodes and it was like, okay, it's time to create a character for Michael Scott who's a viable love interest. And Jen [Celotta] was a big part of that. She was like, "She should be as big a dork as he is. That's the way to do this." It's not aspirational in the sense of she's a really put-together

HUMAN RESOURCES FILE

Amy Ryan

Occupation: Actor

Hometown: Flushing, Queens

Training: Graduate of the New York City High School of Performing Arts (otherwise known as the *Fame* school); hired for the national tour of Neil Simon's *Biloxi Blues* right out of high school (1986)

Previous Employment: A decade on Broadway, starring in plays by Neil LaBute, Arthur Miller, and Tennessee Williams (1994–2005); *The Wire* (2003-2008)

Post-*Office* Credits: Movie roles including *Lost Girls* (2020), *Strange but True* (2019), *Abundant Acreage Available* (2017), and *Birdman* (2014); rave reviews and Obie Award for starring role in Off-Broadway production of *Love, Love, Love* (2016)

Oscar Nominations: One

Tony Nominations: Two

Dundie Nominations: Zero

sophisticate who Michael has to change for. The thing that links them is she's a dork too and she does dorky voices and lame videos. She's a female version of Michael Scott, which is perfect.

AMY RYAN: How do you make it the same but different? I just loved that idea that there's a lid for every pot, you know?

PAUL FEIG: Amy came in the way that Holly the character would come in. She was kind of nervous, 'cause these are such professional comedians, and she's not known for doing comedy. So she came in sort of trepidatious in that way, and I was like, "Play into that. That's exactly who Holly is."

AMY RYAN: There is a weird thing about being a fan of a show and then being employed by that show. I remember doing one episode of *ER* back in the day and being shocked that the hallway was so little. They did all that choreography of running through with gurneys in this tiny hallway. *The Wire* was the same thing, being a big fan of the show and then joining the company in the second season. It takes a minute to just calm down. You're the transfer student from another school. It's like, "Who's going to sit with me at lunch?"

Just how similar was Amy Ryan to Holly? Let's let her answer.

AMY RYAN: I don't know if I really want to admit this, but after however many years playing different parts in movies and theater and other TV shows, I get a call from my high school boyfriend [*laughs*], who's like, "I'm so glad you're finally playing yourself." And I can't really deny that. My nerdy, geeky side was on the rise there. That's the other side of my personality. I like to keep it balanced.

JEN CELOTTA: She was so fantastic, and then we got to keep her around and keep using her. I remember when we wrote the first episode she was in ["Goodbye, Toby" from season four]. Paul had the first half and I had the second half. I'm pretty sure we divided the script up that way. All that Yoda stuff was just pure Paul. I read it and I was like, "Holy shit, this is fantastic." She's Michael, but she's different enough.

> **MICHAEL:** [*Imitating Yoda.*] Sit on floor, put together chair we will.
>
> **[MICHAEL LAUGHS UNCOMFORTABLY.]**
>
> **MICHAEL:** Yo-da.
>
> **HOLLY:** [*Also imitating Yoda, much to Michael's surprise.*] Pass curvy metal piece, you will.

AMY RYAN: And now I'll confess, I had to google Yoda. I mean, I know who he was, but God, what does he *sound* like?

JEN CELOTTA: I was always on the side of "We should evolve him past Jan," even though Jan's ridiculously funny. What if we evolve him past Jan and give him someone to fall in love with? But what if it's just boring and it's not funny and it doesn't work? That's always a challenge. How do you make Pam and Jim interesting and funny once they're together? How do you make Michael funny once he's evolved? Thank God Paul wrote those Yoda scenes, 'cause I feel like it was an instant "Yes, this is—this is going to work."

For all the tiny bits of evolution we'd seen Michael go through, Holly allowed his character to grow in a different direction, to mature without losing any of his Michael Scott–ness.

STEVE CARELL: I think Michael was just a bit myopic and became more aware once he was able to start stepping outside of himself and his own little eccentricities. He could see a little bit more about the world around him.

AMY RYAN: Michael just became a happier person, but he's still crazy. That's what I like about it. He's still making really bad choices along the way and doing things that make other people cringe. It's not like suddenly Holly comes and spreads this magic pixie dust on him and he's a normal person. Holly is someone that he doesn't have to work so hard with, for the first time that we've known him. The message is really, "It's all going to be okay. There is someone for you."

PAUL FEIG: He finally found somebody who found him charming. You go through life when you're trying to find your other, and you think you know what you want and you have all these superficial things that you want. And then when you meet the person who gets you and looks at you with love in their eyes and enjoys who you actually are, it blows everything else out of the water. It's like your parents finding love and you're like, "What, *them*? Why would they possibly have something nice?"

Michael and Holly's relationship was a rocky one. After she's transferred to another branch in season five and they decide to call it quits, Holly returns to Scranton in season seven and the couple slowly start to reexplore their romance, culminating in the "Garage Sale" episode, where Michael proposes to Holly with the help of his office mates.

AMY RYAN: That proposal when I had to walk down the line of everybody holding candles, I couldn't stop crying. I had to tell myself, "This isn't real. These are actors. You are not getting married."

Holly wasn't just surprised to walk into a room with every employee at the Scranton branch holding a candle. Michael covered her desk with candles, which soon set off the fire sprinklers.

BRIAN BAUMGARTNER: There was something about that scene, with the water coming down, it was sort of beautiful.

AMY RYAN: Steve directed that episode, and I remember that first take, which is what's in the show because it was shocking and cold and goofy and it wasn't cinematic.

> **MICHAEL:** [*With a Yoda voice.*] Holly Flax, marrying me will you be?
>
> **HOLLY:** [*With a Yoda voice.*] Your wife becoming, me will I.

Michael and Holly: Love at long last.

AMY RYAN: I don't know who, but somebody on the other side of the monitor said we have to go again, and Steve got up and he fought for it. He's like, "No, this is better. It's not slick. It's not cool. They look terrible, but it's funny." I was so glad for two reasons: because I agreed with him and I really didn't want to get wet again. [*Laughs.*] That water was so cold.

BRIAN BAUMGARTNER: It's how life is, right? It's not the perfect moment that you assume it's going to be. And even though there's a beautiful moment with the candles, there's something that's going to screw it up.

AMY RYAN: But that's the life I prefer to live in. Weird is good to me. Odd is really good to me. That's what makes me laugh through life, when things are slightly off-kilter.

BRIAN BAUMGARTNER: The moment that always stays with me is when he says . . .

> **MICHAEL:** We're moving to Colorado.
>
> **KEVIN:** All of us?
>
> **MICHAEL:** Yep.
>
> **JIM:** Wait, what?

BRIAN BAUMGARTNER: Because with Michael, we all must go. The office has always been his family. But because of you, there's that transition.

AMY RYAN: I think when you find true love then nothing else matters. His old ways aren't necessary, because he's found his true family.

BRIAN BAUMGARTNER: Which is you.

AMY RYAN: Yeah. That's me.

"I Didn't Want to Let Him Go"
The Last Days of Michael Scott

KEN KWAPIS: One thing about [Michael leaving] is it mimics what happens in our lives. We work with people and then they go away. They leave, they get another job, they get married. It was one more example of the show not behaving like a show.

Steve knew exactly how we wanted his story to go. And for his final episode—"Goodbye Michael," which aired on April 28, 2011—he had a plan.

STEVE CARELL: Six months before, I talked to Greg about how I wanted Michael to go out, like what I thought a final arc would be. The idea I pitched was, obviously, he's going to move on and he and Holly would be together. We had talked about that before. But on his last day, I thought there should be a party being planned, but Michael

Steve Carell and Will Ferrell at Michael's last Dundies.

should basically trick people into thinking he was leaving the next day. I thought that would be the most elegant representation of his growth as a human being. Michael lives to be celebrated throughout the whole series. That's all he wants. He wants to be the center of attention, and he wants pats on the back. He wants people to think he's funny and charming and all of those things. But the fact that he'd walk away from his big tribute, his big send-off, and be able to, in a very personal way, say goodbye to each character, that to me felt like it would resonate.

Some of those moments were sweet and sentimental, like when he gives Phyllis a chattering teeth gag gift.

> **PHYLLIS SMITH:** To give me a voice. [*Starts to tear up.*] That was a really hard episode to go through. It's weird. It stays with you after all these years.

Or the letter of recommendation for Dwight, in which he describes the onetime assistant to the regional manager as a leader and a friend.

> **STEVE CARELL:** After all the stuff that Michael has put Dwight through, at his core he loves him and appreciates him and understands how loyal he had been that entire time. For the greater part of the series, Dwight had really been his only advocate.
>
> **GREG DANIELS:** I remember sitting in a Coffee Bean and writing Dwight's letter and literally making myself cry. Clearly, Steve leaving was very emotional for me too, and it hit me during the writing, three weeks earlier than everybody else's breakdowns on set.

He doesn't get a chance to say anything to Pam, who decides to play hooky that afternoon and catch a screening of the movie *The King's Speech*.

PAUL FEIG: *Bridesmaids* [which Paul directed] was coming out in a few months, and we almost put BRIDESMAIDS up on the marquee. But we all decided, "Well, what if it bombs?" So we didn't do it. But Pam almost snuck in to see *Bridesmaids*.

Michael waits as long as he can for Pam to return, but he finally heads to the airport. After seven years, he takes off his mic and says goodbye to the camera guy.

GREG DANIELS: It was kind of a test. Is he over needing the office mates to be his family now? The price for that was not getting to say goodbye to Pam.

But then, at the last minute, Pam races over to Michael in the airport and whispers something to him.

JENNA FISCHER: Paul Feig directed that episode. We were at the airport and Paul said, "Jenna, I want you to just run up and just say goodbye to Steve, your friend. This is your last scene with him. So say goodbye. We're not gonna use the sound. We're just going to have a spy shot on you." So I ran up to Steve and I just told him all the ways I was going to miss him and how grateful I was for his friendship and the privilege of working with him. I'm sobbing and he's sobbing and we're hugging. I didn't want to let him go and I didn't want the scene to end. And then Paul Feig says, "Cut."

PAUL FEIG: I'm actually getting choked up when I talk about it. Just seeing them and you don't know what they're saying and it's just her hugging him. It really landed for me just what the show was.

JENNA FISCHER: And Paul was like, "Jenna, that was brilliant, but can you do it again, just a little faster?" Our first take of that final scene was like five minutes. [*Laughs.*] He was like, "We just need to tighten it up."

Pam's goodbye is the last one you see in the episode, but it was actually filmed three days before we wrapped. The last goodbye was between Michael and Jim Halpert.

JOHN KRASINSKI: I cried so hard when we did that scene. I actually remember the number—we did seventeen takes of not even speaking. I was just dribble-crying. I also remember Steve crying and I was not expecting that. It was so unlike him. Not that he's emotionless, but it was so unlike him to let real life bleed into the moment. And of course, it was a little bit of real life. That's what Greg was so good at doing, capturing these moments in relationships.

STEVE CARELL: It was emotional torture. Imagine saying goodbye for a week. It wasn't "See you later" and you wave and you're out. It was just fraught with emotion and joy and sadness and nostalgia. But it was also really beautiful because it did allow me to kind of have a finality with everybody.

Saying goodbye to Michael Scott was one thing, but we also had to say goodbye to Steve Carell.

BRIAN BAUMGARTNER: What do you think was the bigger loss, Michael or Steve?

GREG DANIELS: Huh. Wow.

MATT SOHN: Boy, that's hard.

BRIAN BAUMGARTNER: That's what she said. [*Laughs.*] Sorry.

JOHN KRASINSKI: I have to be honest and say it was losing Steve, because as much as he was so good on the show, his presence on the set was fantastic. He was as professional as it gets. He was your cleanup hitter; he just crushed everything that was thrown at him.

JENNA FISCHER: It wasn't just the character of Michael that we were losing. We were losing the captain of our ship, Steve Carell. And I don't think I can say enough about how important he was as our leader. His work ethic, his kindness, his generosity. There was no ego. And he was the most important person on set. He had the most lines, the most work. He had to drive the show, and he was so generous.

KATE FLANNERY: He made sure that the show was the star, even though clearly he was the star.

DAVID ROGERS: Losing Steve and not having him there every day, that was definitely the hardest thing. Losing Michael Scott was tough, but the show can still go on. There's still comedy. We have this bench of great characters.

ANGELA KINSEY: I actually went back and found an email that I wrote him during our first week back without him. I was like, "Dear Steve, it was really weird to walk on set today and not see you. I miss our talks about the weekend." [*Laughs.*] Steve used to walk over and talk to us about his weekend, what he got at Target. And I was like, "I just really miss you."

JOHN KRASINSKI: It felt like the end of an era. More than even losing Steve or losing Michael, it felt like the end of that evolution of our show. It's like when you graduate college. Your life isn't over, but that version of your life will never come back. You will never have your college years again or your high school years again.

PAUL FEIG: I loved everybody, but I remember saying, "I'm not going to direct any more episodes." I love all the episodes after Steve left, but I felt like I almost had to leave with Michael Scott. It wasn't a reason like, "How dare you?" It was just this really weird, natural feeling of like, "Oh, it's over." It felt like there was closure for me when that happened.

BRIAN BAUMGARTNER: For weeks leading up to Steve's last day, it was really hard to think about.

PHYLLIS SMITH: It was like somebody punched you in the stomach, you know? I can remember in the trailer, if we started talking about it, we'd start crying. And makeup would be like, "Stop it! Don't talk about it!"

PAUL FEIG: Every time we were going into a scene, especially towards the second half of the week, it was that feeling of, "This is our last scene with Steve." We would do the first few takes and there would be a real sadness about it. I had to constantly go like, "Remember, we love Steve, but we don't necessarily like Michael." I completely got it 'cause I was emotional too. But I was also like, "Everybody can't be weeping because it's not going to track with the rest of the show!"

At the end of that last take, once all our characters had said goodbye to Michael, it was time for us to say goodbye to Steve. Producers, Allison Jones, people who'd been there from the beginning, people who hadn't been there in years—they all arrived en masse at the warehouse set for a big farewell party. We retired Steve's number, number one on the call sheet. For the rest of the show, no other actor would ever be given number one. And we gave him a hockey jersey with number one on the back. That made even Oscar Nuñez emotional.

OSCAR NUÑEZ: I didn't want to cry. I'm Cuban and we just don't do that. So everybody was crying very freely, and when we were in the warehouse and gave him the hockey shirt, I did have to excuse myself and went back behind the boxes and cried. But it's not good crying. It's like breakdown crying, like vomiting 'cause you held it too long. I should let it out more is what you're saying. I get that.

BRIAN BAUMGARTNER: Is that true? You went behind the boxes?

OSCAR NUÑEZ: I had to cry 'cause freaking Paul Lieberstein started crying and then I'm like, "Oh man, this is just crazy."

MIKE SCHUR: I was gone, because I was at *Parks and Rec*, but I came back for his farewell party. When he shot his last scene, Greg did this

Michael's goodbye to Oscar.

thing where he went around and said, "Everyone, tell me your best Steve story." And there were stories that like brought people to tears that no one had ever heard.

GREG DANIELS: I remember when *The 40-Year-Old Virgin* was still in theaters and he was the biggest movie star in the country and we were shooting, I think, "The Dundies." We were in the parking lot of a defunct Black Angus [Steakhouse], and Michael was offering Pam a ride as he was driving off. It's two or three in the morning, and his entire role is to drive the car away from Jenna after saying his line, and we're doing take after take after take. So many people would've been like, "Yeah, put the body double in, goodbye." But he stayed.

MATT SOHN: When you shoot scenes, there are people in the background, and on a lot of shows, they find a way of shooting so that the other actors don't have to be there. But we had a very tiny set, so we didn't really have that luxury. But there was never a time where Steve complained about sitting at his desk, doing monotonous work in the deep background. Steve kept everybody else in check, because the fact that he never complained meant no one else did.

DEBBIE PIERCE: I was going through a situation with my hip and at that time nobody really knew. I was in a lot of pain, and getting up and down on the van [that took cast and crew to various shooting locations] was very hard for me. So one day, we were all gathering into the van, Steve and some of the actors, and I went to go in the back and he looked at me and went, "Debbie, where are you going? Take the front seat." I could reach up on the bar and pull myself up in, so it was just easier for me. It was such a kind thing. He's the star of the show, and he would always hold the door and help us in the van. I was like, "I see some mama's raised a nice young man."

MIKE SCHUR: They've gotta carry big plastic crates full of makeup and hair stuff, and without her asking, Steve just picked up her makeup case and walked with her to the location and put it down. And then he proceeded to do that every single time they ever went on location for seven years. He did it so quietly and so subtly that nobody even knew it. No one. In my memory, everyone heard that story [at Steve's farewell party] for the first time. For seven years, the star of the biggest sitcom on NBC, arguably the most famous television actor of his day, not only ceded the front seat of the van to his makeup person, but also carried her equipment for her every time they went on location.

Schur has a theory that Steve's kindness wasn't just the result of a good upbringing. It was a by-product of having been trained at Second City, the venerable sketch and improv comedy theater in Chicago that's responsible for comedy legends like John Belushi, Dan Aykroyd, Amy Poehler, Gilda Radner, Stephen Colbert, Amy Sedaris, Chris Farley, Julia Louis-Dreyfus, Eugene Levy, Mike Myers, Tina Fey, Jason Sudeikis, and hundreds of others.

Between 1990 and 1994, Steve performed in six Second City sketch revues, including *Truth, Justice, or the American Way* and *Are You Now, or Have You Ever Been Mellow?* Bonus fun fact: Stephen Colbert was originally Steve's understudy.

MIKE SCHUR: People who come from that Second City world are the best people to have on TV shows, because the ethos is everyone's a point guard. It's not about personal glory. It's not about dunking in the most cool way you can dunk. It's about setting up other people to be funny. Sketches only work when you're constantly passing the ball. Having worked with Amy Poehler for many years now, she's exactly the same way. She was the star of a TV show who was never happier than when other people were being funny around her. The goal is to allow other people to shine.

Not only shine but, in some cases, get paid.

MIKE SCHUR: Networks are always trying to slash budgets, right? When something's making money, the question is not "Thank God we're making money," it's "How do we make *more* money?" After season three or four, there was a budget meeting with NBC [about *The Office*], and Greg asked me to come. He was like, "You're going to have to deal with this kind of crap [on *Parks and Rec*] and you should see what it's like." They were trying to slash the budget 'cause they were *always* trying to slash the budget. And one of the things on the table was reducing the size of the cast. 'Cause at that point, how many series regulars were there? Twenty-two or something? It was a lot. By far the largest cast of any show on television, comedy or drama. Greg was like, "I don't think that's a good idea. People invest in these characters. Everyone has a different favorite character." And they were like, "Well, we have to find the money somewhere, and we're only making $780 million a year on this thing." So we went back and had a meeting with Steve, and he just completely shut it down. He was like, "Nope, that is not happening. This is the show. These are the people on the show. This is how the show will be until the end of the show. That's it. That's it."

BRIAN BAUMGARTNER: Wow.

MIKE SCHUR: There were executives in the room and that ended the discussion. He wasn't angry. He wasn't pounding his fist. He was just saying, "No, that's not going to happen. That's a nonstarter. Move on. What's next?" That's the way he is. It was this quiet leadership that he exhibited all the time.

GREG DANIELS: One of the things I got out of working with Steve was that I didn't really have an improv background. And I found that to be really the key to how he worked. It saved us a bunch of times. One of my favorite memories of Steve as a producer is when we were doing "The Dundies." We got a call from the Chili's lawyers and they were like, "We just looked at the script. The part where Pam is so drunk that she throws up is not gonna work for us. We're being sued for overserving patrons." We'd already finished two-thirds of our shoot. What do we do? So I was getting ill in the corner, freaking out, and Steve notices and he's like, "What's up?" I told them the situation, and I completely shut down. I was going to blow my brains out. And then Steve came up with this notion of the manager being interviewed and saying that Pam had a lifetime ban from Chili's [for sneaking booze from other tables] and it solved everything. That was the improv thing. Steve had utter faith that he would be able to find an answer when it was necessary. That's a different way to live than I'm used to. The overthinker doesn't do that.

STEVE CARELL: As an actor, we're lucky if we just get to work and get paid and make a living. Come on, that's all any of us wanted. No one [on *The Office*] aspired to anything beyond that. So there was complete contentment in what we had there. And to work with a group of people that you care so much about, that you can't wait to see the next day.

BRIAN BAUMGARTNER: Were you apprehensive about leaving?

STEVE CARELL: Sure. But I tend to do that, though. Career-wise, I tend to leave. I left Second City when it was the best job in the world. I couldn't imagine it being any better. I was having the most fun of my life. I gotta go. 'Cause I don't want to get comfortable. I did the same thing on *The Daily Show*. I was there for four years or so. Nancy, my wife, we were both correspondents. This is fantastic. Love it. We're having a ball. And we both decided, "Gotta go. Let's just keep it moving on." I sort of did the same thing on *The Office*. Maybe it's out of fear. Maybe it's like, you don't want it to turn a corner in any way. You don't want it to be less than it ever was. I was just so proud to be part of it. And it was very difficult for me to leave because I loved everybody.

Losing Steve (and Michael) wasn't just about losing a friend and leader. There was suddenly a big, gaping hole in our show, and it brought up a lot of scary questions. Chiefly, could *The Office* survive without Michael Scott?

PAUL LIEBERSTEIN: We didn't know how much of a hit we would take with Steve leaving, but we took a pretty big one. When I had meetings with the higher-ups, I think we were just a disappointing line item at the time. They wanted those numbers up. And all of the ratings were falling across the board. Steve left as a giant A-list movie star and incredible talent. We gave him a send-off that was cathartic, but we lost a lot of viewers. We did. In the millions. It may have even happened if he'd stayed. There was no way to know.

BRIAN BAUMGARTNER: I remember feeling way more emotional about him leaving than even the end of the show, because I felt like a kid when Mom and Dad leave or something. It's like, "Well, *now* what?"

PHYLLIS SMITH: I was really nervous about how that void was going to be filled, you know?

CREED BRATTON: I think I probably voiced it with a few people. I said, "You know what? I think it might be time to just stop." I really felt that. I thought, "Without him, how can this possibly go on? How can it go on?"

How can it go on? We were about to answer that question, and what came next decided whether *The Office* would continue in a Michael Scott–less world.

ONE LAST TIME: THE OFFICE EXTENDED FAMILY, SEASON NINE.

11

"Who Should Be the Boss?"

THE SEARCH FOR A NEW DUNDER MIFFLIN REGIONAL MANAGER: SEASONS EIGHT AND NINE

It was the end of our seventh season and Steve Carell was gone. Who should replace him—and even if he should be replaced at all—was on the forefront of everyone's mind.

One thing that helped cushion the blow of Steve's leaving was the arrival of a new (temporary) regional manager, Deangelo Vickers, played by Will Ferrell.

GREG DANIELS: One of the really good ideas that Paul [Lieberstein] had was to bring in Deangelo Vickers. He was like a little palate cleanser.

ANGELA KINSEY: I mean, that was brilliant. That eased the transition.

JENNA FISCHER: I've done movies with Will Ferrell [she costarred with Ferrell in the 2007 comedy *Blades of Glory*] and I always thought, "Wow, [Steve Carell and Will] must have a competition for the greatest-person-to-work-for title." Will is like the nicest man in Hollywood.

KATE FLANNERY: I loved working with Will. Oh my God, just the greatest. He remembered that we'd had dinner in 1994 in New York when he first got hired on *SNL*. I couldn't believe he remembered. I was embarrassed 'cause I [went to the dinner party with] an awful ex-boyfriend who was a real douchebag. Will didn't remember him at all. He was just like, "I felt really intimidated 'cause all you guys were from Chicago." I was like, *what*?

Deangelo was only with us for four episodes in season seven, culminating in "The Inner Circle," in which he nearly kills himself attempting a dunk from the free throw line. The character leaves the office in an ambulance. But it wasn't just Will's character who had a close call.

BRENT FORRESTER: Were you there when Will Ferrell had to dunk the basketball?

Will Ferrell's fateful dunk.

BRIAN BAUMGARTNER: Yes, he dunked over me.

BRENT FORRESTER: Well, the stunt guys had come in and said, "We're just gonna put a harness on him and then it'll go up to a pulley, and we'll yank all this rope and he'll go flying in the air." And Greg said to them, "Gosh, that sounds a little dangerous. Do you want to test it out for us?" They're like, "We don't need to. This is going to be fine. Trust us." So on the first take, Will Ferrell dribbles down the court and he jumps up and he's wearing a harness, and they pull a rope that's attached to a pulley and he just goes flying up at like four times the speed that any human could jump and his head smashes into the basketball rim. [*Laughs.*]

BRIAN BAUMGARTNER: I missed it because his joke was, he makes me sit cross-legged on the ground to dunk over me, so I can't see what's going on. I hear all this happening, but it's happening literally right behind me. I duck my head and roll. I remember just trying to get out of the way 'cause I don't know what's going on.

Will was fine after his head-on collision with the rim. And after he left, we were still left with the question: What comes next?

> **JOHN KRASINSKI:** I knew the show could go forward. I didn't know what the plan was. I couldn't see the forest through the trees. But I trusted Greg.

> **RAINN WILSON:** I had great reservations about the show existing without Steve. Did I think we were going to bomb and fail without Steve? No. Were we going to be hurt by losing one of the greatest comedic actors of all time in the lead character? Of course we were. No one thought otherwise.

> **PAUL LIEBERSTEIN:** There were a lot of good reasons why we could keep going. The show could either find a new direction or it wouldn't work. Ultimately, I wanted to keep going because we had a great cast.

> **ALLISON JONES:** I thought the show should have ended, except for the actors' sake. I was like, "We gotta keep Phyllis employed. They all have to keep their jobs."

Steve's leaving was a big blow to our show. But Greg Daniels, always deciding the glass was half full rather than half empty, saw this as an opportunity to feature more of the cast.

> **GREG DANIELS:** The painful part of my job is you've got to go edit all of the things, cutting the show down. Our rough cuts were thirty-eight minutes long and we had to get it down to 21:03 or whatever. That's an enormous amount to throw out. And it was very painful, because we could get the show down to twenty-six minutes just cutting the

fat. But after that you've got to cut the muscle. There are good scenes not getting in. And once we got five or six years into the show, everyone in the ensemble was capable of carrying an important story. So the best argument to me to continue was, if we didn't have Steve at that point, we still had our SAG Award–winning ensemble. And it would let all these people who didn't have as much screen time have more screen time.

RAINN WILSON: We had a pretty damn great ensemble, better than any other thing that was on TV at the time. It was time for all of us in the cast to step up and carry more weight.

But would we be allowed to carry that weight through what would become our last two seasons? That remained to be seen.

"They Wanted a Big Gorilla"
Who Gets Michael Scott's Office?

JENNA FISCHER: This was the conversation. Who should be the boss? I remember being up in the writers' room and people asking me who I thought should be the boss. And I was like, "Guys, I don't know. I don't know who should be the boss." They were still trying to get anybody's opinion. "Does anyone have a perspective on this?"

GREG DANIELS: We had a lot of thoughts like, do we bring somebody new in or do we promote from within? And I think the feeling was, well, geez, we've got guys already on the staff that are tremendous. We had Krasinski and Craig Robinson [who played Darryl].

PAUL LIEBERSTEIN: With Darryl and Jim, it was just a nonstarter because they were too competent. You needed someone who could make the mistakes.

Craig Robinson as Darryl Philbin.

BRIAN BAUMGARTNER: Craig, did you want Darryl to get the regional manager job?

CRAIG ROBINSON: No. No. No. One time I went up to Paul and I'm like, "Hey, man, just put that in your pocket." I gave him a dollar. [*Laughs.*]

BRIAN BAUMGARTNER: You tried bribing Paul so he wouldn't give Darryl the promotion?

CRAIG ROBINSON: I thought it was interesting that my name got brought up and it was cool. I thought about it, but the thing is, it just seemed . . . like a lot of work. [*Laughs.*]

BRIAN BAUMGARTNER: Jim was the most qualified. I mean, he was lazy.

JENNA FISCHER: He was the most well suited to it on a technical level.

BRIAN BAUMGARTNER: In terms of his interaction with people, his ability to lead and sort of inspire people. But then that messes up story lines in a way.

GREG DANIELS: The difficulty is that these characters are not created to be leads. Dwight, for instance, had been created to be the foil.

BRIAN BAUMGARTNER: Being the boss would change him. Dwight as the boss is not Dwight.

Dwight did get a taste of his dream job in the season seven episode "Dwight K. Schrute, (Acting) Manager," but it was a brief tenure. (It lasted just a single episode.)

DWIGHT: I will never be happier than I am right now. I will also never be less happy. I will be at my current maximum happiness for the rest of my life.

JENNA FISCHER: Dwight is the character who *wants* to be the boss. He's always angling to be the boss but does not actually have the authority. So if you make him the boss, then who is that guy?

PAUL LIEBERSTEIN: We were getting a lot of pressure from the network. The network, who had historically been behind us so much, changed hands to Comcast just as Steve was leaving, and they wanted a big gorilla.

BRIAN BAUMGARTNER: They wanted a big star to come in and take it over.

PAUL LIEBERSTEIN: Which we fought.

BRIAN BAUMGARTNER: Was there a specific name that Comcast wanted to take over?

Craig Robinson

Occupation: Actor, musician

Hometown: Born and raised in Chicago, Illinois

Training: Illinois State University, Class of 1994, B.A. in Music; Saint Xavier University, MEd in Music Education

Previous Employment: Music teacher at Horace Mann Elementary in South Chicago; costarring role in FX series *Lucky* (2003); small roles in shows like *Curb Your Enthusiasm, Friends, The Bernie Mac Show, LAX,* and *Arrested Development* (2004)

Post-Office Credits: Roles in movies like *Pineapple Express* (2008), *This Is the End* (2013), *Hot Tub Time Machine 1* and *2* (2010, 2015); played the "Pontiac Bandit" on the TV series *Brooklyn Nine-Nine* (2014–2020)

Side Project: Keyboardist for Kevin and the Zits (fictional), and singer/keyboardist for funk-comedy five-piece The Nasty Delicious (actual band)

PAUL LIEBERSTEIN: Lots of names were floated. Like Julia Louis-Dreyfus. And James Gandolfini, who we actually met with to explore it. But that was going to be in the part-time range.

As negotiations with Comcast continued about the new lead for the show, a bunch of other famous people made cameos in the season seven finale "Search Committee." A-list actors like Ray Romano, Jim Carrey, Will Arnett, James Spader, and Catherine Tate, along with billionaire investor Warren Buffett, showed up (in character) to interview for the regional manager position.

> **KATE FLANNERY:** I remember Ray Romano. I've gotten to hang with him a few times since, and he said [being on *The Office*] was really scary for him. Because his kids were huge fans and he was like, "I don't want to mess this up."
>
> **BRIAN BAUMGARTNER:** It's not an easy thing.
>
> **KATE FLANNERY:** Do you remember when Warren Buffett came with [his business partner] Charlie Munger? Oh my God. That was insane. He agreed to do the show if we let them shoot this thing with us, which was amazing.

Steve, Rainn, and Kate, all in character, appeared with Buffett in a five-minute spoof of *The Office*, which was screened only once, at the annual Berkshire Hathaway shareholders meeting on April 30, 2011. During the skit, Michael Scott remarks that Buffett is "at least ninety years old and runs a company called Berkshire Hathaway that produces all of Anne Hathaway's movies."

In exchange for the favor, Buffett agreed to do the cameo as an unnamed candidate for the regional manager position.

> **KATE FLANNERY:** He used the fake men's room. He or Charlie, one of them, accidentally used the fake men's room [on *The Office* set],

which is not good because the drains don't work. I know this because of my boyfriend, Chris, who was the set photographer for *The Office*. That's where he always hung out, in the fake men's room, so I always knew where to find him. I guess he couldn't be in there for a while 'cause they literally had to redo the wall.

BRIAN BAUMGARTNER: He just peed into a fake urinal?

KATE FLANNERY: A drainless urinal.

BRIAN BAUMGARTNER: That is crazy. The lesson is, it doesn't matter if you're Warren Buffett or anybody else, it's hard to be a guest star on *The Office*.

KATE FLANNERY: This is true. All the money in the world and it's still not easy.

Obviously Warren Buffett wasn't going to join our show, but Paul and the network had to agree on someone to lead the next season. Some in the cast weren't happy that the network was looking elsewhere.

JENNA FISCHER: This is the only time I've ever really publicly said this, but it's always disappointed me that we didn't trust in our core *Office* group enough to continue the show without bringing in these big guest actors to fill Steve's shoes. I always wondered what that season would've been like. Like if we'd said, "We're enough. The bench is deep enough. The talent is there. We can keep the ship afloat with what we have."

RAINN WILSON: Ed Helms was a lead in *The Hangover*, which was the biggest comedy ever made. We had him and I didn't think we needed to bring in big names. We *had* the ensemble.

PAUL LIEBERSTEIN: We ended up with a part-time James Spader.

Spader was not only a movie star—known for films like *Sex, Lies, and Videotape* (1989) and *Secretary* (2002)—but he'd just ended his run on

Boston Legal, where he had won two Emmys. His first appearance was in the season seven finale, as the one and only Robert California. He shows up to interview for the regional manager position and ends up both impressing and creeping out some of the staff.

> **ROBERT CALIFORNIA:** I will get offered the job. That's a . . . call I've received many times. The slight hopefulness in their voice, the pregnant pause . . . while they wait to hear my response, and then . . . my response.

James stayed on through season eight. As a new cast member, he brought a very different energy to the set.

SEASON EIGHT
Episode Guide

TITLE	DIRECTED BY	WRITTEN BY	ORIGINAL AIR DATE
"The List"	B. J. Novak	B. J. Novak	September 22, 2011
"The Incentive"	Charles McDougall	Paul Lieberstein	September 29, 2011
"Lotto"	John Krasinski	Charlie Grandy	October 6, 2011
"Garden Party"	David Rogers	Justin Spitzer	October 13, 2011
"Spooked"	Randall Einhorn	Carrie Kemper	October 27, 2011
"Doomsday"	Troy Miller	Daniel Chun	November 3, 2011
"Pam's Replacement"	Matt Sohn	Allison Silverman	November 10, 2011

"Gettysburg"	Jeffrey Blitz	Robert Padnick	November 17, 2011
"Mrs. California"	Charlie Grandy	Dan Greaney	December 1, 2011
"Christmas Wishes"	Ed Helms	Mindy Kaling	December 8, 2011
"Trivia"	B. J. Novak	Steve Hely	January 12, 2012
"Pool Party"	Charles McDougall	Owen Ellickson	January 19, 2012
"Jury Duty"	Eric Appel	Aaron Shure	February 2, 2012
"Special Project"	David Rogers	Amelie Gillette	February 9, 2012
"Tallahassee"	Matt Sohn	Daniel Chun	February 16, 2012
"After Hours"	Brian Baumgartner	Halsted Sullivan & Warren Lieberstein	February 23, 2012
"Test the Store"	Brent Forrester	Mindy Kaling	March 1, 2012
"Last Day in Florida"	Matt Sohn	Robert Padnick	March 8, 2012
"Get the Girl"	Rainn Wilson	Charlie Grandy	March 15, 2012
"Welcome Party"	Ed Helms	Steve Hely	April 12, 2012
"Angry Andy"	Claire Scanlon	Justin Spitzer	April 19, 2012
"Fundraiser"	David Rogers	Owen Ellickson	April 26, 2012
"Turf War"	Daniel Chun	Warren Lieberstein & Halsted Sullivan	May 3, 2012
"Free Family Portrait Studio"	B. J. Novak	B. J. Novak	May 10, 2012

JENNA FISCHER: He wanted to rehearse all the time, and we were like, "Oh yeah, we stopped doing that in season three, James." But he was like, "I want to rehearse." And it kind of infused us with this new integrity and a way to work. He would rehearse those scenes with me at reception for forty minutes and we'd be like, "Oh my God, we're *still* rehearsing."

RAINN WILSON: He wanted everything worked out. If you threw something in, if you said, "I want some spaghetti," it would just completely throw him. He'd have no idea what would come next or how to get back to his line. Spader is a great actor, he's one of the great character actors. Look at his œuvre over the last twenty years. He's so present and interesting and odd. But [performing in *The Office*] just involves a very different skill set.

ANGELA KINSEY: I was talking to Kenneth Paul [Schoenfeld], who did my makeup, about the fact that my daughter liked to sleep in bed with me and I felt bad. She was getting older, she was four years old, and I knew I shouldn't let her crawl in a bed and sleep with me, but she's so snuggly. When James came in to get his makeup done, it looked like he went into some meditative trance. He looked asleep. But he suddenly sat up and looked at me and he goes, "Angela, get that baby out of your bed if you ever want a man in there." I was like, "What? You're alive and you're talking? All right, James. I guess."

KATE FLANNERY: I was intimidated by Spader 'cause he's a movie star and there was so much sexual tension between the two of us. So much! Oh my God!

BRIAN BAUMGARTNER: I felt like there was sexual tension between me and Spader.

KATE FLANNERY: Probably even more.

BRIAN BAUMGARTNER: No seriously, between Spader and *anyone* there's sexual tension.

KATE FLANNERY: This is true. In the season eight Christmas episode, there was one take where Meredith thinks she's got a chance with him and he sorta touches her cheek like . . .

ROBERT CALIFORNIA: The lines in your haggard face are paths that lead nowhere. Your hair is the fire of hell. [*Hugs Meredith.*] I sincerely hope you find a sexual partner tonight.

The sexual tension between Robert California (James Spader) and Meredith.

KATE FLANNERY: In one take, I grabbed his ass, and immediately we stopped. I'm like, "I'm so sorry, I'm so sorry. I'm so sorry!" He goes, "No, that was the right thing to do." [*Laughs.*] They didn't end up using it, but I was like, "You grabbed James Spader's ass, Kate. What the fuck is wrong with you?" I was so nervous. I was like, "Oh no, oh no, oh no!"

Robert California was a polarizing figure, both among fans and critics.

EMILY VANDERWERFF: Characters leave. Their replacements are never as good because we were so familiar with the originals. Robert California can never be Michael Scott because we knew Michael Scott for seven seasons. And how *dare* you come in and try to take his place.

BEN SILVERMAN: I don't think we did anyone a favor by bringing in James Spader—neither James nor the show. He's so talented and clearly had *The Blacklist* one second later, but that feels custom-made for him.

Spader went on to star in the critically acclaimed NBC thriller *The Blacklist,* which premiered in 2013 and (as of this writing) is still a network hit.

BEN SILVERMAN: The way he played [Robert California] on our show didn't breathe as well and didn't work as well in our format.

RAINN WILSON: The Robert California experiment was not right. His energy just didn't fit.

Robert California never became the Scranton branch regional manager. Instead, he somehow talked his way into the role of Sabre CEO. He'd visit the branch often, but Michael Scott's old office remained unoccupied.

PAUL LIEBERSTEIN: I really did not want to put a new person in the office, in Michael's chair. I just thought, "We're never gonna get that right." So [Robert California] was part time. We didn't bring in a new Michael Scott. The new manager came from inside.

And that new manager was none other than Andy Bernard, played by Ed Helms.

ANDY: [*Drumroll with hands.*] It's unbelievable. True, I may have been the second choice, but I was the first choice's first choice.

ED HELMS: I was thrilled and super excited and terrified. I meditated a lot on this idea of like, I'm not trying to fill Steve's shoes. I'm walking in a different direction. At the same time, there was a sense that it was going to be leaning harder into an ensemble. Steve really was the organizing principle for the show for so long. So there was a sense that even with Andy in that office as manager, it wasn't necessarily all on my shoulders. We'd be leaning into the whole cast.

GREG DANIELS: Andy Bernard was created to be the Stamford version of Dwight. He's like a preppy weirdo, a different type of weirdo.

Andy takes over the manager's office.

BRIAN BAUMGARTNER: He was also an idiot. Dwight was an idiot too, in his own way. But Andy was positioned to be bad at his job, right?

GREG DANIELS: Right. He punched holes in walls. It would have needed the same kind of moving the character over that we did in season two—

BRIAN BAUMGARTNER: With Michael Scott.

GREG DANIELS: Right. And I believe Paul was doing that with Andy. But it was different 'cause everybody was paying close attention to the show at that point.

EMILY VANDERWERFF: Once Michael Scott leaves that show, it has to become something different, and it never quite figured out a way to become different in an interesting way. It's a tricky thing to do when you have to replace the center of a show. I don't think *The Office* managed it, but I don't think any show ever has. You can't do that.

JENNA FISCHER: That was tricky. But we made it through and we got some great episodes that season, and then we went into season nine where we sort of just didn't have a boss for a while. Andy was our boss, but then he got lost on the boat.

SEASON NINE
Episode Guide

TITLE	DIRECTED BY	WRITTEN BY	ORIGINAL AIR DATE
"New Guys"	Greg Daniels	Greg Daniels	September 20, 2012
"Roy's Wedding"	Matt Sohn	Allison Silverman	September 27, 2012
"Andy's Ancestry"	David Rogers	Jonathan Green & Gabe Miller	October 4, 2012
"Work Bus"	Bryan Cranston	Brent Forrester	October 18, 2012

"Here Comes Treble"	Claire Scanlon	Owen Ellickson	October 25, 2012
"The Boat"	John Krasinski	Dan Sterling	November 8, 2012
"The Whale"	Rodman Flender	Carrie Kemper	November 15, 2012
"The Target"	Brent Forrester	Graham Wagner	November 29, 2012
"Dwight Christmas"	Charles McDougall	Robert Padnick	December 6, 2012
"Lice"	Rodman Flender	Niki Schwartz-Wright	January 10, 2013
"Suit Warehouse"	Matt Sohn	Dan Greaney	January 17, 2013
"Customer Loyalty"	Kelly Cantley	Jonathan Green & Gabe Miller	January 24, 2013
"Junior Salesman"	David Rogers	Carrie Kemper	January 31, 2013
"Vandalism"	Lee Kirk	Owen Ellickson	January 31, 2013
"Couples Discount"	Troy Miller	Allison Silverman	February 7, 2013
"Moving On"	Jon Favreau	Graham Wagner	February 14, 2013
"The Farm"	Paul Lieberstein	Paul Lieberstein	March 14, 2013
"Promos"	Jennifer Celotta	Tim McAuliffe	April 4, 2013
"Stairmageddon"	Matt Sohn	Dan Sterling	April 11, 2013
"Paper Airplane"	Jesse Peretz	Halsted Sullivan & Warren Lieberstein	April 25, 2013
"Livin' the Dream"	Jeffrey Blitz	Niki Schwartz-Wright	May 2, 2013
"A.A.R.M."	David Rogers	Brent Forrester	May 9, 2013
"Finale"	Ken Kwapis	Greg Daniels	May 16, 2013

In the sixth episode of season nine, "The Boat," Andy reunites with his alcoholic brother (played by Josh Groban), and they decide to sail their family boat to the Caribbean for "serious bro time."

JENNA FISCHER: And then we were like, "Oh, here's an answer. It's an empty office."

"This Last Season Is for the Fans"
Finding the Perfect Ending for Jim and Pam

In season eight, we no longer had Steve or a clear vision of how to replace him. Streaming was killing our viewership. The network changed hands. And by the end of the season, Paul Lieberstein retired as showrunner, moving on to develop an *Office* spinoff. With all this uncertainty, we had to find a path forward and decide how much longer the show should last.

CLAIRE SCANLON: Initially, Greg wasn't going to be there. It was going to be Dan Sterling and Brent Forrester as the showrunners. But Greg kept coming, and then it was finally like, "Okay, Greg's just here." Even though he wasn't technically gonna run the show, he was running the show.

GREG DANIELS: I realized how much more pleasurable it is to be the showrunner than to be an executive producer who gives notes that sometimes are taken and sometimes aren't. It's not as much fun.

At first, Greg wasn't sure about coming back officially to run the show for season nine. But then he had a conversation with John Krasinski . . .

GREG DANIELS: John actually motivated me. He came to me and said, "Look, I think we need to do our last season and not continue to keep going, and I want you to do it." And he was the leader. After Steve left, John became more of the cast leader.

JOHN KRASINSKI: I remember, when they came to us for season nine, I had a very honest conversation with Greg. He called me about season nine and said, "What do you think?" And I said, "You have to end the show. You have to end the show before they end it for us. It's coming to an end regardless." I wasn't telling him anything he didn't know.

GREG DANIELS: I definitely wanted to tell the end. If there's going to be an end, I wanted to tell it.

JOHN KRASINSKI: I remember that feeling of, we don't want to be taken out back. [*Laughs*.] Don't take us behind the shed like Old Yeller. I don't want to see behind the shed.

BRIAN BAUMGARTNER: I remember being conflicted, but ultimately I felt like it was the right decision. I mean, we could have gone on forever. I call it the "*ER* syndrome." After Steve left, other people could begin to leave. So it's like, "Are we going to *ER* this? Are we going for twenty seasons?"

JOHN KRASINSKI: The show totally could have gone twenty, because everybody would have slowly cycled out and we'd have just kept to the reality of it. My question is, would people want to see that? Or were we ruining the relationship with the fans?

GREG DANIELS: The *ER* version could have happened. I mean, that was for sure a possibility. There was a question of: Should the show continue with a new cast? I did work out a version of that, which is kind of where Clark Duke and Jake Lacy came in.

Clark and Jake played Clark Green and Pete Miller, respectively, the "New Guys" introduced in season nine, who some in the staff called "New Jim" and "New Dwight."

GREG DANIELS: I thought, "This is a cool way to motivate the ending, to have Jim and Dwight see a version of themselves, younger versions, and kind of feel maybe it's time to move on. Our little story is now happening with a different generation." I think everybody also wanted closure, not to be replaced with a different guy. If the show did do an *ER* kind of thing, part of me was worried about not being able to control it. Who knows when it would end? So I think we made the right choice. I think it was good to have one last hurrah.

Since this was our last season, everything was on the table. And everyone was invited to contribute.

GREG DANIELS: We'd kicked up a bunch of ideas during the whole run of the show. Often I would turn ideas down from writers and I didn't want to just say, "I don't want to do that," I would say, "That is a season six idea. Let's revisit that in three years or whatever." We had a box of ideas.

BRENT FORRESTER: It was really cool in season nine, the way the actors were invited into the writers' room more than usual. "Tell us everything you've ever wanted to do on this show." 'Cause this is our last chance. Jenna and John were invited to have serious creative input. I remember John saying something very cool and interesting. He was like, "We don't have to build an audience now. This last season is for the fans. Imagine them as your primary audience." That informed a lot of creative decisions.

Sometimes things could get weird. There was one episode set entirely on a bus: "Work Bus," directed by *Breaking Bad* star Bryan Cranston.

ELLIE KEMPER: That was the episode where we all almost died.

BRIAN BAUMGARTNER: We almost got carbon monoxide poisoning.

ELLIE KEMPER: To name one of many ways. I don't think I was enjoying it. And now in retrospect I'm like, "That was fun!" You remember that I wet my pants on that bus? I don't know what you

Jim and Dwight on top of the "Work Bus."

guys were doing, I don't know what exactly set me off, but I got a case of the giggles and I wet my pants. I had to change skirts and all of that.

We didn't get to do everything we wanted, like film in the actual town of Scranton, Pennsylvania.

ANGELA KINSEY: That's one of the things that makes me sad. I really wish they had tried.

JENNA FISCHER: Every year they would toy with the idea of taking us there, and it was just always cost prohibitive.

ANGELA KINSEY: It's a lot of moving parts to move a whole cast and crew and set up for a week.

JENNA FISCHER: I know Greg's dream was that we would shoot the St. Patrick's Day parade in Scranton. I remember one year they were really looking into this parade idea, and [the town of Scranton] agreed to move their parade two months earlier so that we could shoot an episode. They were going to have their St. Patrick's Day parade in January. The network just couldn't figure out, cost-wise, how to get the entire cast and crew there.

One thing we had to get right in this final season was Jim and Pam, which was part of the reason that Jenna and John were brought on as producers.

JENNA FISCHER: We were given those titles because we were brought in to discuss the Jim-Pam arc of the final season. We spent a lot of time up in the writers' room, talking about all the beats of that story and what it would be.

BRENT FORRESTER: What's interesting about those romantic long-term arcs, we discovered that you didn't have to advance them every episode. They could just stick around and then six episodes later they could advance. Then we had this crazy turn in season nine where we were going to split Jim and Pam up and the audience hated it so much.

The tension began in season eight with Cathy Simms (played by Lindsey Broad), a temp who replaces Pam while she's on maternity leave.

JIM: No, I'm not going to tell my nine-months-pregnant wife that I find her replacement objectively attractive. Just like I'm not going to tell my two-year-old daughter that violent video games are objectively more fun. It's true, but it doesn't help anybody.

GREG DANIELS: You needed to inject a bit of upset in the tranquility at that point and try and get the intensity back. Something I think is really important about the show is the intensity of it. You want to really *feel* something, right? And in order to make people really feel something, you gotta put a little jeopardy in.

JOHN KRASINSKI: Greg said, "We need to come up with a good Pam-Jim story line." And I said, "I think we should get borderline separated, and I think we can do it and then come back." He was so on board with that.

The episode that put Jim and Pam's marriage to the test was "After Hours," directed by Brian Baumgartner for season eight. During a business trip to Florida, Cathy makes up an excuse to spend time in Jim's hotel room, and the sexual tension is pretty apparent. According to John, there was talk that maybe Jim would go too far and actually have an affair with her.

JOHN KRASINSKI: That's the only time I remember putting my foot down. 'Cause [Greg] was saying, "You're going to actually make out with her in this scene." I remember saying things that I never thought I'd say before, like, "I'm not going to shoot it." I remember Paul Lieberstein was in the room, who I think was very much into it. He was like, "No, you'll do it." Not in an aggressive way, but it was like, he saw the benefit of doing it. I remember saying to Greg, "My feeling is there is a threshold with which you can push our audience. They are so dedicated. We have shown such great respect to them. But there's a moment where if you push them too far, they'll never come back. And I think that if you show Jim cheating, they'll never come back."

But they weren't out of the woods yet. Jim decided to pursue his dream of launching a sports marketing company in Philadelphia. But when it came to moving to Philly . . .

PAM: I don't know if I want this.

JIM: [*Long pause.*] Huh. This is a little out of left field.

PAM: Is it? I just—I liked our life in Scranton.

JIM: And I have started a business in Philadelphia.

To further complicate their relationship, another character threatened to come between them. The idea began with a suggestion from John.

JOHN KRASINSKI: I had this idea that I pitched Greg, and it came from [*Office* camera operator] Chris Workman. He had put down the camera and left it running. And I was like, "Let me see the footage." We went over the footage and it was just feet, and you could hear people talking. I said to Greg, "Dude, you should do that. Have someone in the camera crew put their camera down, not knowing that they're catching a moment, and they left to go to lunch or something." And then it ended up in the episode with the boom guy.

In a scene from the season nine episode "Customer Loyalty," Pam and Jim get into a fight on the phone. And for the first time ever, the camera pans over to the boom mic operator, who puts down his equipment to comfort Pam. As viewers, we'd never put faces to the invisible documentary crew. But in this moment, we realized that Brian the boom guy, played by Chris Diamantopoulos, had been there all along, watching everything unfold. And it was instantly clear that in those ten years, he'd developed a crush on Pam.

BRIAN: Hey, you okay?

PAM: What am I doing wrong, Brian?

BRIAN: Nothing. You're doing the best you can.

JENNA FISCHER: I did many on-camera auditions with various [actors wanting to play] Brian, and then many discussions about who exactly it should be. There was this one actor who was just phenomenal, who looked so much like John Krasinski that we had a whole discussion about whether or not he should look too much like John Krasinski.

GREG DANIELS: I don't know if Brian the boom guy was particularly liked by fans. My guess is that was maybe a misfire. People didn't seem to enjoy that. But that kind of goes back to the idea of nobody wants to see trouble with Jim and Pam. But you can't have a happy ending without an act break. And I feel like that kind of worry was

good in terms of the fans' engagement. I think they knew what was coming. They were very comfortable with the show they were getting, and I needed to worry them that maybe I was going to give them a bad ending so that they were happy when they got a good ending. That was how I was thinking. It may be overly negative, but that was my thought.

EMILY VANDERWERFF: A lot of the final season is about the question of: Are their individual dreams more important than the dreams that became *their* dreams together? There's a beauty to that idea that there's an impermanence to life. That flower growing in the cracks of the asphalt is probably going to get driven over by a car and die. But there's a beauty in seeing it all the same.

That flower in the asphalt doesn't die. Pam and Jim's relationship seems to be in jeopardy until the very end. Even in the penultimate episode—"A.A.R.M.," which aired on May 9, 2013—Pam worries that she made a mistake by asking Jim to stay in Scranton and not pursue his dreams in Philadelphia. But then he surprises her with a video that the documentary crew helped him create, a montage of their best moments together while the cameras were rolling (and sometimes catching them in unguarded moments).

There's a callback to the season two episode "Christmas Party," where Jim hides a note in a teapot, his Secret Santa gift to Pam, and then slips it into his back pocket at the last minute. We never did find out what he'd written. And when he finally hands the note to Pam in this season nine episode, telling her . . .

> **JIM:** It's from the teapot. Everything you'll ever need to know is in that note.

. . . we still don't know what it says.

MIKE SCHUR: I wrote the ["Christmas Party"] episode, with the teapot and the note and everything, and then it was in season nine and I was watching, just as a fan, and I was like, "Oh my God, it's coming back!" I had John write the note himself and I said, "Don't tell anyone what you're writing. Write whatever you want, write whatever you think Jim would write." And I don't know what he wrote. I have no idea. I've never seen it. I don't think he ever told anyone. I don't think Jen ever told anyone. I believe it's like a secret shared by the two of them and maybe the props department.

We watched their story develop over nine seasons. Remember when Greg told Ricky Gervais and Stephen Merchant that he thought of *The Office* as a love story? Writer Claire Scanlon says it was a love story that Greg took very, very personally.

CLAIRE SCANLON: The moral compass of the show was Pam, and whenever he was stuck in what Pam would do, he would actually say, "What would Susanne do here?"

Susanne being, of course, Greg's wife since 1991.

CLAIRE SCANLON: It's like the best love letter. I thought that was like the most romantic thing. He loves his wife so much, he put her in Pam. You think *The Office* is about Michael Scott, but it's also Pam. She is the person you aspire to be as good as or, if you're Jim, be good enough for. To me, the whole series is about growing up. And when a character grows up, they don't need to be in the office.

JENNA FISCHER: I think that's what it was about. Yeah, I do. I mean, it was my job as an actress to view the show through my character. But it's not lost on me that when Pam was ready to break free of Dunder

Mifflin, the show ended. So I thought it was the journey of a girl becoming a woman, finding herself, going out into the world. When we meet her, she's trapped behind this desk, and she slowly moves to sales and then finds the man she loves and starts this family. When she's ready, she fights against leaving, but when she goes, it's all over. The documentary doesn't stop when Michael leaves. They decided to stop making the documentary when Pam leaves.

The characters finally get to see the finished documentary in the "A.A.R.M." episode, when the entire Scranton branch, past and present (well, most of them), reunite at Poor Richard's Pub to watch the doc's world premiere on PBS.

JENNA FISCHER: You were gonna see how it affects these people's lives for them to see themselves in a documentary. And I think that's really great closure for the show as well.

> **PHYLLIS:** Yeah, I'm not ready for this.
>
> **STANLEY:** No one is ready for this. You can't be ready for this. We don't even know what this is.
>
> **OSCAR:** One thing we do know, nothing will ever be the same.

"Nothing will ever be the same." How right Oscar was.

KATE FLANNERY: Well, not only did I stop waiting tables, I met my boyfriend on the show. We've been together fourteen years. And I was the worst picker ever. You do not want to meet any of the guys I dated, particularly in the nineties. I was the worst. But I kind of found myself when I worked on that show, and I surrendered to accepting who I was, as opposed to what I thought I should be.

JOHN KRASINSKI: Without sounding hyperbolic, the show changed my entire life. I was twenty-three when it started, so I hadn't even really formed an identity of who I was. I have an entire lifetime that's all due to that show. I never would be doing any other thing that you've seen me do—writing, directing, acting. But as a person, it gave me this very quintessential building block that I got to stand on to build the rest of my life.

CLAIRE SCANLON: I call it "going to the University of Greg Daniels." He was our master professor.

GREG DANIELS: I think there is something very personal about the show. I mean, part of the whole docu-thing, the realism and the people and the truth and beauty and all that kind of stuff, that was everything I felt was important about writing for TV, and it was able to happen in *The Office.* So after the show was over, I was pretty spent. I was like, "God, I'm done. I don't know if I need anything else."

But there was one more episode to write. The final goodbye, if you will.

GREG DANIELS: Part of how to do good endings is there's growth for people, but almost everybody [on *The Office*] had grown. Angela was the last person who was kind of a dick, right into season nine. So I was like, "Let's put Angela through some shit. Angela deserves a happy ending."

Angela wasn't the only one getting a happy ending. (Must . . . resist saying . . . "that's what she said.") And it was just one of a few surprises in store for us in the finale.

THE FINAL TABLE READ.

12

"It's a Wrap"

THE SERIES FINALE

GREG DANIELS: I remember being on vacation and actually getting tears when I was writing [the series finale]. I felt like we came through this wonderful experience together, and I wanted it to be a together type of ending. I felt very bonded to everybody. And my impression of the wants of the cast was a grand finale with everybody together and not like a dribbling away.

For Greg, the finale was his chance to say goodbye, both to *The Office* cast he'd brought together and the characters he helped shape from the very beginning.

MATT SOHN: He kept writing more and more and more. It was almost as if he didn't want the show to end.

KEN KWAPIS: He was both very emotional about the finale, and I think he was also anxious about it. I think for him the stakes felt really high. I don't want to call it a parting shot, but this was the last chance to say what he needed to say with this series. The cast felt the same way. There wasn't a day on the finale where everybody wasn't expressing what these characters are doing with precision, because you're not going to get to do it after this.

For his final statement on *The Office*, Greg was getting the old band back together again. And one of the first to sign on was Ken Kwapis, who'd directed our pilot and some of the biggest episodes of our first few seasons, like "Booze Cruise," "Casino Night," and "Gay Witch Hunt." His last time directing for us was the one hundredth episode, "Company Picnic," back in our fifth season.

KEN KWAPIS: Greg asked me to come back for the finale. It had been two or three seasons since I worked on the show, but I think Greg wanted to create a sense of coming full circle and returning to the show's origins. I was very flattered and excited, and also very daunted. All of the characters' lives had evolved. And I felt like, even though I knew the show as a viewer, I needed to get a little deeper and get involved in the characters' lives now. I had to go back and watch things in a different way. So many of the characters who began the series in secondary roles, their roles had grown. Everybody had an interesting and complicated story to tell. How were we going to do that? Well, it took longer than a normal show, that's for sure.

Greg had been planning the finale's story, where the documentary crew returns to Scranton, since season three. Dwight is still regional manager at Dunder Mifflin. Andy is now working in the admissions office at Cornell, trying to forget the very public humiliation of his *America's Next A Capella Sensation* audition. Darryl is living in Austin, working at Jim's sports marketing company, Athlead. Stanley escaped to Florida, and Creed faked his own death to avoid prosecution (he was accused, among other things, of trafficking endangered animal meats). Kevin had been fired, as was Toby. But everyone was returning to Scranton for the wedding, an event we'd all been anticipating since Dwight and Angela first hooked up in a doghouse at Jim's barbecue.

It was a beefy script, and that's just what the actors and crew were allowed to read.

KEN KWAPIS: There were forty to fifty pages of alternate ideas that may or may not make it into the final script.

There were a lot of amazing moments that didn't make the cut, like the now infamous *Matrix* prank, where Jim tries to convince Dwight that he's living in a computer simulation—a plot borrowed from the 1999 sci-fi movie *The Matrix* starring Keanu Reeves.

DAVID ROGERS: There's a cat that walks by [Dwight's office], and then the same cat walks by again, like a glitch, and then Jenna goes . . .

PAM: Training the cat was both easier and more boring than I thought it would be.

DAVID ROGERS: And then we had Hank the security guard as Dorpheus, who's Morpheus's brother, and he's wearing the same kind of jacket as Morpheus. All of these guys were going to run out, like Hugo Weaving–type characters. [Hugo Weaving played Agent Smith, the black-suit-wearing villain in *The Matrix*.] We had a whole thing, we just never finished the visual effects. And it was too long. It was going to be the cold open, but we cut it for time.

The Office meets *The Matrix*: Now available to stream on Peacock.

We all gathered together on March 4, 2013, for the final table read. Now, usually at a table read, it would just be the cast members, a few writers, and maybe a couple of producers. But this time there were several hundred people watching, folks who had worked on the show over the past ten years and some friends and family.

MATT SOHN: I was very excited to sit and watch it [as an audience member], but ten minutes before it started, Greg said, "Hey, Matt, could you grab a camera and shoot the final table read?" And I was like, "Really?" He said, "Yeah, it'll be great for us to have." So I shot it as a cameraman and didn't get to really take it in.

The entire table read, all one hour and seventeen minutes of it, was shared online and has been watched by millions of *Office* fans. There were a lot of hilarious moments—like how Rainn was the only cast member to dress in costume, or when everybody else was crying at the end and John glanced at the camera with the perfect Jim Halpert smile—but there was also a lot of emotion.

"I'll say I love you all . . . [*voice breaks*] without falling apart."

—Greg Daniels, during his opening comments at the table reading

JENNA FISCHER: I was crying. That was really emotional. Chris Workman, our camera operator assistant, took a photo of the last table read, and Angela had it blown up and put on a wall in her house.

ANGELA KINSEY: I was starting to really feel it. Oh, they're going to be people I might not see for a really long time. Because that's what happens. You all get on other projects, and people move apart. I knew we'd stay in touch, but just getting to see people, have lunch with them, have a really great conversation by the coffee truck, you know? There's a group of our crew that were really just like family.

BRIAN BAUMGARTNER: We were a family.

ANGELA KINSEY: We *are* a family.

GREG DANIELS: It wasn't just fiction. It was such an emotional friend group that developed over the show. There's this cliché that if you do a pilot with people and the pilot doesn't go, you'll be friends for life. If it goes maybe one or two seasons, you might still be able to talk to each other. But if it goes a long time, you're gonna hate each other. I think it's very rare that it worked out the way it did for us.

"He Was Very Nervous About Lying to NBC"
The Finale's Mystery Cast of All-Stars

Ken Kwapis wasn't the only *Office* alumnus to return for the show's finale. B. J. Novak and Mindy Kaling, who'd both left the previous year to work on *The Mindy Project*, were back, as was Mike Schur, who (reluctantly) featured in the final episodes as an actor.

MIKE SCHUR: I most famously, and most annoyingly to me, played the character Mose Schrute.

BRIAN BAUMGARTNER: Oh my God. We never talked about Mose.

MIKE SCHUR: I assumed it was gonna be your first question.

BRIAN BAUMGARTNER: You weren't happy playing Mose?

MIKE SCHUR: No. I hated it. I hated every second of it. I was wearing wool clothes and had a neck beard and it was always really hot. The joke was I didn't talk, and that's not a funny joke. I had to get up at 4:30 in the morning and drive to the middle of nowhere and wear wool clothes. All I wanted to do was be back in the [writers'] room breaking stories. Shouldn't that be what you want me to do instead of this? Then the joke became with the writers, because they knew how much I hated it, "What if you're shirtless? What if you're on a seesaw? What if you're on a trampoline? What if you're running as fast as you can alongside a car, like a dog?" I was at *Parks and Rec* and they would call me and be like, "We need Mose!" And I was like, "I have a job. I have a life. I have young children." They would just make me do it. They would compete with each other to find the most humiliating possible thing they could have me do.

BRIAN BAUMGARTNER: I love that Mose existed primarily to make the writers laugh.

MIKE SCHUR: Meant specifically to make me miserable. Like riding a moped, trying to jump a bunch of cars [from the season eight episode "Garden Party"]. I don't know how to drive a moped. No one taught me how to drive. They were like, "Just get on and rev the thing." Because the point was, if I wipe out or slip and fall and break my pelvis, it'll be really funny. The subtext was always the worse this goes, the funnier it'll be.

A few new faces were added to the cast for this last episode. During the Q&A session for the fictional documentary, a woman in the audience (played by Joan Cusack) asks a question of Erin about her birth mother.

> **JOAN:** Don't you hate her? I mean, I would just imagine that you were so angry at her that you would hate her.

The employees of Dunder Mifflin come together for one final reunion.

> **ERIN:** Maybe sometimes. But not like *hate* hate. More just like, "Mom, I hate you!" And then she would say, "Go to your room, young lady."

Just as Erin realizes that the mystery woman is her mom, a man (played by Ed Begley Jr.) steps forward and takes the microphone.

> **ED:** Erin . . . Same question, but about your dad? [*They hug.*]

ELLIE KEMPER: Erin never really had a permanent family. I just loved that the writers arranged for her to meet her birth parents.

CRAIG ROBINSON: Oh my God. When Erin was reunited with her parents? I'm gonna cry thinking about that. I didn't know what was going on. It was pretty heart-wrenching.

ELLIE KEMPER: By the way, do you know I still have Joan Cusack's cardigan? I either complimented her cardigan or said it smelled good or something. This was on the last day. She took it off and gave it to me.

BRIAN BAUMGARTNER: She gave it to you to use for a minute? Or was she like, "Here, take this forever"?

ELLIE KEMPER: She said, "You can have it." But maybe she literally meant "you can borrow it," and then I never gave it back. It's very possible I misinterpreted that.

The finale's cast also included quite a few people not accustomed to being on the other side of the camera.

BRENT FORRESTER: You may have noticed that Greg cast tons of people who worked behind the scenes.

Writer Brent Forrester was one of those people, the first "audience member" to ask a question of the Q&A panel.

BRIAN BAUMGARTNER: Is that your acting debut?

BRENT FORRESTER: It certainly is.

> **BRENT:** How did it feel to see your lives played out on TV?

BRENT FORRESTER: Before I went on camera, I turned to you and said, "How do you act? I have to deliver a line. What is actiiiiiiing?!" We had two minutes for you to tell me how to deliver a line. You kind of translated it into "just imagine it's really happening."

GREG DANIELS: I put a lot of people on. Every writer was on. [Writers Amelie Gillette, Allison Silverman, Dan Sterling, and Steve Hely all asked questions during the Q&A.] My wife was on. [Susanne was the Q&A moderator.] Part of that is I wanted ordinary people, 'cause it's a documentary, and if they are a little bit uncomfortable in front of the camera, great. The boom's in the shot, the nonactor is looking weird, that all works.

Jen Celotta finally achieved her dream of playing a Schrute. Her character name was listed as "Jen Celotta Schrute" on the call sheet, and she appeared at Kevin's bar with the other Schrute relatives.

Greg Daniels and "Jen Celotta Schrute."

JEN CELOTTA: I said no to every other offer. Like Person #3 in Line and Waitress #4. I said "Schrute or nothing" for like five years. And then Greg called me, mostly because I think he wanted all his pals back for the finale. He was like, "Fine. You can be a Schrute."

BRIAN BAUMGARTNER: How'd it go?

JEN CELOTTA: Awesome. They kept wiring me, unwiring me, wiring me, unwiring me, because there was some Pam-Jim scene that needed to happen and the light was fading. So I didn't get to do my scene with dialogue that I was really excited to do. I was really, really nervous because I was like, "This is going to be terrible." But when they pulled the mic off, I was kind of sad. And then they're like, "I think we're going to get it," and they put the mic back on. And then they were like, "No, we're not." I went through an emotional roller coaster.

Kate Flannery got a moment on-screen with her favorite crew member, photographer Chris Haston.

KATE FLANNERY: They let my boyfriend, Chris, dance with me during Dwight and Angela's wedding. I'm with the tall red-faced guy. It was a nice gift, just subtle and wonderful, and it really meant a lot.

The frat boy who mocks Andy in the steak house is actually Greg's former driver/assistant, Jonah Platt. Jennie Tan, the *Office* superfan who ran the OfficeTally blog, emailed Greg and asked if she could be in the finale, and he said absolutely, giving her a speaking role in the Q&A. (She's the one who asks Jim and Pam if their relationship is "like Harry Potter.") The after-party guests who pose for a group photo include editor/directors David Rogers and Claire Scanlon, script supervisor Veda Semarne, first AD Rusty Mahmood, and prop master Phil Shea. Matt Sohn's voice made a guest appearance, as the crew member interviewing Dwight in his Dodge Challenger SRT8 during the cold open.

MATT SOHN: I was assured that they were going to replace my voice with a more masculine documentarian voice. They told me, "We'll change it in the edit." Lo and behold, there's my first and only acting credit for anything.

The woman at the warehouse party who tells Phyllis the mugs are for PBS executives is Allison Jones, casting director extraordinaire.

ALLISON JONES: Oh God, I was horrified. I remember Greg wanted everybody who had worked on the show to be in the finale. And I said I'd only do it if Phyllis was right there with me, 'cause I just don't know how to do this. So I had a line with Phyllis, and now of course I think I was terrible. The whole situation was terrifying for me.

BRENT FORRESTER: What Greg was doing was creating a kind of yearbook for himself, where he managed to photograph all these people that he cared about. So when he watches that episode, it's an emotional reunion for him too.

There was only one person missing from this group, a guy who'd been away for a few years and was sorely missed. Could we have a finale without Michael Scott?

GREG DANIELS: It was essential to me that Steve come back. So I approached him very early, and he didn't think there was enough of a reason for Michael to return. The happy Michael who had grown as a person didn't care about fame anymore.

STEVE CARELL: I felt like Michael's story had definitely ended. And when the show was wrapping up, I was reticent about coming back.

GREG DANIELS: I think he was really anxious that it not be all about him. Everybody who put in these other two years [after he left], this is the end of all of their stories. So he didn't want to do too much.

STEVE CARELL: I just didn't feel like it was right for Michael's return to take anything away from that. That was everyone else's ending. Michael had already had his. But at the same time, I felt like I should, out of respect for all of you guys and out of my love for everybody, acknowledge the ending of this thing. So that was my reasoning behind it. I wanted to do as little as possible while still being there to support it.

GREG DANIELS: He really liked the idea of coming back for Dwight's wedding, like he thought the character had learned something. He didn't need self-promotion at this point. He didn't need to come back to be on the documentary. He came back for his friend Dwight, which was like a very deep human relationship.

STEVE CARELL: I just didn't want it to take away from anything. That was my biggest fear.

KEN KWAPIS: Aside from the excitement of getting the whole gang back together again, it speaks a lot to Michael's character that he would show up for the wedding. It just emotionally felt like, with Michael's evolution over the course of the series, it made perfect sense that he wasn't going to miss that.

Dwight's wedding was the perfect excuse to bring Steve back. There was just one catch. They didn't want anyone to know about it.

DAVID ROGERS: We lied to everybody about Steve.

Well, almost everybody. Editor Dave Rogers was one of the chosen few to get the news about Steve's imminent return.

DAVID ROGERS: I remember Greg felt really bad about lying to people. He was lying to family and friends. I remember telling Greg, "Listen, it's like a surprise party. Someone asks, 'Are you throwing me a surprise party?' and you say, 'No,' and then two hours later, 'Surprise!' That's what this is. I know it's hard, but we have to keep it a secret."

They lied to everyone else, including most of the cast and crew.

MATT SOHN: I didn't tell anybody except my wife. But I tell her everything.

Okay, a few people found out.

JENNA FISCHER: John and I had been up in the writers' room talking about the finale, and we were sworn to secrecy. So I feel like I knew for a pretty long time and I knew that there was a lot of trickery going on. He was not written into the final script at the final table read. There was a scene between Dwight and Steve, but it was written between Dwight and Creed.

GREG DANIELS: We had the whole fake table read with Creed somehow taking all of Michael's lines. Yeah, that was pretty exciting. We were lying to everybody about Steve coming back. NBC didn't know. I bald-faced lied. I made the line producer lie. I said to him, "I'll take care of you if you get fired because of this." He was very nervous about lying to NBC.

KEN KWAPIS: It's still remarkable to me that it was kept a secret. I was pestered by different newspeople and, you know, honed my fibbing skills.

CLAIRE SCANLON: Greg had such a guilty conscience about it. He was like, "Oh, these people are asking if Steve's coming back and we have to lie and say no." And he's like, "Ken, don't you feel like an awful person for lying to everybody?" And Ken's like, "Not at all. I feel nothing. I don't care." [*Laughs.*]

BRIAN BAUMGARTNER: The reason they had to lie was because they didn't trust the network to keep the secret.

DAVID ROGERS: We even had the footage of Steve transferred somewhere else. Normally we do all our stuff at the Universal lot. That's where we would mix. But we took his scenes and we got them transferred somewhere else. We didn't want NBC execs to have access to the dailies because we didn't want them to run promos like, "Steve Carell returns!" Steve didn't want that.

CLAIRE SCANLON: He didn't want them to ruin it. And they would have. You *know* Steve would have been in the promos.

BRIAN BAUMGARTNER: NBC didn't notice that scenes were missing?

DAVID ROGERS: We just sent them edited versions without Steve footage. You pull out the scene of Jim and Dwight and the Steve reveal.

> **DWIGHT:** [*Turns around.*] Michael. I can't believe you came.
>
> **MICHAEL:** That's what she said.

DAVID ROGERS: And after that, there's the wedding march where Steve is just standing. I cut an alternate version for the network.

Many of the cast members didn't know that Steve would be in the episode until the day of filming.

ANGELA KINSEY: That morning, I was walking into the hair and makeup trailer and they said, "Steve's here right now. He's in hair and makeup." I was like, "You're kidding me." I mean, he was there a few hours and then he was gone. And listen, thank you, Steve Carell, 'cause you definitely gave my story line a nice ending.

The network had to wait a little bit longer.

BRIAN BAUMGARTNER: But you had to deliver it at some point.

DAVID ROGERS: We delivered it that morning. At nine A.M. that morning.

Nine A.M. on the morning of May 16, 2013, exactly nine hours before the show would air on the East Coast.

CLAIRE SCANLON: NBC never knew until the morning it aired. They were so pissed.

A very Schrute wedding.

DAVID ROGERS: I showed it to Lauren Anderson [senior VP of prime-time programming at NBC] that day and she was upset. She was pissed that she wasn't part of the secret. But the show was going to get promoted and people were going to tune in regardless. It's not like it needed, "Hey, here's the series finale of *The Office* and who knows who might show up!" [*Laughs.*]

In the end, it was exactly what the finale needed: just enough Michael Scott to make it feel like a proper family reunion.

DAVID ROGERS: There's just enough footage of him as a surprise that you're blown away. My mom cringes at Michael Scott. But she watched that finale moment, and she would rewind and rewatch the reveal of Michael showing up at least fifty times. She's like, "David, I can't stop watching it."

"I Can't Wait to Show My Daughter When She's Older"
The Last Scene

After shooting on location for almost two weeks—from an AT&T office building used for the Scranton Cultural Center to a Scottish pub in L.A. for Dwight's bachelor party to Disney's Golden Oak Ranch in Newhall, California, for Dwight and Angela's wedding—it was time for our family to come back to the office.

KATE FLANNERY: I remember trying to be as present as possible, to try and enjoy all of it. We took two weeks to shoot the finale, and I felt like it was the shiny object. We were going to all these different places, it was the shiny object to distract us from the fact that this was ending. [*Laughs.*] So the very last day was when we were actually back in the office itself. And that's when it started to feel much more intense and real. We had been on the farm, which was nuts. You couldn't even get cell service out there. It was just us. It felt like we were distracted. And now we're here, and there's a reverence and a sense of honor in finishing this lovely journey together. I remember John called us all into his trailer and we all took a shot. Do you remember? That was so awesome. That was just the actors. [*Sighs.*] So good.

PHYLLIS SMITH: That was a tough night, especially when Creed started singing.

In the final moments of the finale, Creed emerges from a closet—where he's been living—and plays an original song for his office mates, "All the Faces."

CREED BRATTON: [*Plays the first chord of "All the Faces."*] You're going to start crying already, huh?

BRIAN BAUMGARTNER: I just love that you didn't know until the table read.

CREED BRATTON: I didn't know. No one told me that I was going to get to sing my song. You know about John holding the mic? I couldn't hide the mic for the guitar itself, so then John said, "Well, I'll just hold the shotgun mic under my arm."

BRIAN BAUMGARTNER: Because he was the closest?

CREED BRATTON: He was the closest to me. He was sitting there, looking at Pam, but all the time he's holding it right there next to the sound hole.

BRIAN BAUMGARTNER: It gets me every time. It's just one of those moments. I'll never forget all of us sitting there.

CREED BRATTON: It was magical, it was really magical. I was just worried—can I get through the song? I knew it well enough. It's one of my oldest songs. I get all emotional, and sometimes I'll cry onstage when I'm singing it. When I play it live, I always say, "I'm leaving you now, just like our show left you." And they're like [*imitates a crowd crying*]. Before I even hit the first note, they're gone. [*Laughs.*] I love making people cry.

Everyone got to do one last talking head to the camera, a final reflection in the office.

CLAIRE SCANLON: There's this one Pam talking head that I can't wait to show my daughter when she's older.

> **PAM:** But it would just make my heart soar if someone out there saw this and she said to herself, "Be strong, trust yourself, love yourself. Conquer your fears. Just go after what you want and act fast, because life just isn't that long."

CLAIRE SCANLON: It was so powerful. Even thinking about it makes me misty. As a woman, you were just not seeing that on TV, you know? It was such a powerful message. And Jenna just delivered it beautifully. And now she has a little girl that she can show that to as well. Just the whole ending was sad and special, and it's all a blur because we were pulling all-nighters when we were doing it.

Pam gets the final talking head, and it's arguably one of the most emotionally powerful monologues in the entire series.

Saying goodbye to Dunder Mifflin: Filming the last talking heads.

PAM: I thought it was weird when you picked us to make a documentary. But all in all . . . I think an ordinary paper company like Dunder Mifflin was a great subject for a documentary. There's a lot of beauty in ordinary things. Isn't that kind of the point?

ANGELA KINSEY: Watching Jenna do that talking head, all of us crammed in that little room right off the main stage that had a little TV in it. We called it Video Village. It's about the size of a small restroom. And we were all crammed in on this little sofa. Right after she did it, Ed Helms said, "Circle that one for me," which is what we would say to our script coordinator, to circle the ones that we thought were great. It really felt like that was goodbye. It was goodbye to Scranton, goodbye to Dunder Mifflin, goodbye to those people.

JENNA FISCHER: They had originally scheduled [Pam's talking head] to be the very last thing we shot. Ken thought it would be a good idea, and I think it was John or somebody else who said, "Oh man, we don't all want to be wrapped." Greg said something like, "Oh yeah,

Pam taking her painting off the wall.
Finding beauty in ordinary things.

yeah, we've got to have the last scene be with everybody." So we shot my talking head, and I think you guys were all out there watching. After I finished, we shot the B-roll of me taking the picture off the wall and all of us walking out the door.

The picture, of course, was Pam's painting of the Scranton branch building, the one that Michael Scott bought at Pam's art show (all the way back in the season three episode "Business School").

JENNA FISCHER: We did it . . . I don't know how many times, five or six maybe. We were crammed in the elevator.

KATE FLANNERY: I remember Greg saying, "One more take." We were all two hours late for our own wrap party. People were texting and calling, "Where are you?" It's like no one wanted it to end.

JENNA FISCHER: There would be this moment where we'd wait to see if they were going to say, "Cut, going again," or "Cut, that's a wrap." I'm getting choked up just thinking about that. Those seconds of waiting, and every time I just wanted them to say, "Cut, going again." 'Cause I knew when they said "that's a wrap" that *that was a wrap*. That was it. I'd never shoot *The Office* again. And when they said,

"That's a wrap," I just burst into tears and started hugging the closest people I could find.

RANDALL EINHORN: Greg always talked about in the last episode, whatever it is, it'd end with "that's a wrap," and the camera would turn around and it'd be Ricky Gervais sitting there [in the director's chair]. [*Laughs.*]

KEN KWAPIS: I remember a different ending to the finale. As I recall, all the characters decide they need to take the plant that's been in the bullpen for nine seasons. Planty. Somebody suggests that Planty needs to be liberated. So everyone marches out of the office with two or three characters carrying Planty, and everyone's chanting "Planty, Planty!" The entire ensemble goes outside to the parking lot and they plant Planty. And the original ending, as Greg and I discussed, was everyone wanders away, feeling a little sad but, you know, festive. Greg's original plan was that there'd be a dissolve through to the next morning, and you just see the empty parking lot at dawn with this plant and its new home. I'm not surprised that Greg decided to end with Pam's drawing. But I must say, I loved the idea of a show that ended with a shot of an empty parking lot and a plant.

Pam's painting and Planty weren't the only ones to escape the office. More than a few props were purloined on that last day of shooting. Like Kevin's ever-present jar of M&M's.

Those who were there from the very beginning: Howard Klein, Jenna Fischer, Ken Kwapis, Greg Daniels, and Teri Weinberg.

BRIAN BAUMGARTNER: I put it on my desk at home. A year passed and I looked and realized the M&M's were going down. I'm like, "Hmm, that's odd." I'm definitely not eating them. I know how old they are. Months pass and the M&M's are going *way* down. Nobody in my house is touching them. The only solution I could come up with was my house cleaner was grabbing a handful of them.

JOHN KRASINSKI: It looks like a communal pot.

BRIAN BAUMGARTNER: So I panicked and threw them away, because I realized I was potentially poisoning her.

JOHN KRASINSKI: It's a great science experiment. M&M's lasting for a hundred years is probably something we should look into.

BRIAN BAUMGARTNER: We probably should. But I had to throw them away. The jar is still there, there are just no M&M's in it.

JOHN KRASINSKI: I took the name plate [from Jim's desk] for sure, but I wanted something that is undeniably from our set. [After the last scene was shot,] we went right to the party, and I super shadily ran back in five minutes after everybody was gone and stole the Dunder Mifflin sign.

BRIAN BAUMGARTNER: The one inside?

JOHN KRASINSKI: Yeah, from the front that we always used to walk by and do the talking heads in front of. I was a little ashamed that I didn't tell anybody, but I really wanted it. So I got to the party and I was like, "Greg, what did you take?" And he goes, "Oh, I'm really bummed. Someone took the Dunder Mifflin sign, that's what I wanted." And he goes, "Do you know who took it?" And I went, "No." [*Laughs.*] I legit to his face was like, "No, that is terrible. If you want it, that should be yours. Good news is you've got tons of other stuff." I remember he was talking about donating the set to the Smithsonian or something. He had that plan. And I was like, "He has plenty!" But then the longer I thought about it, I was like, "You lied to your TV dad."

BRIAN BAUMGARTNER: Do you have it on your wall now?

JOHN KRASINSKI: Oh yeah, it's in my office. I got it framed. It looks great.

"Don't Be Sad It's Over, Be Happy It Happened"
The After-Party

With our show officially in the can, there was just one thing left to do: the after-party.

On March 16, 2013, an "official" after-party (more for the media than ourselves) was held at the Unici Casa Gallery in Culver City, California. But afterward, we all went to a private gathering at Chateau Marmont.

KATE FLANNERY: The public party was like, eh. But the private one was fantastic. We got that suite [at Chateau Marmont], and we were all toasting Greg Daniels, who was so uncomfortable with that, but it had to be done. I remember getting up and getting to express gratitude and the things that you don't normally get to on a set. 'Cause it's all business, you know? It's fun, but it's all business.

The after-party was just the beginning. We wanted to go out with a bang, and there was no better place for that than the town with a closer connection to *The Office* than any other.

John and Oscar at Kevin's bar.

Scranton, Pennsylvania, was always a very specific, very special part of our show. Back when we started *The Office*, Ken Kwapis and Greg were devoted to getting the details exactly right, down to the Froggy 101 stickers and the Herr's potato chips in the vending machine. It was about capturing the reality, making it feel like these were real characters existing in an actual paper company in some Pennsylvania town. So it made sense that we'd go to Scranton for an all-day (and all-night) blow-out farewell party.

JOHN KRASINSKI: Brian, I remember you were instrumental in making that whole thing happen. You were sort of an ambassador for it.

BRIAN BAUMGARTNER: I said, "We have to do this."

JOHN KRASINSKI: I remember one day on set you were like, "Here's the deal. We have to do it in Scranton, nonnegotiable."

The people who actually made it happen were Michele Dempsey and Tim Holmes, cochairs of the Office Convention (which debuted in 2007 and ran for more than a decade) and the Office Wrap Party. They were both born and bred in Scranton.

MICHELE DEMPSEY: If you're from here, you don't pronounce the *T*.

BRIAN BAUMGARTNER: Right. It's *Scranon*.

The idea of doing a wrap party in "Scranon" was first suggested to Greg during the 2007 Office Convention.

TIM HOLMES: Greg was on one of the last flights out of Scranton. We had a moment with him where we just said, "If we can't do something like this every year, at least consider doing a wrap party here, you know? Just get on an airplane, party at thirty thousand feet, and let's do it here."

For the next several years, Tim and Michele would drop little notes to Greg, just reminding him of their offer. Michele even pitched it to the boss.

MICHELE DEMPSEY: I met with Steve Carell and he's like, "I'd love to be in a parade in Scranton. I hear you have a big parade." I was like, "Steve Carell, you want a parade in Scranton, you've got a parade in Scranton. You just say the word." And we did. We had a parade.

The parade ended up being part one of our massive wrap party in Scranton. It was May 4, 2013.

TIM HOLMES: Easily twenty thousand people on the streets in a very small area. Everything is looking good. I take a nice little picture of the parade route. We've got everybody in these beautiful open cars and everything. First guy we have going down is Craig Robinson. He's on the back of a pickup truck, and he just starts dancing. He starts waving the crowd to come in. "You're too far away! Come on in!" That's how it happened. We lost total control. We were literally elbowing eighteen-year-old girls away from John Krasinski.

RAINN WILSON: It was insane. It was absolutely nuts. We should do that again. If they did it now, like it would be millions of people descending on Scranton.

GREG DANIELS: Yeah, it was epic.

JOHN KRASINSKI: It was like thousands and thousands of people. I thought it was going to be the town of Scranton that came out, who thought it was cool that we shot in their town. Even that late in the game, it was still not clear to me how big our show was. I remember when *Cheers* shot in Boston, 'cause they didn't actually shoot in Boston, but they shot a scene there and we went down to see it. There were maybe a couple hundred people outside, watching them shoot this scene. Not thousands. When we came to Scranton, we had *thousands* of people, like waves of people. I remember thinking, "God, there's people back there, sixty rows back, that can't even see us."

Scranton, PA, May 2013.

KATE FLANNERY: They did not have a lot of police and there was so little security. I couldn't believe people were literally on the cars. I'm like, "Please watch your feet." And then I'm telling the guy who's allegedly in charge of my car, "Would you tell them? I don't want to be the person policing the fans." I didn't want someone to get their foot run over 'cause they're running over to a moving car.

Steve Carell didn't take part in the parade, but he did fly in for a Q&A with the cast at PNC Field, Scranton's minor league baseball stadium, which was the only venue big enough to fit everybody who wanted to be there. The episode wasn't airing for another week, so fans had no idea that Steve was even in the finale, much less that he'd show up in Scranton to be part of our goodbye.

JENNA FISCHER: The moment that Steve walked out on that baseball field, oh my gosh. The crowd just erupted.

MICHELE DEMPSEY: That stadium is what happiness looks like. That's what joy looks like.

TIM HOLMES: Joy personified.

MICHELE DEMPSEY: Everybody's faces just lit up, including Steve's. He came out and you could tell, even at that level of fame, he genuinely appreciated that those people were there.

After the Q&A, we went to the Backyard Ale House for a pint or two . . . or three.

JOHN KRASINSKI: While we were shooting, I was very disengaged to the fact that it was ending. I didn't really let my brain be like, "Oh my God, only two weeks left, only two episodes left, only two scenes left only," whatever. A big thing that helped was when we went to Scranton. Getting together and having a life experience that felt like we were memorializing it, that helped. Because I don't know if I would have been good having the finale just come out and being like, what do I do? Do I call you and be like, "What'd you think about last night's episode?" I didn't know what to do. So that really helped when we went to Scranton. That was a really special experience for me.

BRIAN BAUMGARTNER: I want to show you something.

JOHN KRASINSKI: [*Looks at photo.*] Is it me behind the bar?

BRIAN BAUMGARTNER: This is my favorite picture of me and you and Jenna, behind the bar in Scranton.

JOHN KRASINSKI: Wow.

BRIAN BAUMGARTNER: I'm now showing John a picture of him holding an iPad with the lyrics of "Roxanne" on it. That's what I was singing to a giant crowd of people.

JOHN KRASINSKI: Can you send these to me? All this stuff.

BRIAN BAUMGARTNER: Sure!

JOHN KRASINSKI: I don't know that I ever would have [bartended] if the love for the show didn't always feel so warm. It never felt fanatical or sort of mercenary or something negative.

BRIAN BAUMGARTNER: It was authentic.

JOHN KRASINSKI: Everybody in that bar felt like they respected the fact that they got to have this moment, where we were all celebrating the show together. Cast and fans alike were all together. It felt so organic, rather than like a PR stunt. There were only like fifty or sixty people in the beginning, and then by the end there were like five hundred. Obviously texts had been sent. I remember even Steve stuck around for the end. And I thought he would bail. Not because he's a bad person at all. He's the nicest person ever, but of all the actors, I imagined that he would get his ear chewed off. But he was so psyched and he kept saying like, "Dude, look at this." Imagine being at home right now and getting a text that said, "You should probably come because Denzel Washington is at the bar." If I was a kid in high school, I'd be like, *"What?!"* Steve got back behind the bar, didn't he?

BRIAN BAUMGARTNER: Yeah, he sure did.

JENNA FISCHER: Did you get super drunk at that bar? Because I really got super drunk at that bar. Ellie and I closed down that party. Ellie's always the last person to leave a party. She's very proud of this fact.

BRIAN BAUMGARTNER: Not that night. I promise you I was there as late.

JENNA FISCHER: No, you were there after me and Ellie. I remember walking back to the hotel with her, riding in the elevator with her. I turned to her and said, "You really are the last person to ever leave a party," And she said, "I like to make that my goal." I think that she thinks the best stuff happens right at the end. I like to be the first person at a party. I like to be the first guest because then I get a chance to talk to everyone as they come in, and then I can scoot out and be home and in bed at a reasonable hour. That's how I do a party.

BRIAN BAUMGARTNER: You're more grandmotherly.

JENNA FISCHER: Oh, I've always been that way, from the time I was very young. I'm waiting to be seventy-five so that I make sense to people.

MICHELE DEMPSEY: When I'm an old lady on a rocking chair in the old folks' home, I'll still be telling people about that night. I heard Steve Carell say to a little group of people at the wrap party, "Don't be sad it's over, be happy it happened." When I'm on my rocking chair, it's how I'm going to feel about my life too. *The Office* gave us this and that's priceless. It makes ordinary people feel like they have meaning, right? That we all are important.

Is *that* the reason people still watch *The Office* today, so many years after it's stopped being Thursday night "appointment TV"? Why does it still mean so much to people? The show may've ended, but our relationship with it was far from over.

THE OFFICE CAST LOOKS BACK ON A SUNDAY AFTERNOON IN SCRANTON.

13

"Beauty in Ordinary Things"

THE LEGACY OF *THE OFFICE*

BRIAN BAUMGARTNER: 57.1 billion. That's how many minutes people watched *The Office* in 2020, according to Nielsen. That's about four billion more minutes than people watched the series in 2018.

PAUL LIEBERSTEIN: What? Holy . . .

There haven't been new episodes of *The Office* since 2013. But somehow, it's become a bigger cultural phenomenon than it ever was during its initial run. A survey by research firm Maru/Matchbox found that more people signed up for a video streaming service in 2021 to watch *The Office* than any other licensed TV show, including heavy hitters like *Grey's Anatomy* and *The Simpsons*.

RAINN WILSON: Oh my God, that's nuts. People just need to get a life. Listen, people, I love you all. Thank you for watching *The Office*. But there are so many other great shows out there.

Rainn is right, but rarely do even the best of those shows achieve anything approaching the success of *The Office*. Consider this: Every TV pilot made has only a 6 percent chance of airing on television, according to *Variety*. Of those that do get picked up—there are roughly five hundred original, scripted TV series made every year—only 35 percent will air longer than a single season. An even lower percentage of shows get syndicated. And of those that do get a second life in repeats, just a handful continue to get discovered by younger audiences.

So how did *The Office* pull off this hat trick? How does a show about a tiny paper company in Scranton, Pennsylvania, made during an era when you still had to memorize phone numbers and a subscription to Netflix involved using a mailbox, become a timeless phenomenon?

We're still trying to figure it out. We're still shocked when complete strangers, some who were barely out of diapers when *The Office* first aired, walk up to us like we're old friends.

BRIAN BAUMGARTNER: I can't go into a bar without getting multiple drinks [bought for me]. It comes to the point where I have to say, "No, I'm good. I gotta stop now, guys." I am such a huge sports fan, and I'll play in these celebrity golf tournaments and meet all of these athletes who want to hang out with me because of the show. It's just so crazy.

PHYLLIS SMITH: At least people call you Kevin. When people shout "Phyllis," I have to think for a moment: "Have our paths crossed? Do I know you?" Did I go to school with them or what? But in reality, they do know me, because I've been in their bedrooms and their living rooms and their kitchens, before they go to work and as they go to sleep. We are a part of their lives, you know? I'll meet someone and they'll ask, "We've met before, right?"

GREG DANIELS: You guys in the cast feel it more than I do, 'cause I walk around and it doesn't come up all the time. But if I walk around with Paul [Lieberstein], it comes up. I was just walking down the street with Paul the other day and I heard this squeal of car brakes. Somebody turned his car around and did a U-turn 'cause he saw Paul out of the corner of his eye, and he jumped out to tell him how much the show meant to him.

ANDY BUCKLEY: I have a ton of fun with it now. I purposely walk around wearing my David Wallace glasses or a Dunder Mifflin shirt. Like if I'm doing a corporate speaking thing, I know why I'm there. It's not 'cause of my incredible *Silk Stalkings* performance. It's so much more fun for photos if I'm in the Dunder Mifflin shirt.

We've had a few celebrity fans over the years. And like so many others, they'd discovered us long after the show ended. John Legend joked on Twitter in 2018 that he once invested in the Michael Scott Paper Company. Jennifer Garner and her kids binged *The Office* in 2020, and she shared an Instagram video of her crying after watching the finale, saying that the show "gave me some really big feelings." And then there's a certain beloved U.S. president, one Barack Obama.

OSCAR NUÑEZ: Steve came in with this letter and he was like, "You guys might want to read this." It said something like, "Dear Steve, I just want you to know that at the White House, *The Office* Thursday is family night." It was a letter that the president sent to Steve Carell because the Obamas are fans of the show.

BRIAN BAUMGARTNER: That's kind of a big deal.

OSCAR NUÑEZ: Steve said he showed it to his children, and they were little and they're like, "Can we touch?" And he's like, "Nope, just look. Just look." [*Laughs.*]

JOHN KRASINSKI: It's the difference between fans who feel like they're a part of something and fans who just watch something. There are very few things that I watched when I was a kid that I felt connected to. It was more like, "Oh, I liked the movie *E.T.*," but I never felt like the people [who starred in the movie] and I shared a life moment together. If I'd ever met Chris Farley, I would have said that, 'cause I watched *Tommy Boy* so many times, and he didn't know he was my best friend, but he was my best friend. Probably the closest I ever came was meeting Conan O'Brien when I was his intern.

John, along with Ellie Kemper, Mindy Kaling, and Angela Kinsey, was an intern on *Late Night with Conan O'Brien.*

JOHN KRASINSKI: Because I was like, "I think you're the most talented person I've ever come in contact with." I think that our fans see me, and instead of going up to an actor to get a picture, they're actually seeing a friend of theirs that just happens to be in the same city. No one looked at Jack Ryan—

John began playing the iconic Tom Clancy character in 2018 on Amazon Prime.

JOHN KRASINSKI: —and was like, "Oh my God, my buddy Jack Ryan! You're an actor, I didn't realize." They do think that with Jim. They think they know him. I had one woman who insisted we went to school together. I was like, "I don't think we did." And she went, "Yes, we did." So I went, "Where did you go to school?" She said some school and I went, "I did not go to that school." And she went, "Yes, you did!" I was like, "Okay," and then I left.

"She's Got a Dwight in Her Class"
Why Kids Can't Get Enough of *The Office*

BRIAN BAUMGARTNER: Do your kids watch *The Office*?

STEVE CARELL: Never.

BRIAN BAUMGARTNER: No? Come on.

STEVE CARELL: I completely get it. Like, why would you? That's just weird to watch your dad do that thing. Although my daughter's a freshman in college, and she's taking a course in communications and [*laughs*] the subject matter is the paradox of comedy or something. They are studying an episode of *The Office*, which she's never seen. She texted me like, "That was really funny." [*Laughs.*] Oh, thanks, hun. But she said, "It's so weird. I never thought I would be studying something that my father was in for a course."

Kids aren't just learning about *The Office* from their college curriculum. They're discovering it on their own. Which is kind of confounding, given that they're growing up in a world that couldn't be more different from our show. Why are younger generations so fascinated with a TV show about working adults who somehow survived without smartphones or social media?

Steve Carell looks down at his *Office* family with pride.

STEVE CARELL: That was always a shock to me. When we were making the show, I thought, "Well, people who've worked in an office environment will have a context. I think they'll have something in here they can relate to." But the fact that not only teenagers but also preteens have taken to it? It's shocking that these younger generations . . . God, I sound like I'm eighty years old. But it almost seems to have been passed down from their older siblings. Like, "I'm seventeen, I'm going to college next year. Hey, twelve-year-old brother or sister, check this out."

ANGELA KINSEY: My daughter is eleven and she'd never seen the show. She grew up on the set. She was born in season five. She was there every day. I had a little baby nursery trailer right on the set. But when she came back to school this year—she's in fifth grade—she said, "Mom, everyone in my class watched *The Office* over the summer. Everyone." I see kids I've known since kindergarten in Dunder Mifflin shirts. She was like, "Can I watch it now?" I was like, "Okay, all right, fine." I think there's some content that might not be appropriate, but we'll muscle through it together. She's into it and my stepsons are into it. They're eleven and nine. They love it. And I feel like they see me in a different way now. My own kids are like, "Wow, you did that?" I'm like, "What do you guys think I do when I leave here?" "Mom, you did something other than get me some Goldfish [crackers] and pretzels? Wow."

JOHN KRASINSKI: A four-year-old came up to me at the airport and was like, "It's my favorite show." And I was like, "Do you get any of it?" And they're like, "Yeah, it's totally universal." [*Laughs.*]

BRENT FORRESTER: I watched the whole thing, from beginning to end, with my daughter when she was fourteen, and that gave me an emotional connection to the show that was even greater than what I had when I was there. It makes me very proud to be part of that. It makes my daughter look up to me just a little bit, which is extremely unusual and rare. I'll take it.

OSCAR NUÑEZ: When we started doing those Office Conventions, people were coming in with eleven-year-olds and they're like, "Look, my kid watches the show." Sometimes it was eight-year-olds. Is that good? And they're like, "Yeah, they love it. It's fine."

RAINN WILSON: Here's where I feel really bad sometimes. I had a little girl come up to me and say, "I've watched every episode of *The Office* fifteen times." This girl was like fourteen and her mom was there. I was like, "You are the world's worst mother. Your daughter could have learned Italian. She could have learned to play the tuba. You literally could write a doctoral thesis in that many hours. That is crazy."

CLAIRE SCANLON: My peers didn't watch [*The Office*] when I was working on it, but they're watching it now with their children because their children are making them. Nine-year-olds love Dwight, and they grow into it and then they want to be Jim and Pam. It's like role-playing.

GREG DANIELS: At first, I didn't understand why it would be appealing to kids. But it's actually really similar to the experience of being a kid in school. Your teacher is your boss, and you're sitting at your little desk next to somebody else who you may or may not like, and you're compelled to listen to whatever boring crap is coming down from above.

> **KEVIN MALONE:** Sometimes I feel like everyone I work with is an idiot. And by sometimes I mean all times. All the times. Every of the time.

KATE FLANNERY: Michael Scott, he's the boss, but he's like the teacher. I think kids can relate to having to sit next to someone that they didn't necessarily pick but they're kind of stuck with for years.

CLAIRE SCANLON: You see a lot of the same dynamics in school. There's a bully and there's someone who stands up for the little guy. It's all played out in *The Office*.

STEVE CARELL: They're archetypes. And even though [these characters] are grown and some are middle-aged, teens can relate to those archetypes.

EMILY VANDERWERFF: I talked to a twelve-year-old girl who loves this show. She's watched it four or five times, and it's a thing she can watch with her parents. It's a thing she can watch with her friends. But one of the things she told me was, she's got a Dwight in her class. These relationships scale. These relationships are in her seventh grade class and they're in a nursing home. Literally everybody alive has a relationship like that with somebody. As soon as you get past the very basic "being a little kid and only caring about your own needs" phase and start to realize other people exist and have their own needs, then you start to realize there are Dwights in the world, and Michaels and Jims and Pams and Ryans. That specificity applies to all age groups.

VEDA SEMARNE (SCRIPT SUPERVISOR): The characters are kind of misfits. And they're all very flawed, which gives you that kind of cringe feeling when you watch it. Especially Michael Scott and his obvious need for love and respect from everyone. You can identify with them and in different ways. I think that's what kids relate to, you know? They're all dealing with pretty difficult issues and identity issues and things that kids have to deal with, finding the right friends and being part of things or being left out of things. All those issues are important to kids.

Love and Tragedy: The happy couple (and Michael Scott).

BRIAN BAUMGARTNER: I think the show appeals to young people who feel marginalized either because of their age or bullying or they don't quite fit in. *The Office* appreciates people of all shapes and sizes and denominations and creeds. And it does it in a funny way.

AMY RYAN: I have friends who tell me their kids watch it for its soothing effects. If they're having a bad day, they go and pop in *The Office* and it lifts them.

GREG DANIELS: The society we live in is so often winner-driven and celebrity-driven and rich-people-driven. To have this slice of ordinariness matters.

EMILY VANDERWERFF: In the last fifteen-ish years, American capitalism has gone insane. Everything is awful now. And I say this from a position of relative privilege, but we live in a world where it feels like capitalism no longer cares about the average worker. *The Office*, when it started, was a show that captured the drudgery of workaday life. But it's become an escapist fantasy. There are no Dunder Mifflins left. If you made *The Office* today, you'd have to come up with some other business that they all work at. People ask why this show is so popular with Generation Z. I don't know that they're cognizant of this, but if you're seventeen years old, you're going to graduate into a workforce that doesn't have jobs like this for you. It just has a lot of gig economy work, driving Ubers or renting out your apartment on Airbnb, stuff that is by definition unstable and does not provide firm ground to stand on. Say what you will about Dunder Mifflin. I bet all of those people had a solid health plan. Now we live in a world where Dunder Mifflin seems like a great place to go. It seems like Oz, and that's weird and fucked up and says something about our society. It also says something about our society that this show is so popular that we can be like, "Oh, look at this escapist fantasy about working at a paper company."

"It Was Built for Streaming"
Why Fans Come Back to *The Office* Again, and Again, and Again, and . . .

A big reason *The Office* appeals to so many generations, young and old, is that it never felt like a show that belonged to a certain era. Sure, it had a few pop culture references—"Lazy Scranton," the *Saturday Night Live* "Lazy Sunday" homage, and Michael declaring, "I am Beyoncé, always"— but watching it never seems like unlocking a time capsule from a bygone decade.

RAINN WILSON: You watch other shows like *Desperate Housewives* and it looks so dated. But in *The Office,* no one's fashionable. People are wearing that same kind of Sears and JCPenney crap in Scranton now as they were twenty years ago, as they were forty years ago. You can't even tell what time it's set in. Is it contemporary? Is it the nineties? Is it the eighties? Is it ten years ago? You can't really tell. There are a few Obama jokes in there, but there's a timelessness that Greg wove into *The Office.*

KEVIN REILLY: There were no hairstyles. There's no "Oh, that was an eighties outfit," or "Ooh, look at that palette or music choice." *The Office* was just drab. And the drab then is the same as the drab today.

MIKE SCHUR: We used to try constantly to put pop culture references in the show. And Greg was like, "No, this show needs to feel timeless. Like it could be happening at any moment in time from the seventies until like 2050." And I remember thinking at the time, "All right, you're pretty high on yourself there, bud, thinking that this show is going to matter [in the future]." And now look, it's twenty years later and it matters just as much. My son doesn't know that that show isn't on the air. He was born in season four and he's now eleven, and he just watched every single episode and every kid in his grade watches every single episode. It doesn't feel dated.

PAUL FEIG: *Monty Python and the Holy Grail* is one of my favorite movies, because every scene that comes up, you're like, "This is my favorite scene. Oh wait, no, *this* is my favorite scene." That's what *The Office* is. You love these characters and you remember these moments and you can watch them over and over again, because they're not trying too hard and they're not *joke, joke, joke*. The humor is behavioral and beautiful and relatable.

PAUL LIEBERSTEIN: In a way, it was built for streaming. The best streaming is lightly serialized. We were doing that with no knowledge of what streaming was. That was just how we thought the show would be best. We told stories over years and we told them in mini-arcs.

Mini-arcs are basically stories within the series that play out over the course of four to six (and sometimes more) episodes, like Jim's transfer to the Stamford branch or Holly's brief tenure as Scranton's new HR rep.

PAUL LIEBERSTEIN: As a viewer, if I'm watching something on streaming and I have to wait too long for a conclusion, I get really angry and I'm out. *The Office* had these six-episode arcs. [Each season] was kind of built around, "Okay, what's happening over these six episodes?" Which is perfect for streaming. It's very satisfying to watch six episodes, see the beginning of something and see the end of it. Like Michael Scott Paper Company, where he takes a journey over six episodes. By the end of it, we're back to where we were.

BRIAN BAUMGARTNER: You can pick up where you left off, and it's not like you're scrambling to catch up with the story.

PAUL LIEBERSTEIN: Exactly. There are a few different ways people are watching now. Sometimes you watch an episode or a series of episodes, sometimes you have a certain amount of time and you stop mid-episode. We had very few of those bullshit forced resolution scenes where you got to the end and now this has to happen, you know? So even if you have just three minutes left in an episode . . .

BRIAN BAUMGARTNER: It's not going to be some tedious "we sure survived that crazy thing" wrap-up.

PAUL LIEBERSTEIN: Right. It's still going to be enjoyable.

Jim's "mini-arc" at the Stamford branch.

MIKE SCHUR: We did two hundred episodes. There aren't many shows that do that anymore. That era is over. How many more shows are going to even do a hundred? We're in an era of six-episode, eight-episode, ten-episode seasons. Even shows that last ten years, they'll do eighty episodes or something. I think the reason why so many people have discovered *The Office* and have really sat with it is because you can watch a new episode every night.

EMILY VANDERWERFF: There's a rhythm to *The Office*, there's a quietude to it. There's something soothing about it, like watching one of those little clackers go back and forth. I'm gonna use a word that a lot of people will think is a criticism, though it's absolutely not, but there's a predictability to it.

RAINN WILSON: Greg always said, "It's 90 percent funny, but 10 percent truthful and moving." You don't want to go more than 10 percent, 'cause then it starts to get sentimental and maudlin. But if it has that 10 percent per episode of reality, of truth and real connection, then that grounds the show. That gives it a lot of heart. Also, the style of the comedy never tells you when to laugh or even that you *have* to laugh. There's no laugh track. You can choose to laugh at something or not. Maybe the third time you watch it, you find it hysterical and you hadn't the previous time. There's a great amount of detail in there, so it stands up to repeated watchings.

MIKE SCHUR: You can't end an episode without learning something new about someone. In the "Christmas Party" episode with the Yankee swap gift exchange, my original idea for a present for Angela was one of those Joel Osteen self-help-y Christian books. And there was no story with Angela's gift. It was just like, what would someone get Angela? And Greg was like, "It should be something else." And I was like, "Okay, why?" He was like, "'Cause we already know that she's a religious person. You're not learning anything new by that gift." And I was like, "God, I'm so annoyed right now. There are so many things going on in this episode and this isn't even a story point, and you're telling me to *rewrite* it?" Then someone else mentioned those ugly photos where they take babies and dress them up in clown costumes or whatever. And I was like, "I can imagine Angela being into that." It ended up being a key plot point later on [in the season two episode "Conflict Resolution"].

ANGELA: I got this poster for Christmas and I feel I want to see it every day. It makes me feel like the babies are the true artists, and God has a really cute sense of humor.

MICHAEL: Come on. Seriously, that?

OSCAR: I don't like looking at it. It's creepy and in bad taste, and it's just offensive to me. It makes me think of the horrible, frigid stage mothers who forced the babies into it. It's kitsch. It's the opposite of art. It destroys art, it destroys souls.

MIKE SCHUR: That's why you do it this way. Even if it doesn't matter in that episode, it might end up mattering a whole lot twelve episodes later. I think people settle into the show and watch it because it feels like you're eating the richest dessert a tiny bit at a time. You can really follow people's psychologies and their lives as they grow over the course of nine years. A show like that is very rare.

KATE FLANNERY: There are so many subtle things, you can watch it a million times and see different things that you didn't see before if you weren't paying attention. There's so many Easter eggs and weird little things. Like the "Weight

Sunscreen is like a joke: A little goes a long way.

Loss" episode [from season five] where people still have questions about Meredith's skin. There's a whole story line where Meredith got sun poisoning on a fishing boat and it got worse and worse as the week went on and it never got explained. I remember Steve [Carell] thought it was brilliant that they just didn't worry about explaining it. 'Cause how many times do you work with people that you're not that close to and something's going on and you're like, "I don't even want to know." You know what I mean?

CLAIRE SCANLON: I always get so frustrated working on anything new where they underestimate the sophistication of the audience. I feel like so many shows are like, "We need to signpost that." Or in other words, you need to announce to the viewer what you're gonna do. Show them what you did and then remind them what you just did. You're going to signpost it all the way through. It's always better to be a step ahead of the audience. They will catch up. They are smart and they can sniff out phoniness so quickly, you know? Most of the stuff I've done in reality TV, you can't cheat. You can't fabricate something. You can't make someone into a bad guy who isn't. Your audience is way too sophisticated. The same is true for scripted television. If you're pandering, it never works.

JOHN KRASINSKI: It wasn't born out of a fad or a trend or where things were headed. It was its own thing and remained its own thing. And it never changed, in my opinion. Greg never changed the DNA of the show to reflect what people are into. His whole thing was like, "We'll just keep the show in our small pond. And if you want to come and visit our small pond, you can visit any time." I think my taste level became solidified on that show, probably without me even knowing. I see what's possible now in everything I do. I never would have directed and written [the 2018 feature film] *A Quiet Place* if it wasn't for Greg. Because I remember him saying to me one day, "Don't look at this as a comedy. Just be in the moment. Your character doesn't know he's funny. *We* get to decide. So we're not making a comedy, we're just telling the best story we can. And if you end up laughing at what we're doing, great. If you cry at a moment with Pam, great. But just tell the best story." When I got offered *A Quiet Place,* I was like, I don't know anything about horror. I remember actually sitting down before I wrote the script and saying, "I'm not gonna make a horror movie. I'm not gonna make a genre movie. I'm going to tell the best story I can about this family. And if you end up getting scared at moments, that's on you. Because my only job is to tell you the most concise and strong story I can. And then every emotional thing that you feel is coming from you and how you're experiencing it." I never would have had the guts to do that, because I would've said the same thing I said to Greg that day, which was, "I don't want to mess this up. I want to make sure I'm really funny in the scene for you." And he was like, "No, no, no. I don't want you to be funny. I want to tell the best story and let other people decide whether the scene is funny."

GREG DANIELS: The approach we took valued character comedy and behavior as opposed to jokes. Jokes kinda don't last that long. But you fall in love with the characters and you always have something to see. It gave so much re-watchability to it. You can watch the entire show looking at one character, and it's interesting 'cause they're doing their own thing, being funny in the background.

PAUL FEIG: There are few shows in my life that you just want to watch over and over again. *Taxi* was that way. *All in the Family* and *Seinfeld.* But *The Office* is always going to be that because it's just comfort food, you know? It's so relaxing to sit with these people. I love the fact that we didn't have any score. There was no music on the show. Our sound mixes were always about like, where do we put the phone ringing? We were always placing phones ringing in the background. It just became this really low-key, relaxing, happy place that you can go to.

ANGELA KINSEY: You turn it on and you know where everyone's going to be. You know where Pam is at reception, you know where everybody sits in accounting. Those people become like your extended family. And you're just sort of checking in with them. I have people tell me all the time that they put it on at the end of a long day or a bad day, or maybe if there's something they're anxious about. They put it on and it's just comfort.

ED HELMS: Dunder Mifflin is kind of aggressively mundane, but when you look closely and you get in the hearts of these people, it's enormously complex and beautiful and familiar all at once.

ALLISON JONES: I think everybody can relate to working in an office like that and not everybody can relate to [the TV show] *Friends*. You can insert yourself into *The Office* very easily. There must be some comfort in that.

JEN CELOTTA: I read that [pop superstar] Billie Eilish has watched the entire series, every episode, at least eleven times, and she has it on the background sometimes when she's in her tour bus.

An aggressively mundane "Costume Party" at Dunder Mifflin.

"Most of the Things That I Know Are Because of *The Office*"

BILLIE EILISH ON HER STRANGE *OFFICE* ADDICTION

Billie Eilish, a woman who was four years old when the British version of *The Office* premiered, is an American pop singer with several number one singles, including the theme to the James Bond movie *No Time to Die*. In 2020, she was the youngest artist ever (at eighteen years old) to win four of the top Grammy categories—record, song, album of the year, and best new artist—in a single year. And in 2019, she recorded "My Strange Addiction," a song that included snippets of dialogue from our seventh-season episode "Threat Level Midnight." The episode, you may recall, is when we finally see the filmed version of Michael's action-adventure screenplay *Threat Level Midnight*, eleven years in the making. Some of the dialogue included in Billie's song include Steve (as Michael Scott, playing secret agent Michael Scarn) saying, "No, Billy, I haven't done that dance since my wife died."

Brian Baumgartner and Steve Carell got on a Zoom call with Billie (and, we'd soon learn, her mom) to find out why a Grammy-winning teen is so fascinated with a paper company in Scranton, Pennsylvania.

STEVE CARELL: *It's so nice to actually say hi.*

BILLIE EILISH: *Oh my God. It's so crazy to hear your actual voice and look at your face. It's crazy. Fucking crazy. Wow.*

BRIAN BAUMGARTNER: *Who is your favorite character on The Office?*

BILLIE EILISH: *That's a trap.*

STEVE CARELL: *Just say Dwight and get it over. Do it! Dwight is everyone's favorite.*

BILLIE EILISH: *Honestly, I think it's Michael.*

BRIAN BAUMGARTNER: *That's fair.*

STEVE CARELL: *Terrible taste.*

BRIAN BAUMGARTNER: *He only did seven seasons, but that's fine.*

BILLIE EILISH: *Oh my God. This is crazy.*

STEVE CARELL: *Where are you? Are you in L.A.?*

BILLIE EILISH: *I am. I am sort of in L.A.*

BILLIE'S MOM: *We're in Palmdale.*

BILLIE EILISH: *This is my mom, by the way.*

BILLIE'S MOM: *Hi.*

**BRIAN BAUMGARTNER
AND STEVE CARELL:** *Hiiii!*

BILLIE'S MOM: *Billie watches your show all the time.*

BRIAN BAUMGARTNER: *Is it your strange addiction? Is The Office your strange addiction?*

BILLIE EILISH: *Definitely. That's why I had to use [your voices] in that song. Because I was telling the truth. It was a fact. [Laughs.] This is crazy. I don't know if you guys understand how huge this is for me. Thanks for talking to me.*

STEVE CARELL: *Well yeah, it's a pretty big deal that you get to do this. I'm just saying. [Laughs.] It's such a pleasure.*

BRIAN BAUMGARTNER: *When did you start watching The Office? How old were you?*

BILLIE EILISH: *I think I was twelve.*

BRIAN BAUMGARTNER: *Twelve. And why?*

BILLIE EILISH: *I've seen it fourteen times now, all the way through, which is really crazy. And honestly, every time I watch it, because I've been getting older, I understand something new. If you ask my parents, most of the things that I know are because of The Office.*

STEVE CARELL: *No, no, don't say that.*

BRIAN BAUMGARTNER: *Don't say that. Oh no.*

STEVE CARELL: *That's terrible. No, no!*

BILLIE EILISH: *It's fucked up. It's fucked up. What can I say?*

STEVE CARELL: *This is what we've created!*

BRIAN BAUMGARTNER: *I know. What has happened? No!*

STEVE CARELL: *No. Dammit. No!*

BILLIE EILISH: *But like my parents will reference things that I only understand because of The Office. There are literally words, Steve, that you said in the show that I thought were real words, but they were fake.*

STEVE CARELL: *I know what you're thinking. "Dinkin flicka." [Laughs.]*

BILLIE EILISH: *Definitely that one.*

In "Casino Night," "dinkin flicka" was one of the phrases that Darryl taught to Michael "to help him with his interracial conversations."

BRIAN BAUMGARTNER: *Oh, that's amazing. So you've watched [the entire series] fourteen times?*

BILLIE EILISH: *Yeah.*

BRIAN BAUMGARTNER: *Have you started the fifteenth time yet?*

BILLIE EILISH: *I have not. I had to take a break so that it's like, it's all fresh.*

[Everybody laughs.]

STEVE CARELL: *You might want to take ten or twelve years so it's really fresh. I have not actually seen all the episodes of The Office. So you have me by like fourteen.*

BRIAN BAUMGARTNER: *Do your friends watch it?*

BILLIE EILISH: *Yeah. My best friend is the same level of obsessed with it as I am.*

BRIAN BAUMGARTNER: *What is it that you love about it enough to watch it fourteen times?*

BILLIE EILISH: *I dunno. I feel like it's not stressful. So many shows, you really have to pay attention closely to understand. I don't know if it's because I've seen it so many times. I'll set my phone down—I watch it only on my phone, like my tiny little phone. I don't ever watch it on a TV or anything. I put my little phone on a table and then I clean my room or I'll leave the room or I'm in the shower.*

STEVE CARELL: [Laughs.] *That's the best way to do it, put it on and then leave the room.*

BILLIE EILISH: *I'm listening, though, because I've seen it so many times that I can fully envision exactly what the scene is. My brain is like, "Oh yeah, I know what's going on." Even if I'm on a plane and I see three rows ahead of me somebody watching The Office, I can tell what scene it is and what episode it is from what [the characters] are wearing.* [Laughs.]

BRIAN BAUMGARTNER: *Does it give you comfort?*

BILLIE EILISH: *Totally. It makes me feel like, I don't know, it's like a safe space. I think it takes me away from the reality of my life.*

"Better Than Any Medicine"
How *The Office* Comforts, Heals, and Makes Viewers Feel Part of a Family

PAUL FEIG: It just makes you feel good about your life and it makes you feel good about other people. It makes you tolerant of other people in a weird way, because you're watching such a diverse group of folks that have no reason to be together, other than the fact that they are trapped within this building. You don't choose to be there, other than I guess you could leave if you want it, but you can't really. There's just something very lovely about that. People will be watching this show for as long as the planet exists.

EMILY VANDERWERFF: There's another thing about this show that kept coming up when I talk to people who are fans. They were like, "This is my go-to for when I have anxiety. This is my go-to for when I have depression. This is my go-to for when I'm struggling." Real life feels huge all the time. Real life is hard to deal with for anybody, and that probably goes for Steve Carell too, even though he's a very successful actor and seems like a very nice man. But I'm sure he has days when he just doesn't want to get out of bed. I talked to so many people who said, "When I am anxious, this is the show I turn to." It's another world to escape into.

JENNA FISCHER: I am most proud of the show being a thing that comforts people when they are in pain or suffering grief. I hear so often from people who are sick or have lost a child; they tell me that the first time they laughed after this loss in their life was watching our show. I am so honored to be a part of something that brings comfort to people. And I get it because I have suffered losses in my life and I have turned to entertainment to get me through. Hearing that people just have it on in the background and that it's part of their home life as they cook dinner and things like that—it's just deeply meaningful to me. All I wanted was a job. I just wanted to be a working actor. Never in my wildest dreams did I ever think that I would be part of something so special and so meaningful. I try to live up to that responsibility.

BRIAN BAUMGARTNER: I was recently doing something in South Carolina and I went to the children's hospital there. They asked me to come and say hi to some of the kids, and of course I said yes. I was there with a few other people and we were going from room to room. There was someone there who was kind of prepping, going in and making sure that we were allowed to go into the next room, that there wasn't a nurse there or whatever. She came back and told me, "Okay, this next room . . . he doesn't know that you're here. And we haven't told his mom and dad." I go walking in and there's this boy on the bed and there are tubes. I mean, he's clearly suffering a tremendous amount, and he's lying there in bed and he's watching *The Office* on TV.

JENNA FISCHER: And then you're going to walk in?

BRIAN BAUMGARTNER: They didn't even tell me! I walked in the room and I saw what was happening and saw his face and I went, "Yeah." I mean, this is what it's about, right? This is why I'm doing this and not theater anymore.

CRAIG ROBINSON: People have these stories of, you know, "My mother had cancer and we watched *The Office* and we got through this." It'll be these incredible heart-wrenching stories like, "Our family doesn't talk, but we bond over *The Office*." Why the hell is this show still relevant after being off the air for so many years? I think that's a big part of it. People really connect through the show with family members or whoever.

GREG DANIELS: We used to have a lot of visitors from different Make-A-Wish type things. I always thought that was indicative of something. People with all these health problems would get so much solace out of the show. I always was proud of that, but I didn't really know what it was. But it seems like it was a valuable thing to have made. We did a good job making it, and people like it and it provides something good for them.

CLAIRE SCANLON: I'm not a religious person, but I can see why people go to the church of *The Office*. Because I do think it espouses the best version of religion. It's not about getting rich. It's not about being popular. It's about being happy and being kind to others. I mean, do you see people being so kind to each other on other shows?

RAINN WILSON: We weren't trying to do this, but I do believe that *The Office* was a spiritual show. When I talk to people, any time I'm recognized, people will say, "Thank you for the show. My parents were getting a divorce or my little brother had cancer, and we would watch it together and we would cry. It got me through some of the hardest times." Every day there are people writing on my Facebook, "[*The Office*] got me through such hard times. I was going through depression, I had anxiety and mental health issues, and *The Office* got me through that." We made something that ultimately made people laugh and got their minds off their problems. That's really what people need now. At the end of the day, it's not a cynical show. It's people that do love each other, as weird as it is, and it's been a positive force in the world.

BRENT FORRESTER: A great writer named Mike Reiss, an original *Simpsons* guy, told me that the secret to every hit network TV show is the subtext of family. I believe that's true, and it's definitely true of *The Office*. And it's true of the actors on *The Office* as well. You can feel that love that they have for each other and the respect they have for each other's performances. There are certain shows that make you feel good about liking them. People liked *Frasier* more than they actually liked it because it made them feel smart. *The Office* has a little bit of that. It has to do with behavior over banter, and a priority on realism. These were phrases that flowed through the *Office* writers' room and are the hallmarks of good taste in drama and comedy. So the young people know that they have good taste by liking it.

RAINN WILSON: All great television is about unlikely families, and *The Office* is the most unlikely family. And you love to be with that family. There's something really soothing about showing up, hearing that theme song.

OSCAR NUÑEZ: No matter what Michael Scott did, he was still protected and loved in the office. No matter how awful he was, we knew his little brain was broken and he really didn't mean it. We all protected each other through all our foibles, the backstabbing, the insanity. There were always people looking out for each other. [My character] made out with Angela's fiancé, and I was still, "Angela, you can stay with me." Dwight was crazy, but Jenna loved him and took care of him. They were BFFs. So those things were very sweet. The only relationship that never worked was Michael and Toby. Toby can never win Michael Scott over. Other than that, it was fine.

CLAIRE SCANLON: It's giving equal time to lots of people who don't normally get that. I mean, just the fact that the show's moral compass is a woman. Everyone's got their stories, whether you're a Latino

An *Office* family "Fun Run."

gay man or an African American heavyset man or heavyset woman. What other prime-time show had some of the heartfelt moments that Phyllis got? I keep coming back to that word, "humanity," but it really is a utopian society. It's not shocking that kids are gravitating towards that today, because I think we see just the opposite every day in the news and it's so disheartening. I want to go live in Scranton, in the world of *The Office*.

RAINN WILSON: I've talked to so many young people that have said, "I want to work in an office just like in Dunder Mifflin." They're thinking somehow, out in the workaday world, that it's going to be even remotely like *The Office*. [*Laughs.*] The most wrong-headed thing known to man.

ED HELMS: There's something I think that makes people want to be a part of that Dunder Mifflin family when they watch it. It's mundane, but it's gettable, it's understandable, and it doesn't change. The people in that office go through so many things, but you never question whether they're going to be there the next day. You never question whether they love each other still.

JENNA FISCHER: People always ask us if we're all really friends in real life. And I don't even think saying that we're friends in real life accurately communicates how deeply I feel for everybody [from the cast]. It's like a love of family. I can't explain it. Do you think if we'd made the show in the age of smartphones and whatnot, that we would be as deeply connected? It was the circumstances of us being trapped on set for the first season with no working computers, no phones, no internet, nothing. Just a troupe of actors and artists trapped in a room for twelve hours a day, playing. I mean, we improvised constantly and played constantly. We never absorbed ourselves in our phones or emails or anything. I think that lent itself to something, to part of the magic. If you tried to put us all in a room today, we'd just be at our desks on our phones.

BRIAN BAUMGARTNER: In a world that's in constant upheaval, I think *The Office* might be just what we need.

CREED BRATTON: If you wanted to work with people and make relationships, you'd want to be at Dunder Mifflin. Not at an impersonal Staples, because you get lost. *The Office* is like Mayberry in a way. It's *Green Acres*. There are trees outside. It's autumn and they go to work at Dunder Mifflin and see the seasons go by, and babies are born and people fall in love and out of love and it's sweet. We need that stuff in our lives. We're losing a lot of it, unfortunately.

JEN CELOTTA: There's something happening right now where everybody is so fragmented and so divided. You can kind of retreat into *The Office* when things are chaotic outside. I know these people, they're like me. I feel safe here. I felt that way with the Mr. Rogers movie. I was like, "Oh God, just come hug me, Mr. Rogers, again and again." There's like a weird thing that's almost subversive. It makes you feel you can kind of disappear with them and stay with them for a while.

"A Single Little Dandelion Growing Through the Asphalt Crack"
Truth and Beauty and the American Dream

Talking about what made *The Office* so remarkable isn't an easy task, especially for the people who created it. Mark Twain once compared analyzing comedy to dissecting a frog: "You learn how it works," Twain wrote, "but you end up with a dead frog." (Some sources attribute the frog anecdote to E. B. White.) Greg Daniels has a similar analogy.

GREG DANIELS: There's that parable of the centipede. They have hundreds of legs, and when the centipede tried to think about how it was that his legs all work properly, they all got tangled up and he couldn't walk anymore. There's something that always makes me worried when I talk about comedy. I don't want to lose the ability to do it.

But let's try anyway. The secret to *The Office*'s success and longevity may be contained in the very last lines of the show, written by Greg Daniels, which Pam shares in her final talking head interview. We quoted these lines earlier, but let's bring them back:

> **PAM:** I thought it was weird when you picked us to make a documentary. But all in all . . . I think an ordinary paper company like Dunder Mifflin was a great subject for a documentary. There's a lot of beauty in ordinary things. Isn't that kind of the point?

Was it the point? Did Pam stumble upon the single idea that defined why *The Office* mattered (and continues to matter) to so many people?

PHYLLIS SMITH: That is beautiful.

BRIAN BAUMGARTNER: Greg's pretty smart.

JOHN KRASINSKI: My brain just exploded again.

MIKE SCHUR: There were a bunch of phrases that became mantras early on [in the series]. Greg's number one most repeated one was "truth and beauty." He was like, "Everything that we make should be true and it should be real." The attempt should be to find the beauty in whatever you're doing in the writing and the acting and the directing and the set design and the costumes and everything. Truth and beauty, truth and beauty. It just got deeply ingrained in us. He gave us an analogy for what the show was in the first season. He was like, "Imagine a completely paved parking lot in an office park, with just cracked asphalt and yellow parking lines. It's stretching out as far as you can see. You're walking across it and it's a hot day and you're in a corporate industrial wasteland. Then you look down and there's a crack in the asphalt and there's a single little dandelion growing through the crack. That's what the show is. It's finding that dandelion. Finding that little tiny glimmer of truth and beauty and happiness in an aggressively unbeautiful landscape."

GREG DANIELS: That was my thing with Randall [Einhorn]. I would go, "Truth and beauty, truth and beauty."

BRIAN BAUMGARTNER: And what did that mean to you?

GREG DANIELS: I'm not sure where that came from. Some Romantic poet, somebody like John Keats or something. I don't know. And I don't even know what he meant by it.

In "Ode on a Grecian Urn," an 1819 poem by the English Romantic poet John Keats, he wrote, "Beauty is truth, truth beauty,—that is all / Ye know on earth, and all ye need to know."

GREG DANIELS: But the way I used it with Randall was, let the camera seek out truth. That's what it's trying to find. That's the point of a documentary, right? What's the *truth*? Not like a cynical, negative truth. Where's the beauty? It's another principle of photography, finding the little weed coming through the crack in the concrete. You know what I mean? Where are you going to find something that's inspiring but in a truthful way?

On *The Office*, there was truth and beauty everywhere, from the cameras barely capturing Jim and Pam's first kiss with a long shot through the window blinds, to Michael falling in love with Pam's painting of Dunder Mifflin, to just the simple ways these characters found dignity and joy in the tedious nine-to-five world of a low-level paper company.

KEN KWAPIS: I wonder if the show's continued popularity has to do with the fact that it does feel so real to people. It doesn't feel like a show. Most of us do work in really dreary jobs and feel trapped in the workplace. And I feel like the show really honors that experience. I have a younger brother who works at a store in our hometown. And when you go in, behind the counter of the store there are all the *Office* bobbleheads. All of them. I think, in a weird way, it's less about the fact that I worked on this show and more about the fact that working people connect with these characters.

EMILY VANDERWERFF: *The Office* lives in those little tiny moments of solidarity, of friendship, of love. When we talk about striving for the American dream, the American dream is not just "I'm going to get the biggest house," or "I'm gonna get the best car" or "marry the most beautiful person, the most handsome person." The American dream is you find a place where you belong and where you feel like you have people who care about you, who want the best for you, and you're all working toward a common goal. Too often American pop culture forgets that. It's about getting the best house and the best car and the most beautiful spouse. That's fine, that's fun. That's a wish-fulfillment fantasy. I want superpowers too. But there is a beauty in that solidarity, in that meeting of minds, in the way that a collective of people becomes something greater than itself. That is its own kind of American dream. And I think that *was* an American dream. I don't know if *The Office* consciously did this, but it tapped into it. And I think that's why it was so meaningful for so many people. I think that's why people keep coming back to it. It is a kind of dream we forget to have for ourselves too often.

BRIAN BAUMGARTNER: Michael's journey is essentially the journey of the show for the first seven seasons. Whatever he's searching for,

Realizing the American dream.

there is a fragment of the American dream there. He's searching for a family, and ultimately his love of the people he works with transitions and becomes Holly.

PAUL FEIG: Yeah, totally. He's looking for success and he's looking for love and he's looking for acceptance, and that's kind of all any of us really want. Maybe even in that order. But we're all trying to find it in whatever situation we end up in. Some of us get to pick the situation we're in, but most of us don't, you know? That's what's so lovely about *The Office*. We drive past these places every single day. Anywhere you are, every time you're driving, you go past these industrial parks. Every one of these places is filled with people who have hopes and dreams. This show is like, if you just took a camera and you're driving down the street and tossed a coin and said, "Let's stop here, let's just go and see what they're all about." You would find a million interesting stories. You'd find the funniest people in the world. You'd find the saddest people in the world. You'd find happy people, all that stuff. So yeah, it really is the American dream portrayed in a way that makes you not feel bad about your life.

So maybe that's it. *The Office* was looking for the American dream and found it in the least likely place possible. The show's appeal certainly had a lot to do with how it was constructed, and the cast of ordinary-looking people who weren't always winners, and the mix of subversive, cringe-y humor with sincerity, and of course the love stories. But the real spark at the center, the show's beating heart, was something less tangible, an idea that was only whispered behind the scenes and wasn't spoken out loud until the very end: truth and beauty in the ordinary things.

GREG DANIELS: I think that idea was very connected to the whole fabric of the show from the get-go. And it may be why it resonated. It's saying that real life matters, and real people are interesting. I mean, that's sort of the point of a documentary, right? The voice of the show is a very humanistic voice. If there's a message there, it's about the importance of decency and caring for each other, and that ordinary lives are worthy of being on TV.

Thank you for visiting Dunder Mifflin.

Acknowledgments

We realize this is the part of the book everybody is most inclined to skip unless they think they might be mentioned in it. But you're really missing out if you don't read it all. For instance, you'd never learn about Linh Le, a woman who we're pretty sure has superpowers. Without her endless patience, humor, and organizational skills, this book probably never would've existed, or at best would've been a pile of Post-its and a notebook full of illegible scribbles. She held us together when all hope seemed lost. Linh, in the words of Kevin Malone: "You. Are. Awesome."

A lot of amazing, talented people took part in the podcast that inspired this book, and we're grateful for their time and willingness to share their stories with us. We're going to list them all, and you should read every single name, even if you think there are no surprises here. Maybe we snuck in a name that doesn't belong. Can you spot the non-*Office* name?! (See, we told you it was going to be worth it.) A big thank-you to Greg Daniels, Kevin Reilly, Paul Feig, Allison Jones, Ricky Gervais, Stephen Merchant, Teri Weinberg, Steve Carell, John Krasinski, Rainn Wilson, Jenna Fischer, Angela Kinsey, Phyllis Smith, Kate Flannery, Ed Helms, Creed Bratton, Andy Buckley, Oscar Nuñez, Amy Ryan, Craig Robinson, Ellie Kemper, Melora Hardin, Paul Lieberstein, Mike Schur, Jen Celotta, Lee Eisenberg, Bill Russell, Brent Forrester, Ken Kwapis, Randall Einhorn, Dave Rogers, Claire Scanlon, Matt Sohn, Veda Semarne, Laverne Caracuzzi, Debbie Pierce, Kim Ferry, Emily VanDerWerff, Billie Eilish, Tim Holmes, and Michele Dempsey. (Did you catch the mystery name added to make sure you're paying attention? You did if you're a Celtics fan.)

There are so many more people not included in this list, people who played vital roles on the show, both on- and off-screen, but either due to time constraints or unprecedented historical happenings (hello, pandemic), we weren't able to connect for interviews. We love you and you'll always be part of the *Office* family.

An extra-special thanks to the amazing podcast team who helped us create both our first *Office* podcast and the *Deep Dive*: Joanna Sokolowski, Julia Smith, Benny Spiewak, Tessa Kramer, Alyssa Edes, Emily Carr, Russell Wijaya, Diego Tapia, Margaret Borchert, Christian Bonaventura, Liz Hayes, Hannah Harris, Alec Moore, Seth Olansky, Bart Coleman, Ellen Horne, Charles Michelet, Sheldon Senek, Joe Berry, Rich Boerner, Matthew Rosenfield, Alex Mauboussin, Lucy Savage, Syeda Lee, Judson Pickward, Jack Walden, Jonathan Mayor, Andrew Steven, David Lincoln, and of course, Bill Russell, five-time NBA Most Valuable Player. (Editor's note: Bill Russell actually had nothing to do with either the podcast or the book you're currently reading. We regret the error.)

Thanks to Ian Kleinert, our literary agent, who we prefer to think of as our wartime consigliere, and our fearless leader, Custom House's editorial director Peter Hubbard, who's like the Gandalf of editing, and the rest of the amazing team at Custom House/HarperCollins: Molly Gendell, Jessica Rozler, Alison Hinchcliffe, and Michelle Crowe. Thanks to the tireless support of Kevin Anderson & Associates, especially Eric Spitznagel, who helped us piece together this jigsaw puzzle of interviews. Your prose is as beautiful as your soul. (*Wait, did we sign off on that? Peter, please cut that line before we go to print, okay?* [PH: The line stays!])

Thanks to the incredible team at NBC who helped us secure photos and cover art: Pearlena Igbokwe, Masami Yamamoto, Rebecca Marks, Eric Van Der Werff, Jason Hoffman, and Geoff Hansen. A big thanks to Chris Haston, who took a great deal of these photos. We feel seen.

We'd now like to dispense with the royal "we" so that two of our authors can offer some personal thanks. We recommend reading them both in their entirety to unlock the special "clues" hinted at earlier in the book. (Remember to use your special Office Oral History decoder rings!)

Brian Baumgartner still remembers that moment, back in October 2019, when he "met at Propagate's offices in Hollywood with an idea, to tell the story of *The Office* from the perspective of all the key players. This is the result. I want to thank Ben Silverman and Greg Daniels for their belief in me. Thanks to my team: Ryan Zachary, Megan Smith, Ben Jaffe, and Ted Gekis. And to my biggest fans, my parents. I literally wouldn't be here without you. Most importantly, thanks to my family for their unwavering support, their perpetual energy, and above all, for their patience. From multiple trips to New York and Scranton to late-night recording sessions and edits, they were always there to keep me going and help me through. This book is for them."

Ben Silverman would like to acknowledge "all our friends and allies in the UK including Henrietta Conrad, in whose home I first discovered the show; Charles Finch, my partner in running William Morris during the height of Cool Britannia and who introduced me to the best of Europe; Ricky and Stephen, who gave us this opportunity; the brilliant Greg Daniels, the heart and soul behind the show; and of course Brian Baumgartner, my collaborator and partner. Lastly, nothing would be possible without the great taste I was surrounded by my entire life, from both my parents, Mary and Stanley, and now my children, Meyer and Madeline, who motivate me along with my life partner, Jennifer, to tell and share our history."

Last, but absolutely not least, we want to thank our partners at Propagate. You know who you are, but we're going to share your names anyway. Howard Owens, Drew Buckley, Greg Lipstone, Isabel San Vargas, and especially Leili Mostajeran, Diego Tapia, Hannah Harris, Christian Bonaventura, and Max Evans for their work on the book.

Congratulations! You read the entire acknowledgments. Your commitment to *The Office* has been recognized, and your honorary Dundie will be delivered to your home address in the coming weeks.